RACIALIZED POLICING

To Aislean—
My dear friend
and colleague.

In solidarity)
Elizabeth

D0815845

RACIALIZED POLICING

ABORIGINAL PEOPLE'S ENCOUNTERS WITH THE POLICE

ELIZABETH COMACK

FERNWOOD PUBLISHING ▪ HALIFAX & WINNIPEG

Editing: Robert Clarke
Cover art: Jackie Traverse
Cover design: John van der Woude
Printed and bound in Canada by Hignell Book Printing

MIX
Paper from
responsible sources
FSC
www.fsc.org   FSC® C013916

Published in Canada by Fernwood Publishing
32 Oceanvista Lane, Black Point, Nova Scotia, B0J 1B0
and 748 Broadway Avenue, Winnipeg, Manitoba, R3G 0X3
www.fernwoodpublishing.ca

Fernwood Publishing Company Limited gratefully acknowledges the financial support
of the Government of Canada through the Canada Book Fund and the Canada Council
for the Arts, the Nova Scotia Department of Communities, Culture and Heritage, the Manitoba Arts
Council, the Manitoba Department of Culture, Heritage and Tourism under the
Manitoba Publishers Marketing Assistance Program and the Province of Manitoba,
through the Book Publishing Tax Credit, for our publishing program.

Canadian   Patrimoine   The Canada Council for the Arts   NOVA SCOTIA   Manitoba   MANITOBA ARTS COUNCIL
Heritage   canadien   Le Conseil des Arts du Canada   CONSEIL DES ARTS DU MANITOBA

Library and Archives Canada Cataloguing in Publication

Comack, Elizabeth, 1952-
Racialized policing : aboriginal people's encounters with
the police / Elizabeth Comack.

Includes bibliographical references.
ISBN 978-1-55266-475-9

1. Racial profiling in law enforcement--Canada.
2. Police-community relations--Canada. 3. Native
peoples--Canada. 4. Police--Canada. 5. Racism--Canada.
I. Title.

HV7936.R3C66 2012   363.2'30897071   C2011-908400-7

CONTENTS

FOREWORD

Racism is a difficult concept to swallow in the twenty-first century in Canada. Racism is at the heart of everyday life for those who are victims of it, and yet it exists as a preposterous taboo from society's past to those who unwittingly perpetuate it. This book delves deep into the psyche of society's attitudes towards racism, towards the racialization of issues, social structures, and, importantly, of the police.

While exploring and analyzing interactions between the police and people of colour in Canada, Elizabeth Comack makes excellent use of statistical data to provide the reader with an insightful and informative backdrop for an understanding of racism. It is far too easy for the public, police, lawyers, prosecutors, and judges to place unmoving faith in the system of justice, particularly when we believe we have rights at our disposal, as guaranteed by the Canadian Charter of Rights and Freedoms. It is possible, on first glance, to believe that fairness and equality go hand in hand with justice and law enforcement, and it would be remarkable and wondrous if such a system did indeed exist. This book exposes the human element of justice, the attitudes and subconscious generalizations that culminate in differential justice, differential treatment, and the imbalance of socio-economic and criminal circumstances between peoples of Canada. The normalization of abuse leads to less tolerance, less recognition, and more scorn against those who try to assert any issue with the status quo.

Whether the abuse is racism, sexism, or discrimination on any other abhorrent ground, it takes a leap of faith to make the right connections between these and the behaviours of the police and, further still, courage to expose it. This is a task that we are all challenged with if we value the aspiration of a free and democratic society.

Donald E. Worme, Q.C., IPC
November 2011, Saskatoon

PREFACE AND ACKNOWLEDGEMENTS

The impetus for this book came from two sources. One was a study I conducted in 2008 and 2009 in collaboration with Nahanni Fontaine, justice director for the Southern Chiefs' Organization (sco). The study was one of several I carried out as part of a larger project funded by a Social Sciences and Humanities/Community University Research Alliance (sshrc/cura) grant entitled "Transforming Aboriginal and Inner-city Communities," undertaken by the Manitoba Research Alliance <manitobaresearchalliance-tiac.ca/>. My previous research on social justice issues, in combination with the work that Nahanni was doing as the sco Justice Director, led us to see a pressing need to document Aboriginal people's encounters with the police with the aim of producing a collective narrative about those experiences. By publicizing the study through posters at Aboriginal organizations and an announcement on an Aboriginal radio station, we hoped to secure twenty-four interviews. Phone calls came quickly to the sco office and my university number, and we began scheduling interviews. As it happened, the first interview occurred in June 2008 on the opening day of the Matthew Dumas inquest, which became the second impetus for the book.

Nahanni had been actively involved in supporting Matthew's family after he was tragically shot and killed by a Winnipeg police officer in January 2005. She continued that support through the course of the two-week-long inquest. I also sat through most of the proceedings, and it became evident that the inquest would not address fundamental issues relating to the impact of race and racism on policing. Indeed, in his opening statement inquest counsel Robert Tapper said that "race had nothing to do with this." As with most legal proceedings, the focus of the Dumas inquest was on individual actions and behaviours, with the result that Matthew was held responsible for his own death. That was just not good enough — the institutional and organizational nature of the policing of Winnipeg's inner-city communities, home to so many Aboriginal people, had to be brought into view.

When the Dumas inquest came to a close, Nahanni and I proceeded with our study. The interest of people in telling about their experiences with the police was beyond our expectations. We ended up with seventy-eight interviews — and could have done even more but decided we had ample information for the study. The issue then became how best to honour the participants and their stories. We debated whether to follow our initial plan of writing up a research report, but decided on a book instead. A book would give us the space to present our findings in detail and would enable us to locate the experiences relayed to us by participants — as well as the death of Matthew Dumas — in their broader context, including the historical role of policing in the colonial project and how relations between racialized groups and the police have played out in other parts of Canada. Although our plan was to write a co-authored book, Nahanni ended up taking on a new job with the Manitoba government as a Special Advisor on Aboriginal Women's Issues for the cabinet's Aboriginal Issues Committee. So her time was limited. Fortunately, I was given an administrative leave in January 2011 from my position at the University of Manitoba, which afforded me the time to spend on the book.

Writing a book can be a solitary enterprise, with countless hours spent in front of a computer, researching and writing. That was certainly the case for this book. But the final product would not have been possible without the support, guidance, insights, and talents of a number of people.

My friend and study collaborator, Nahanni Fontaine, has taught me much about standing up for social justice and having the courage to speak out when others are so quick to judge and disparage you for your convictions.

Jessica Dumas, Matthew's sister, graciously allowed me access to the documents and other materials that had been gathered in relation to her brother's death and to interview her about Matthew's life. I recognize that reading the chapter about Matthew was not an easy experience for Jessica, and appreciate her readiness to do so and provide me with feedback.

Donald Worme has spent the better part of his life working as a legal warrior for his people. I am truly honoured that he took the time from his other commitments to write the foreword for the book.

My friend Jackie Traverse put her talents to work (once again) and produced an amazing piece of artwork for the book's cover.

Several people also took the time to read the manuscript and to provide thoughtful feedback. They include my mother and biggest supporter, Agnes Bardal Comack; my dear friend, Kirk Baldwin; my University of Manitoba colleagues Steve Brickey and Rick Linden; and Joyce Green, Professor of Political Science at the University of Regina. Special thanks are due to my friend and colleague, Jim Silver, Professor of Politics and Co-Director of the

Urban and Inner-City Studies Program at the University of Winnipeg. Jim and I have worked together on various projects now for over eight years. I have come to rely heavily on his keen insights and political sensibilities and to marvel at his energy and tenacity in working for social justice.

As a university professor I have the privilege of working with some incredibly talented students. One in particular is Evan Bowness. As my Research Assistant, Evan not only helped me with the literature review for this project, but also had the tedious tasks of making sure all the sources were in the bibliography and cleaning up my formatting mistakes.

Once again, I have the pleasure of acknowledging the folks at Fernwood Publishing: Errol Sharpe, Wayne Antony, Beverley Rach, Jessica Antony, Curran Faris, Candida Hadley, Nancy Malek, Debbie Mathers, and Brenda Conroy. This is the ninth time that I have worked with Fernwood on a book project. It is the seventh time that I have worked with Wayne Antony as my publisher. As always, I have relied on Wayne's critical thinking skills to provide me with invaluable feedback on my writing. I have also relied on the skills of Robert Clarke, who I have taken to calling "my" copy editor. Robert continues to teach me about the intricacies of the writing process and how to go about making my words more accessible.

While writing on the topic of racialized policing has been a challenging endeavour, I am ever mindful that ours is a social order in which poverty and social exclusion are all too prominent features, and that race and racism play a key role in reproducing that order. Breaking the silence on the issue of racialized policing takes great courage, and so my biggest thank you goes to the individuals who have taken the risk to tell about their encounters with the police.

Chapter One

RACE AND RACISM

On the early afternoon of January 31, 2005, Winnipeg 911 operators received a call about a robbery that had just occurred at a residence in East Kildonan, an older suburb of the city. The perpetrators were reported to have left the scene in a taxicab. After the police determined that the cab was headed towards Winnipeg's North End, one of the city's inner-city communities, they quickly flooded the area with officers and began doing spot checks of likely suspects. An eighteen-year-old Aboriginal man named Matthew Dumas was walking down a North End street when a police cruiser with a lone officer in it pulled up. When the officer called to him, Matthew took off and ran down a back lane. The officer followed in pursuit. Less than fifteen minutes after this first encounter, Dumas lay dying on a sidewalk. A bullet from a police-issue revolver was lodged in his abdomen.

Following normal protocol for cases in which police officers take the life of a civilian, the Winnipeg Police Service (wps) Homicide Unit conducted an investigation into the shooting death. The investigation found no basis for criminal negligence or liability on the part of the officers involved. Some three years later an inquest was held into the death. Held over a two-week period in June 2008, the inquest proceeded in typical fashion. Civilian and police witnesses were called to testify before a provincial court judge. Several lawyers were also present — an attorney appointed to represent the Crown, counsel for the Dumas family, and counsel representing the Winnipeg Police Service. The focus of the inquest rested squarely on individual actions and the application of standard police operating procedures. The net result was that members of the Winnipeg Police Service were exonerated. Instead, Matthew Dumas was the one held responsible for his own death. The presiding judge concluded, "Mr. Dumas' behavior and choices drove the events that led to his death on January 31, 2005." In her report the judge also wrote that she "found nothing in the evidence to support the claim that Mr. Dumas' death was a result of racism" (Curtis 2008: 67).

This book is premised on a counterclaim: that the death of Matthew Dumas had *everything* to do with "race" and racism. Race and racism are what brought Dumas and the police officer who shot him together in

ily encounter. Race and racism not only pervade the everyday
Aboriginal people, but also inform the wider public discourse and
onal processes — including the practices of law enforcement officers charged with policing Winnipeg's inner-city communities. Until we
acknowledge and address this reality, more Aboriginal people are at risk of
encountering a fate similar to that of Matthew Dumas.*

I do want to make clear at the outset, however, that this book is not
about police bashing. Quite the opposite. Policing is an incredibly difficult
and challenging job, and for the most part police officers carry out their duties with care and professionalism. Because police are one of the few state
agencies that can be counted on to make house calls and are available on
a 24/7 basis, the duties of patrol officers are "of a mind boggling variety"
(Bittner 2005: 116). Police officers are not only called upon to attend to all
manner of social problems and issues, but, as William Westley (2005: 139)
observes, their job includes doing the "dirty work" of society. Officers deal
with people who are in crisis, intoxicated, emotionally disturbed, injured,
sick, dying, or dead — and sometimes just plain angry.

Nevertheless, policing is a controversial subject these days. It gener-
ates considerable public debate. One issue in this debate is whether or
not police officers engage in *racial profiling* — that is, whether they rely on
racial stereotypes to single out certain individuals and groups in society as
being more suspect and therefore subject them to increased scrutiny and
harsher treatment. On one side of this debate are those who argue that a
person's race is an important signifier of his or her propensity for criminal
involvement, and thus the police are justified in basing their decisions and
actions on racial criteria. Those on the other side of the debate suggest
that the question of race should have no part to play in policing because
all citizens should be treated equally by law enforcement officers. Another
version of this debate is over the matter of whether individual police officers hold racist beliefs or attitudes that inform their interactions with the
public. While some would contest this notion, arguing that police officers
are highly trained professionals who carry out their role in an objective
and neutral fashion, others point out that any racist beliefs or attitudes on

---

*   The critical race literature tends to place "race" in quotation marks each time
the word is used as a way of drawing attention to its contested meaning. After
careful consideration I have chosen to not follow this convention, but would
nonetheless encourage readers to be mindful that race is a socially constructed
concept with variable meanings.

the part of members of a police force are simply a reflection of the racism that prevails in the wider society and should therefore not be treated as a special area of concern.

How are we to make sense of these issues? My response is to suggest that to fully appreciate the ways in which race and racism invade the practice of policing — in other words, to understand policing as *racialized* — we need to go beyond the individual or interpersonal level and adopt a more macro or systemic perspective. While racial profiling and individual racism are significant issues and must receive attention, we need to broaden our gaze to include the ways in which race and racism play out in institutional practices and systemic processes. My aim, therefore, is to locate the death of Matthew Dumas — and Aboriginal people's encounters with the police more generally — in their broader, racialized milieu. More specifically, I utilize the notion of *racialized policing* to capture this wider context in which police carry out their work as "reproducers of order" in society.

Criminologists have paid considerable attention to police encounters with people of colour, especially in urban centres such as Toronto (Smith 2007; Tanovich 2006; Tator and Henry 2006; Wortley and Tanner 2004, 2005; Mosher 1998; James 1998, 2008; Henry 1994). Police encounters with Aboriginal people have not received the same level of scrutiny. This book represents an effort to rectify this omission. While I do necessarily consider the issue of racial profiling, my discussion focuses on Aboriginal people's encounters with the police by drawing on both the historical record of Aboriginal-police relations and contemporary cases — specifically, the shooting of J.J. Harper by a Winnipeg police officer in 1988 and the revelation of a practice known as "Starlight Tours" in the city of Saskatoon in the 2000s. In addition I draw upon interviews conducted with Aboriginal people in Winnipeg's inner-city communities. These interviews have produced a collective narrative of Aboriginal people's encounters with police that illustrates the wider context of racialized policing — and this context is crucial to a full understanding of the circumstances that led to the death of Matthew Dumas.

To undertake this investigation, though, we need first to map out the particular understandings of race and racism — and related terms such as racialization, everyday racism, and racial formation — that inform the analysis.

UNDERSTANDING RACE AND RACIALIZATION

The notion of race is not as straightforward as it might first seem. Its meaning has changed over time. When the term first appeared in the English language in the early sixteenth century, it was used primarily to distinguish between different nation-states, such as England and France. In the English case, for instance, Anglo-Saxons were described as a "race" of people (Miles 1989: 31; Banton 1987). With the growth of scientific inquiry in the nineteenth century, race came to be understood as a means of demarcating different groups on the basis of their phenotypic characteristics (especially their skin colour). Science was used to demonstrate "not only the number and characteristics of each 'race,' but also a hierarchical relationship between them" (Miles 1989: 32). These biologically based categorizations soon extended to include a range of intellectual, physical, and social capabilities of each group (such as intelligence, industriousness, and criminality). As one example, social Darwinism, in conjunction with its claims of an evolutionary process of "survival of the fittest," conceived of original races as pure and biologically determined. These supposed innate or essential "differences" between groups of people provided the basis for establishing a hierarchy of races, each having a variable capacity for "civilization" (Miles 1993: 2). Typically, white Europeans were positioned at the top of this racial hierarchy, thereby providing a justification for their supposed racial superiority and the corresponding racial inequality experienced by other racialized groups.

This view of race as a biological category or an ascribed characteristic on which difference is based informed the emerging social science disciplines, including criminology. Nineteenth-century criminologists Cesare Lombroso and William Ferrero, for instance, adopted social Darwinism to argue that criminals were primitive, "atavistic" throwbacks to an earlier stage of evolution. Atavism was associated with moral inferiority; atavists were "innately driven to act as a normal ape or savage would but such behaviour is deemed criminal in our civilized society" (Gould 1981 cited in Linden 2000: 187). In Lombroso and Ferrero's view, Black people constituted an "inferior race." Because they supposedly had not advanced as far along the evolutionary continuum, Black people were considered to be more prone to the "savagery" represented by criminal activity.

During the first half of the twentieth century, advances in scientific knowledge demonstrated conclusively that the world's population could not legitimately be categorized into distinct, biologically based racial groups (Miles 1989; Miles and Torres 2007). Nonetheless, the idea of race continued to hold strong purchase in public discourse. The term became part of common-sense understandings, as both a way of demarcating groups of people on the basis of features such as skin colour, culture, religion, and language, and a way of indicating corresponding ways of acting on these distinctions.

Several writers argue that because the concept of race has been so soundly disproven to be a distinct, biologically based entity — that is, that there are no "races" per se — then our focus should be on the meanings that are attached to it. In other words, race is not a biological category but a *social construction*. Viewing race as socially constructed — in effect, as a discourse or way of making sense — draws attention to its variable social meanings and to the social relations reproduced in the process. As Robert Miles (2000: 137) notes, race is "an idea created by human beings in certain historical and material conditions and is used to represent the world in certain ways." The idea of "race," then, is one of the ways (gender is another) in which individuals are differentiated from each other.

In Miles's (1989: 75) terms, differentiating between people on the basis of race is to engage in a process of *racialization*: "those instances where social relations between people have been structured by the signification of human biological characteristics in such a way as to define and construct differentiated social collectivities." Racialization, therefore, involves the production of difference; it is the process of constructing racial categories, identities, and meanings. With its root in a verb as opposed to a noun, racialization has the advantage of shifting the focus from the people being racialized to those *doing* the racializing. As George Dei (2009: 237) explains, "The process of racializing is thus external and strategic, and it is not the responsibility of the person who is targeted." Emphasis is on the doing or making of difference rather than the categories of difference in and of themselves. Attending to this process of racializing leads to yet another set of questions. Why do particular meanings of race become socially significant, and what are the historical and contextual processes and practices through which individuals, groups, and nations become racially differentiated?

Engaging in racialization, recognizing difference between people, does not in and of itself constitute a problem. Difference can be acknowledged and celebrated without imposing hierarchy. Rather, it is the attachment of negative meanings to this difference that is problematic. In these terms, the idea of race becomes *ideological* when it is used as a rationalization for the dominance of one racial group over another (Miles 2000: 137); in other words, when it is used to promote racism.

Racism and Othering

Miles (1989) defines *racism* as "ideas that delineate group boundaries by reference to race or to real or alleged biological characteristics, and which attribute groups so racialized with other negatively evaluated characteristics." But more than this, racism is a social practice connected to *power*; it is the use of racial categories to define an Other. The idea of race, in this sense, is an effect of power. This effect is evidenced when the process of racialization becomes a "representational process of defining an Other" (Miles 1989: 75).

It is when racialization involves "Othering," then, that racism occurs. At its core, this process of Othering entails establishing a binary between Us and Them. As Stuart Hall (1997: 258) elaborates, the practice "facilitates the 'binding' or bonding together of all of Us who are 'normal' into one 'imagined community'; and it sends into symbolic exile all of Them — 'the Others' — who are in some way different — 'beyond the pale.'" Othering, therefore, is the exercise of a particular form of power by those who are racially privileged. Allan Johnson (2005: 103) explains "privilege" as a position that "grants the cultural authority to make judgments about others and to have those judgments stick. It allows people to define reality and to have prevailing definitions of reality fit their experience. Privilege means being able to decide who gets taken seriously, who receives attention, who is accountable to whom and for what."

Drawing attention to racial privilege — to the ability to make judgments about Others "stick" — showcases how those on the privileged side of the "Us versus Them" dualism are able to avoid such markings. In other words, in societies in which white people are the dominant group, whiteness goes unmarked. Whiteness becomes the unacknowledged norm or standard by which all Others are measured. As Richard Dyer notes:

> Research... repeatedly shows that in Western representation whites are overwhelmingly and disproportionately predominant, have the central and elaborated roles, and above all are placed as the norm, the ordinary, the standard. Whites are everywhere in representation. Yet precisely because of this and their placing as norm they seem not to be represented to themselves as whites but as people who are variously gendered, classed, sexualized and abled. At the level of racial representation, in other words, *whites are not of a certain race, they're just the human race.* (Dyer 1997: 3; emphasis added)

According to this viewpoint, racism comes to be understood as a particular discourse or ideology that offers an explanation of how the world works. Racism organizes, preserves, and perpetuates the power structures of a society (Henry et al. 2009); it rationalizes, legitimizes, and sustains patterns of inequality (Barrett 1987: 7). Hall explains, racist ideas are "not a set of false pleas which swim around in the head. They're not a set of mistaken perceptions. They have their basis in real material conditions of existence. They arise because of concrete problems of different classes and groups in society. Racism represents the attempt ideologically to construct those conditions, contradictions, and problems in such a way that they can be dealt with and deflected in the same moment" (Hall 1978: 35).

Racism, therefore, involves more than just holding particular negative beliefs or attitudes about certain groups in society or acting towards individuals on the basis of racial stereotypes. Racism has a systemic basis. Racist discourse not only has its basis in material conditions but is also supported by — and reinforces — institutional and social practices in society that privilege certain racialized groups over the Others.

Racism does not exist in isolation from other social relations; specifically, those based on gender and class. In combination, race, gender, and class provide the basis for our location in society; they are also factors that mediate our experiences. Speaking about the connections between race and gender, for instance, Patricia Monture-Angus (1995: 177–78) comments, "It is very difficult for me to separate what happens to me because of my gender and what happens to me because of my race and culture. My world is not experienced in a linear and compartmentalized way. I experience the world simultaneously as Mohawk and as woman.... To artificially separate my gender from my race and culture forces me to deny the way I experience the world."

Rather than as compartmentalized or additive factors, then, race, gender, and class need to be understood as interlocking features of our social existence; they operate in relation to each other and inform people's perceptions, interactions, and experiences.

Everyday Racism

Racism occurs at the level of everyday experience — that is, as people go about their daily lives. While individuals vary in their situations and the conditions they face (for instance, according to their race, gender, and class positioning in society) and over their life spans (the experiences of young people may well be different from those of adults), one defining feature of everyday life is that it is familiar; it involves routine or repetitive practices. Moreover, the course of everyday life produces both the biographies of individuals (their life stories) and the social relations in which they are situated (with family, friends, and others).

With "everyday life" goes "everyday racism," which Philomena Essed (2002: 188) defines as a complex of practices (both cognitive and behavioural) that integrate racism — and its underlying power relations — on a daily basis. These daily situations become part of the expected, of the unquestionable. They are what the dominant group in society sees "as normal." To this extent, everyday racism becomes part of our common sense — "a way of comprehending, explaining, and acting in the world" (Omni and Winant 1994: 60). Racist comments or interactions may involve, Tania Das Gupta points out, "a few words exchanged, words not exchanged, gestures, glances, tone of voice, rumours, coincidences, inclusions and exclusions" (2009: 19). On their own, these comments or interactions may not seem overly problematic. Considered collectively, they can reveal a pattern of marginalization and exclusion.

Racist beliefs and actions that infiltrate everyday life thereby become part of a wider system that reproduces racism and racial inequality. For this reason, racism cannot be reduced to single incidents or specific events. At the same time, it cannot be reduced to the proclivities of individuals, as situations and even physical spaces can be subject to racialization.

Racial Formation

While the notion of everyday racism enables us to appreciate how racism is a routine feature in the lives of all of us — including, especially, racialized groups such as Aboriginal people — the concept of racialization also points to more systemic processes. For this purpose, Omni and Winant (1994: 55–56; see also Winant 1998) use the term "racial formation," which connotes "a process of historically situated *projects* in which human bodies and social structures are represented and organized." A racial project is "*simultaneously an interpretation, representation, or explanation of racial dynamics, and an effort to reorganize and redistribute resources along particular racial lines*. Racial projects connect what race *means* in a particular discursive practice and the ways in which both social structures and everyday experiences are racially *organized* based upon that meaning" (Omni and Winant 1994: 56). This theory of racial formation draws attention to the interconnections between the cultural representations of race, on the one hand, and the institutional and organizational forms in which racism is normalized, on the other. In particular, it showcases the role that nation-states have historically played in the production of race, racism, and racial inequalities.

One of the more powerful prevailing racial projects in Canada involves the discourse of multiculturalism. Canada has often been described as a "nation of immigrants." Historically, the country was built up by means of large influxes of immigrant groups, including the Prairie settlers who populated the West and workers of various kinds who took up positions in the urban industrial centres. Unlike our American neighbours to the south, characterized as a "melting pot," Canada has been called a "mosaic," in which diverse racial and ethnic groups have been able to make the country their home while retaining their unique cultural traditions and heritage.

This image of Canada as a diverse, multicultural — indeed, racially tolerant — nation has readily inspired national pride. It could be described as the "official version" of Canada's racial history. In both official state discourse and the public imagination, our society is represented as the "Great White North," the "True North Strong and Free," the "land of opportunity" in which democracy and "equality of all" prevails. As Carl James (2008: 380) notes, "This paradigm of cultural democracy holds that in Canada race does not determine how groups or individuals are perceived and treated; hence, minority and/or immigrant people can expect to have lives devoid of racism and discrimination."

The discourse of multiculturalism has been formally imbedded in Canadian law. Canadian Parliament enacted the Canadian Multiculturalism Act in 1988, which includes the declaration that multiculturalism is "the policy of the Government of Canada" and in particular that it is the government's policy "to ensure that all individuals receive equal treatment and equal protection under the law, while respecting and valuing their diversity" (par 3[1][3]) and that all federal institutions shall "generally carry on their activities in a manner that is sensitive and responsive to the multicultural reality of Canada" (par 3[2][f]). These statutory commitments are consistent with the Canadian Charter of Rights and Freedoms enacted in 1982. Section 15 of the Charter declares: "Every individual is equal before and under the law and has the right to equal protection and equal benefit of the law without discrimination based on race, national or ethnic origin, colour, religion, sex, age or mental or physical disability." Section 27 provides: "This Charter shall be interpreted in a manner consistent with the preservation and enhancement of the multicultural heritage of Canadians." Moreover, sections 25 and 35 of the Constitution Act 1982 are designed specifically to recognize and protect the rights of Aboriginal peoples (Stenning 2003a: 15–16).

This emphasis on multiculturalism supports Canada's claim to be what David Goldberg (cited in James 2008: 381) terms the "raceless state"; a nation-state, unlike the United States, in which race is not considered to be a problem or an issue. As Goldberg argues, "This claim to 'racelessness' masks the historical conditions that account for the contemporary issues and problems related to racism, and simultaneously contributes to the silencing of voices about racism" (James 2008: 381). It also makes any claims of racism and discrimination an individual matter; if racism is recognized at all, it is understood as an individual expression of overt feelings or actions (Henry et al. 2009).

Despite the official version of Canada as a raceless state — a racially accepting, peaceful, and civilized country — it is not difficult to find evidence to the contrary. As Rick Ponting (1998: 270) notes, "Like the tap root of the common dandelion, racism's roots extend deep below the surface of Canadian society." For example, the depiction of Canada as a "nation of immigrants" often fails to acknowledge that Canadian immigration law was historically informed by a "White Canada" policy that was "racist in orientation; assimilationist in objective" (Elliot and Fleras 1996: 290). To this extent, Canada was consciously and deliberately populated quite literally as the "Great White North." Intent on preserving the British character of the nation, the Canadian state devised policies and practices that excluded certain people from entry while encouraging "preferred" immigrants: white immigrants who were considered to be of "superior stock." Section 38(c) of the Immigration Act of 1910, for instance, enshrined in law a class of immigrants considered to be "undesirable." Among those who could be denied entry were:

> any nationality or race of immigrants ... deemed unsuitable having regard to the climatic, industrial, social, education, labour [conditions] ... or because such immigrants are deemed undesirable owing to their peculiar customs, habits, modes of life, methods of holding property and because of their probable inability to become readily assimilated or to assume the duties and responsibilities of Canadian citizenship within a reasonable time after their entry. (Cited in Jakubowski 2006: 100)

While the state required a ready supply of cheap labour for the great projects of industrialization and nation-building, it only allowed certain groups entrance to the country when their labour was required. Chinese labourers, for example, were brought to Canada under labour contracts during the period of the construction of the Canadian Pacific Railway (1800 to 1885). In 1885 a head tax of $50 was imposed on all Chinese labourers entering the country as a way to stem the tide of their immigration. The tax was increased to $100 in 1900 and $500 in 1903. In 1923 the Canadian government passed the Chinese Exclusion Act, which effectively prohibited all Chinese immigration until its repeal in 1947. Selective and racist immigration practices were also directed at Japanese and East Indian people during this period of Canadian history (see Jakubowski 2006; Comack 1986; Ward 1978).

The characterization of Canada as a "nation of immigrants" makes it easy to forget that Canada is also a "white settler society" whose origins lie in the displacement and dispossession of the original inhabitants of the land. In this regard, one of the most significant racial projects undertaken by the Canadian state was the colonization of the Aboriginal population. If we are to understand the wider, racialized context in which Aboriginal-police relations occur, we need to attend to this historical project of colonialism. Indeed, it was within this particular context that Aboriginal people's encounters with the police first occurred.

RACIALIZATION AND POLICING

Attending to the notions of race and racism — and racialization, everyday racism, and racial formation — sensitizes us to some of the dynamics involved in uncovering the complicated and complex ways in which these conditions have come to pervade the practice of policing in Canada. One of the key ways in which this issue has been examined is in the racial-profiling debate, especially as it has played out in Ontario in relation to the claim that police use race as a primary variable in their decisions to stop and search, arrest, and charge people of colour. The offence known as "driving while Black" epitomizes these practices. While this debate has had the benefit of drawing attention to issues relating to racialized policing, the notion of racial profiling individualizes the problem. The idea slips too easily into arguments that rest on simplistic claims such as "police are racist bigots" or that the problem is one of "a few bad apples." Shifting the focus to racialized policing calls attention to the role of the police in the "reproduction of order" (Ericson 1982) — for instance, to how race and racism inform the cultural frames or stocks of knowledge adopted by police in their work. Moreover, in reproducing order, police work involves not just the policing of individuals but the policing of spaces. When police concentrate their attention and activity on spaces deemed to be "disorderly" and "dangerous," they contribute to the process of racialization and the construction of racial hierarchies. In short, "place becomes race" (Razack 2000, 2002). When we apply racialized policing to the matter of Aboriginal-police relations, we are led to investigate the role that it has played in the colonial project of constructing a white settler society.

Situating Aboriginal-police relations in a historical context involves challenging the "foundational narrative" of the nation's history to map out the role of policing in the colonial project of creating Canada as a white settler society. Specifically, the North West Mounted Police (NWMP) occupied a central role in managing and containing the Aboriginal population as white settlement advanced. Colonialism, however, has not disappeared but has taken on new forms in contemporary times. Poverty and social exclusion, violence and alcohol use, becoming tangled up in the net of the criminal justice system: these experiences have come to dominate the lives of too many Aboriginal people. Similar to the role played by the NWMP in the colonial project of creating the white settler society, contemporary police forces have been assigned a central role in the management and containment of Aboriginal people. As a consequence, relations between Aboriginal people and the police have been rife with conflict and controversy.

One event that has come to symbolize the strained relationship between Aboriginal people and the police is the shooting death of Aboriginal leader John Joseph Harper on a Winnipeg street in March 1988. Harper's tragic death became one of two incidents — the other being the murder of Helen Betty Osborne in The Pas, Manitoba in 1971 — that led to the establishment of the Aboriginal Justice Inquiry of Manitoba (AJI) in April 1989. The AJI was headed by Justice Alvin Hamilton and Judge Murray Sinclair. At the time Hamilton was an associate chief justice of the Manitoba Court of Queen's Bench and Sinclair was a newly appointed associate chief justice of the provincial court who had the distinction of being the first Aboriginal judge to be appointed in Manitoba since Confederation.

Given its stated purpose of examining the relationship between Aboriginal people and the justice system in Manitoba, the Aboriginal Justice Inquiry covered a broad scope. Intent on learning directly from Aboriginal people, the two commissioners visited over thirty-six Aboriginal communities (some of which were only accessible by air travel and winter roads) and held hearings in seven other Manitoba communities and five provincial jails. Some one thousand people made presentations at the community hearings.

In addition, the inquiry conducted research projects on a range of subjects and commissioned a number of background papers. It also made trips to the United States to observe the operation of tribal courts there (Hamilton and Sinclair 1991a: 5–6).

The AJI released its two-volume report in the summer of 1991 (Hamilton and Sinclair 1991a, 1991b). The report stands as an indictment of the criminal justice system's treatment of Aboriginal people — in all of its stages. The commission's findings with respect to Harper's death and its aftermath, along with other sources, reveal the ways in which race and racism played out in the case.

More recently, the freezing deaths of three Aboriginal men — Neil Stonechild, Rodney Naistus, and Lawrence Wegner — and the experience of Darrel Night in Saskatoon set off a tidal wave of controversy revolving around the issue of Starlight Tours: the police practice of picking up people and taking them to some remote location and dropping them off, leaving them to find their own way home. Aboriginal activists and organizations declared the practice to be evidence of the racism that was rampant on the Saskatoon police force. Meanwhile, the police and their supporters denied any wrongdoing and posited that Starlight Tours were a myth perpetrated by "special interest groups." Unfortunately, in the broader context of racialized policing, Starlight Tours may well have become normalized as a strategy that police use to reproduce order when dealing with troubled and troublesome people.

Saskatoon is not the only Prairie city in Canada where troubling relations between Aboriginal people and the police prevail. Manitoba's largest urban centre, Winnipeg, has garnered a reputation as crime- and violence-ridden, especially in its inner-city communities where levels of poverty are high and a large proportion of the province's Aboriginal people reside. Just as AJI commissioners Hamilton and Sinclair (1991a: 594) concluded two decades ago, reports of Aboriginal people about their experiences with police provide a collective narrative that documents "a problem of considerable magnitude." When interviewed, Aboriginal men report being regularly stopped by the police because they "fit the description." While Aboriginal men are assumed by police to be involved in the drug trade and/or affiliated with a street gang, Aboriginal women found in the racialized space of the inner city are regularly assumed to be involved in the street sex trade. Racialized frames contour police interactions with Aboriginal people. So too does the use of racist, sexist, and other forms of disrespectful language.

Just as concerning are the troublesome police practices reported by

Aboriginal people. The improper uses of the drunk tank, beatings and physical violence in the form of the "phone book treatment," banishment and "red zoning," and Starlight Tours figure prominently in the interviews about encounters with police that I carried out with Aboriginal residents of Winnipeg's inner city. Not surprisingly, mistrust and animosity readily flow from such practices.

These forays into the historical and contemporary manifestations of Aboriginal people's experiences with the police provide the necessary context for an understanding of the death of Matthew Dumas in January 2005. The official version that emerged from the inquest into Dumas's death was premised on the claim that "race had nothing to do with this." Moving beyond the immediate event and bringing into view the broader dynamics of encounters between Aboriginal people and the police lead to the opposite conclusion. The issue is not simply about how the police behave, however problematic that may be on some occasions. Rather, the issue is much broader. It has to do with how race and racism are embedded in everyday experiences and institutional practices and implicated in our society's prevailing patterns of marginalization and social exclusion.

Chapter Two

RACIAL PROFILING VERSUS RACIALIZED POLICING

Police encounters with racialized groups — especially members of the African-Canadian community in Toronto — have been a subject of considerable discussion and debate in recent years. African-Canadian residents of Toronto claim that police engage in discriminatory practices against members of their community. The form of discrimination known as "driving while Black" became the experience of Toronto Raptors basketball star Dee Brown, who reported being pulled over by police in 1999 simply for being a Black man at the wheel of an expensive vehicle. Brown was arrested after blowing over the legal alcohol limit in a breath test. In his defence he argued that police had no reasonable cause for stopping his vehicle in the first place, and that his arrest was the result of racial profiling. A judge agreed with him. In April 2003 the Ontario Court of Appeal took judicial notice of the existence of racial profiling and ordered a new trial in the case. In its ruling the court said: "Racial profiling provides its own motivation — a belief by a police officer that a person's colour, combined with other circumstances, makes him or her more likely to be involved in criminal activity" (cited in Makin 2003).

Other incidents involving police shootings of Black people and the alleged mistreatment of Black youth led members of the African-Canadian community in Ontario to argue: "We have two systems of justice within the criminal justice system. One is for the majority group in our society — people who have money, connections, etc. — and the other is for the racial minorities" (Commission on Systemic Racism in the Ontario Justice System 1998: 200). In response, government-sponsored task forces and inquiries, journalistic reporting, and research by criminologists have all endeavoured to assess the issue of whether discrimination is perpetrated by the police in particular and the criminal justice system in general against Black people. Much of this focus has been on the issue of racial profiling; that is, the issue of whether police officers utilize race as a primary variable in their stop and search, arrest, and charging practices.

Racial profiling by police has received considerable attention in the United States (Harris 2002; Fridell et al. 2001) and Britain (Solomos 1988; Gilroy 1991; Holdaway 2003). When the issue finally emerged in Canada it was, in the words of William Closs and Paul McKenna (2006: 146), "explosive," generating lively debate. On the one side are those who maintain that racial profiling by police is indeed a practice that occurs (and with some regularity) among Black people, especially young males. On the other side are those who argue that the police have been falsely accused of racial profiling and that the evidence presented to support the charges is so unreliable that it constitutes "junk science."

While some scholars suggest that racial profiling by police has been proven to the point at which there is no need for any further discussion as to its existence (Tator and Henry 2006; Tanovich 2006), I propose that the focus of the debate produces a frame that is too narrow or confined for understanding the complex ways in which race and racialization play out in relation to policing. Instead, I argue that the notion of "racialized policing" broadens the focus to encompass the role of police in the wider society; specifically, as "reproducers of order." Poverty and social exclusion are logical outcomes of the way in which our society is organized. So too are related problems, such as certain forms of crime and violence. The police have been assigned the daunting task of responding to the "disorder" that results from these social conditions. In the process, policing itself has become a racial project. In surveilling the social spaces that police are assigned to govern, race and racialization are put into everyday policing practices as officers bring to bear the cultural frames of reference or stocks of knowledge that inform their work.

GOVERNMENT INQUIRIES

In the last few decades a number of government-initiated inquiries have investigated the issue of race and policing in Ontario. In 1988, for instance, in response to public protests spawned by the fatal police shooting of two Black men, the Solicitor General of Ontario appointed Clare Lewis as chair of the Race Relations and Policing Task Force. The task force's report, released in 1989, affirmed the perception of racialized groups: "They do not believe that they are policed fairly and they made a strong case for their view which cannot be ignored" (Ontario 1989: 14). The report, extremely critical of the state of race relations in Ontario, made fifty-seven recommendations for improvement, including the creation of the Special Investigations Unit

(SIU), initiatives aimed at increasing the representation of visible minorities in Ontario police services, improved community relations, and the collection of use of force statistics. As a result of this report, Ontario introduced a new Police Services Act in 1990. The Act represented a major overhaul in the approach to policing in the province.

The police killing of teenager Raymond Lawrence in May 1992 — which coincided with the acquittal of U.S. police officers in the beating of Rodney King, an event that had been captured on a civilian's video camera and sparked riots in Los Angeles — again generated public protests in Toronto and prompted the New Democratic Party government to take further action. Ontario Premier Bob Rae appointed a special adviser on race relations, Stephen Lewis, to develop a comprehensive action plan. After consulting extensively with African-Canadian and other racialized communities in the province, Lewis released a report in June 1992 that contained three key elements. First, the report recognized "the reality of systemic discrimination" as a pervasive feature of Ontario society. As Toni Williams (2001: 204) notes, "This recognition marked a departure from reliance on the language of 'multiculturalism' and 'race relations' to name and frame the experiences and concerns of people from racialized communities." Second, while Lewis acknowledged that other racialized groups were subject to systemic racism, his report identified Black people as especially vulnerable. According to Williams (2001: 205), "With this move, Lewis made it more difficult to marginalize black people's complaints about systemic racism by pitting their negative experiences against the allegedly more positive experiences, or perhaps more muted complaints, of people from other racialized communities." The third element of the Lewis report was to broaden the focus on policing to include a comprehensive investigation of the other stages of the criminal justice system (see Ontario 1992).

Some four months later the Ontario government established the Commission on Systemic Racism in the Ontario Criminal Justice System. The six-person inquiry had the mandate to examine the extent to which systemic racism affects the administration of justice in Ontario, with a specific focus on "anti-Black" racism (Ontario 1995). In carrying out its mandate, the Commission undertook an extensive program that involved consultations with community members and criminal justice professionals and research to examine the practices, procedures, and policies in three major components of the criminal justice system: the police, courts, and correctional institutions.

SYSTEMIC RACISM AND RACIALIZATION

The work of the Commission was framed by a particular construction of "systemic racism": as "patterns and practices... which, although they may not be intended to disadvantage any group, can have the effect of disadvantaging or permitting discrimination against... racial minorities" (Ontario 1995: Appendix A). In their report the commissioners maintain that the starting point of their analysis of systemic racism is racialization. Acknowledging that the notion of race is itself an idea or a myth, they explain racialization as "the process by which societies construct races as real, different and unequal in ways that matter to economic, political and social life" (Ontario 1995: 40). The commissioners go on to note that racialization can be either explicit, official, and supported by law or an implicit and unofficial feature of a social system; either way, "The process of adopting and perpetuating racialization within these social systems constitutes systemic racism" (Ontario 1995: 56).

From the commissioners' standpoint, racialization is "instilled" into social systems by the personnel working within them. This action can take one of two forms: overt racism; and covert, subtle, or implicit racism. While overt racism involves acting in ways that are personally hostile towards members of racialized groups, the covert, subtle, or implicit brand does not involve specific racist motives or intentions but has the same effect. For instance, the use of racially abusive language can be motivated by a desire to intimidate or control (and not by racist beliefs per se), but will have the effect of reflecting "society's judgments about the superiority of white people and inferiority of others" (Ontario 1995: 47).

Racialization can also be inserted into systems "when the standards or criteria for making decisions reflect or permit bias against racialized people" (Ontario 1995: 50). These standards or criteria can be either formal and explicit in laws, policies, and procedures or informal, arising from accepted ways of doing things. Bias in one part of the system can affect other parts. In the case of the criminal justice system:

> Each stage of the process depends on choices made in other parts of the system. Judges, for example, can impose penalties only on people who come before them for sentencing. People who appear before judges are neither a comprehensive sample of Canadians who commit crimes, nor a random sample of offenders. Who appears before a judge for sentencing depends on earlier decisions of members of the public, police officers, lawyers, justices of the peace, and sometimes other judges. (Ontario 1995: 51)

In addition to personnel and decision-making criteria, the organization or delivery of services can also encourage racialization. As the commissioners note, if the personnel within the criminal justice system (police, lawyers, judges) are mainly white, but large proportions of accused persons are from Aboriginal, Black, or other racialized communities, there may be a perception that the system supports racialization.

Finally, the commissioners state that systems manage personnel, decision-making, and service delivery through operating norms that include not only formal rules, procedures, and policies but also informal rules that are "the often unspoken understandings about how the day-to-day work of the institution is conducted." These operating norms contribute to "a complex and dynamic culture" that influences and is influenced by the individuals who work within the system. Operating norms may tolerate racialization in three different ways: passive toleration (lack of awareness of biases); disregard (awareness of racism but it is ignored); and collusive toleration (differential treatment is explicit and promoted by the system) (Ontario 1995: 54–56).

THE COMMISSION'S FINDINGS

The Commission released its 445-page report at the end of 1995. In their report the commissioners observed that, compared to white people, Black people stand a disproportionate chance of being charged and imprisoned in Ontario, and that this overrepresentation had skyrocketed within a period of six years, with 204 percent more Blacks jailed in 1994 than in 1986 (from 4,205 to 12,765 admissions), compared to an increase of 23 percent for whites (from 49,555 to 60,929 admissions) (Ontario 1995). Based on a survey of the general population, the Commission found a widespread perception among Black (58 percent), Chinese (31 percent), and white (36 percent) Torontonians that judges do not treat Black people the same as white people (Ontario 1995: i). While many judges and lawyers interviewed flatly rejected the possibility that systemic racism was a problem in the Ontario criminal justice system, others acknowledged differential treatment based on race as well as class or poverty: "Four in ten defence counsel (40%) and three in ten (33%) provincial division judges appointed since 1989 perceived differential treatment of white and racial minority people in the criminal justice system" (Ontario 1995: i–ii).

Police Stops: Use of Discretionary Power

With regard to the police, a survey of 1,657 Metropolitan Toronto residents about their experiences of being stopped by police in the previous two years found that more Black (28 percent) than white (18 percent) or Chinese (15 percent) residents reported being stopped by the police in the last two years (Ontario 1995: 352). More Black (17 percent) than white (8 percent) or Chinese (5 percent) residents reported being stopped more than once in the past two years. Many more Black respondents (39 percent) than white (9 percent) or Chinese (14 percent) respondents believed that the officers who stopped them did not treat them fairly (Ontario 1995: 352).

When broken down by sex and race, the data showed that Black men were particularly vulnerable to being stopped by police. About 43 percent of Black male respondents, but only 25 percent of white male and 19 percent of Chinese male respondents, reported being stopped by the police in the past two years. Also, significantly more Black (29 percent) than white (12 percent) or Chinese (5 percent) men reported being stopped by the police two or more times in the past two years (Ontario 1995: 352).

Analysis of the male sample by age as well as race revealed distinctive patterns. Among men aged eighteen to twenty-four, Black (50 percent) and white (48 percent) men were equally likely to report being stopped by police in the past two years, while Chinese men (22 percent) were less likely to report being stopped. However, Black men (50 percent) aged eighteen to twenty-four were much more likely than both their white (24 percent) and Chinese (11 percent) counterparts to report two or more stops in the past two years. Every Black man aged eighteen to twenty-four who reported being stopped by the police said he was stopped more than once. By contrast, about half of the white or Chinese men in this age group who reported being stopped had experienced tat act on more than one occasion (Ontario 1995: 355). Similar patterns existed for older age groups, with Black men being most likely to have experienced a police stop in the past two years.

When the data on police stops were analyzed in a subsample of male university graduates, Black males (48 percent) with a university degree were much more likely than white (19 percent) or Chinese (11 percent) male university graduates to report being stopped by the police in the past two years. Black male graduates (39 percent) were also much more likely than white (11 percent) or Chinese (7 percent) male graduates to report two or more stops (Ontario 1995: 355).

Perceived Fairness of Police Stops

The Commission's report also noted that many of the Black respondents strongly believed that police stopped them partly or wholly because of their race. Reflecting the notion that police target African Canadians simply for "driving while Black," some of these respondents believed that they were stopped because they were driving an expensive car. One respondent, for example, said that police stopped him "because they saw a Lexus with a black driver. We were not speeding or anything. They had no real reason to stop us." Others believed that police suspected them of selling drugs. One man said he was stopped because "if you are black and you drive something good, the police pull you over to ask about drugs." In some cases, respondents believed they were stopped because they were accompanied by a white woman. Interestingly, some white people mentioned race as the reason for the police stopping them, but it was the race of their companion that was the factor. One young white male said that he was stopped "because my friend was driving my Mercedes and he's black" (Ontario 1995: 356).

In interpreting these findings, the commissioners rejected the individualistic explanation that "all Metro Toronto Police officers are overt racists who consciously stop black people simply because they are black" (Ontario 1995: 357). If that were indeed the case, according to the commissioners, then one would expect more Black people — including women — to report police stops and the differential between Black and white respondents to be much higher. As the commissioners noted, "The racial difference in the number and perception of reported stops suggests that the cause is not 'a few bad apples' among the police" (Ontario 1995: 357; see also Tator and Henry 2006). Rather, they suggest that racialized characteristics, especially those of Black people, in combination with other factors — such as sex (male), age (youth), make and condition of a vehicle (if driving), location, dress, and perceived lifestyle — provoke police suspicion. One of the outcomes of this racialization, according to the commissioners, is that "these stops (particularly if unpleasant and also if frequent) breed distrust and suspicion of the police among black and other racialized people" (Ontario 1995: 358). In sum, the commissioners concluded:

> Systemic racism, the social process that produces racial inequality in how people are treated, is at work in the Ontario criminal justice system. Commission findings leave no doubt that the system is experienced as unfair by racialized people and, at key points in the administration of justice, the exercise of discretion has a harsher

impact on black than white people. The conclusion is inescapable: the criminal justice system tolerates racialization in its practices. (Ontario 1995: 106)

The Exercise of Discretionary Power

While the Commission should be credited for its efforts to address the systemic nature of racism in the criminal justice system, much of the research undertaken for the Commission — particularly with regard to the police — focused on the exercise of discretionary power. This individualized focus derived very much from the commissioners' view that "system personnel [are] the means by which a social system applies and transmits racialization" (Ontario 1995: 56).

In this regard, Williams (2001) notes that the Commission succeeded in producing "formal knowledge of how discretionary power may be abused in ways that produce racial inequality, and it showed how the abuse of power may become embedded in routine practices." Nevertheless, she also suggests that the difficulty with the empirical studies carried out for the Commission is that they were founded on a "formal equality model" that relies on demonstrating differential treatment by focusing on the outcomes of discretionary power and the practices of those who exercise it. In the process, this approach explains systemic racism in terms of attitudes, beliefs, and assumptions that decision-makers hold (either explicitly or subconsciously), and it sees solutions to the problem as resting in education and consciousness-raising — as opposed to necessitating more substantive, systemic change. Williams also makes the point that, given broader observations that law enforcement processes treat most people badly, realizing formal equality — that is, treating all individuals alike, regardless of their race — may not be the desired end: "To put the point bluntly, equality may be a hollow goal if it means nothing more than a criminal justice system that (mis)treats poor black people no worse than it (mis)treats poor white people" (Williams 2001: 213).

This tendency to focus on the use of discretionary power by criminal justice personnel became even more pronounced in debates generated by a series of *Toronto Star* articles alleging racial profiling of Black people by the Toronto police.

THE *TORONTO STAR* ARTICLES

While the Commission on Systemic Racism in the Ontario Criminal Justice System concluded that racism exists in virtually all levels of Ontario's criminal justice system, it was the publication of a series of articles on race and crime by the *Toronto Star* in October 2002 that became a new flashpoint for the issue of racial profiling by police (Rankin et al. 2002a, 2002b, 2002c, 2002d).

Through a Freedom of Information request, the *Toronto Star* gained access to data from the Toronto Police Service's Criminal Information Processing System (CIPS). The police database included information on 483,614 incidents in which an individual was arrested, charged, or ticketed for an offence dating back to 1996 — with almost 800,000 criminal and other charges recorded in the data. Under the direction of Michael Friendly, a psychology professor and director of Consulting Services for York University's Institute for Social Research, the *Star*'s investigative team used the data to conduct an in-depth study of how minorities are treated by police. Because Toronto police are prohibited by their governing board from analyzing these data in terms of race, the *Star*'s analysis represented one of the first times that such an analysis of police-generated data had been undertaken in Canada.

The *Star*'s analysis of the CIPS data focused on two issues: arrests for simple drug possession and traffic offences. In both cases the *Star* argued that Black people were being treated more harshly than whites, leading to the conclusion that Toronto police engaged in racial profiling.

The charge of simple possession was selected because it was a relatively minor crime and a "high discretion" charge, "meaning police officers at the scene of an arrest, and in a police station, have considerable leeway on how they handle a suspect" (Rankin et al. 2002a). More than 10,000 arrests for simple drug possession had occurred during the six-year period. While the majority of individuals arrested for simple possession (63.8 percent) were classified by police as being white, about one-quarter (23.6 percent) were described as Black. (The remaining skin colour classifications in the database are "brown" and "other," which together accounted for about 12 percent of simple drug possession charges.) The *Star* also reported that whites were more likely to be released at the scene (76.5 percent of the time) compared to Blacks (who were released 61.8 percent of the time). Of those taken to the station, Blacks were held in custody to await a bail hearing at a rate twice that of whites (15.5 percent versus 7.3 percent).

The analysis of the CIPS traffic data focused on "out-of-sight" offences. These are offences that the police cannot detect without stopping the driver first, such as failing to update a driver's licence or driving without insurance. In the absence of any other charge one would assume that such police stops would be random in the population of drivers. The *Star's* analysis of 7,500 out-of-sight violations found that skin colour was listed in about two-thirds (4,696) of the cases in which drivers were ticketed only for this type of offence. Black drivers made up 34 percent and white drivers made up 52.1 percent of those cases in which the race of the driver was listed. According to Census figures, however, Black people represent just 8.1 percent of Toronto's population, while whites account for 62.7 percent. Further, Black males between twenty-five and thirty-four years of age were issued 39.3 percent of the tickets for out-of-sight violations in that age group, yet they represented only 7.9 percent of Toronto's population in that age category. These differences were taken as evidence of racial profiling by police (Rankin et al. 2002b).

A FIRESTORM OF CONTROVERSY

Charles C. Smith (2007: 23) notes that the *Star* articles "resonated with the experiences of African Canadians" because they spoke to a long-standing issue between people of colour and the police in Toronto. Nevertheless, while the findings reported in the *Star* articles may have reflected a "common truth" for African Canadians (Smith 2007: 24), the allegation of racial profiling by Toronto police officers generated a firestorm of controversy.

Toronto Police Chief Julian Fantino disputed the findings of the *Star* report. "We don't treat people differently," he stated. "Nor do we consider the race or ethnicity, or any of that, as factors of how we dispose of cases or individuals." Fantino emphasized, "We don't do racial profiling" (Rankin et al. 2002a). Toronto mayor Mel Lastman commented, "Police only arrest bad guys…. I don't believe the Toronto police engage in racial profiling in any way." The chair of the Toronto Police Services Board called the *Star's* allegations "reckless" (cited in Sewell 2010: 76). Alleging that the articles inflicted severe damage to the reputation of its members, the Toronto Police Association responded by launching a $2.7-billion class action libel suit against the *Toronto Star*. The suit sought damages in the amount of $300,000 for each of the 7,200 members of the force. (The lawsuit was eventually dismissed on a pretrial motion. The judge was satisfied that the statement of claim disclosed no cause of action, as the allegedly defamatory comments and innuendos in the articles could not reasonably be understood as intended to apply to every officer of the Toronto Police Service (Tanovich 2003–4: fn5).)

Some Toronto police officers had their own personal experiences of being racially profiled by their fellow officers, and they were not as critical of the *Star*'s conclusions. At an informal focus-group meeting of thirty-six Black Toronto police officers in October 2003, these officers agreed that "the stereotype that black motorists in expensive cars and neighbourhoods receive extra attention was true." One officer described how a colleague referred to Black citizens on bicycles as "chimps on bikes." While the majority of the officers at the meeting reported having experienced racial profiling first-hand, three officers said they had been stopped more than once in the course of a week; six officers mentioned being stopped more than twelve times in a year (Tanovich 2006: 35).

To counter the claims made in the *Star* articles, the Toronto Police Service commissioned an independent review of the newspaper's analysis. The review, conducted by criminal lawyer Alan Gold and University of Toronto sociology professor Edward Harvey, was released in March 2003 at a Toronto Services Board meeting that had been advertised as an opportunity for the Black community to express its profiling concerns (Tanovich 2006: 34). The report described the *Star*'s analysis as "junk science" or "claims and conclusions illogically based upon incomplete or inaccurate data." It deemed the allegations of "systemic Police bigotry" to be "bogus, bogus, and bogus." The reviewers, roundly denying that racial profiling was a problem in the Toronto Police Service, argued that "the *Star*'s completely unjustified, irresponsible and bogus slurs against the TPS must be put down once and for all" (Toronto Police Service 2003).

In a related article that was part of a special forum on racial profiling in the *Canadian Journal of Criminology and Criminal Justice*, Gold (2003) raised the issue of the differing meanings attributed to the term "racial profiling." While some use the term to refer to "the handful of police officers" who "may unfortunately and illegally be bigots," Gold said, others apply the concept to situations in which a police force is seen to be promoting racism "through teaching materials or other shared police knowledge" such as training videos in which the drug traffickers are always Blacks or Hispanics or "operational instructions to watch the highways for older cars driven by black males" (2003: 393). Gold questioned whether this scrutiny reflected "politically correct hypersensitivity," but nonetheless noted that such materials were no longer in use by police departments.

Gold also pointed out that the practice of criminal profiling was itself a form of "junk science" because the use of profiles — the drug-courier profile, sex-offender profile, smuggler profile — had been found to be a very poor predictor when applied to searching out offending individuals. Racial profiling, according to Gold, is a "subspecies" of criminal profiling. It involves "profiling where race or ethnicity replaces all other characteristics" or "the profiling (i.e., identification of target criminals) based upon one characteristic: race." In Gold's view, equating racial profiling with racism is "logically irrelevant." He cited how the example of "deciding that driving an old car is part of the drug-courier profile does not depend on a hatred of old cars" (2003: 394). In Gold's view:

> There is a difference between believing in racial profiling in drug offences because one believes that a disproportionately high number of blacks have been found to use drugs in the past, or believing the stereotype that blacks generally use drugs, or being a racist towards blacks and attributing excessive drug use accordingly. The last situation involves a bigot, who can be identified, as any bigot will be. The first two cases involve the same erroneous reasoning as is implicated in profiles generally and are simply instances of the same junk science as drug-courier profiling and battering-spouse profiling. They do not involve racism (although the second example does involve false, stereotypical reasoning) and it is difficult to see why they cannot be dealt with as ordinary matters requiring countervailing education. (Gold 2003: 394)

Gold also suggested that racial profiling had no relevance to situations in which police have already identified an offender as belonging to a particular race: "If the police stop only black males because the perpetrator of a homicide has been described by witnesses as a black male, this practice is absolutely irrelevant to any claim of racial profiling" (2003: 395). For this reason, he maintained, a distinction needed to be made between proactive and reactive policing. In proactive policing, Gold argued, "statistics on police stops must obviously exclude stops involving the police looking for a racially identified perpetrator." At the same time, in reactive police work — for instance, in response to community concerns for a greater police presence — statistics can easily become skewed. As such, researchers need to "distinguish between situations in which the police are 'using race' and where they are 'finding race'" (2003: 395).

For Gold, the only valid data that could support a finding of racial profiling are those that involve "proactive police decision making in a context that is completely racially neutral" (2003: 396). At the same time, he goes on to comment that the *Star* analysis makes the false assumption that the statistic for each racial minority and for whites should be the same. In other words, the percentage of Black people stopped by police should be equivalent to their percentage in the population.

> Unless it is claimed that all social groups are otherwise equal in all relevant social and economic factors, that all groups are evenly and randomly distributed geographically and socially, how can it possibly be expected that state institutions, including the police, will interact with them on a statistically identical level? Do welfare institutions, banks, public transportation, or any other social institutions interact with the various races in society on statistically identical terms? (Gold 2003: 397)

His argument is contradictory. On the one hand, Gold suggests that "completely racially neutral" contexts exist in a contemporary, racially diverse society. That is clearly not the case. Researchers are hard-pressed to find contexts that are "completely racially neutral." As Michael Omni and Howard Winant (1993: 5) point out, "Our society is so thoroughly racialized that to be without a racial identity is to be in danger of having no identity at all. To be raceless is akin to being genderless." In the same way that identities are framed and informed by race (as well as gender and class), the social contexts in which we move will also, unavoidably, be racialized (and gendered and classed). Indeed, Gold demonstrates an awareness of this condition when he says that social (or racialized) groups are not "equal in all relevant social and economic factors."

For Gold, however, the main issue is about "police identifying criminals," and success in this regard is measured though outcomes:

> Suspects correctly and incorrectly identified as criminals; searches that correctly found contraband versus those that did not are the basis for reliable conclusions.... Racial profiling is all about using race to decide whom to suspect as a criminal. If it is as undoubtedly an erroneous basis as we believe then its very failure will give it away. (2003: 398)

If the police are somehow wrong in relying on race, this failure will be reflected in unsuccessful outcomes; that is, the acquittal and withdrawal rate for racialized individuals should be higher than it is for white accused.

One problem with this reasoning is that Gold fails to consider that "crime" is a legal construction. As labelling theorist Howard Becker (1963) pointed out many years ago, who gets defined as criminal is a social creation. It is the result of a lengthy process of rule-making, detection, apprehension, accusation, judgment, and conviction. Crime categories, then, are not unproblematic, unitary things that are simply employed in the "correct identification" of criminals. Rather, crime categories represent one way of ordering or making sense of social life. Much of police work, in other words, involves making a judgment as to who might be suspicious and whether their actions or behaviours should be deemed as "criminal."

Consider this example. A Winnipeg high-school principal was walking down the hallway of the school one morning when he noticed a young male Aboriginal student standing outside, smoking a cigarette (which was against school policy). The principal took the young man to his office to talk about the infraction. Knowing that the youth had been having troubles at home, he asked him how things were going. The principal was aware that because of the unstable home situation, the youth had been crashing at a friend's house. The youth told the principal that the night before — at 1:30 a.m. — he had been walking down an inner-city street on his way back to his friend's place when a police car pulled up alongside him. There had apparently been a burglary in a nearby home just that evening, and the police were on the lookout for suspects. The youth had no priors. As he told the principal the next day, he was holding three garbage bags as he made his way down the street. Knowing that his friend's mother was likely to ask him to leave soon, he was making preparations for transporting his belongings.

The police took him to the District Station and charged him with possession of burglary instruments (the garbage bags). His dad eventually came and retrieved him at 3:30 in the morning. In this case, being in possession of garbage bags on an inner-city street late at night was translated into a criminal offence in the judgment of the police officers involved. Had the Aboriginal youth been an older white man or woman walking down the same street at the same time of day, the incident might well have played out very differently.

Another problem with Gold's reasoning is that it justifies police practices that involve the "oversurveillance" of racialized groups. A self-fulfilling prophecy is produced in which greater surveillance leads to more crime being detected, which reinforces the practice of increased surveillance. As the Ontario Human Rights Commission noted:

> If a particular group is stopped more often, even if they are committing less crime than the rest of the population, the fact that they are scrutinized more frequently will result in higher charge rates. This then becomes the justification for profiling. Some scholars therefore argue that, at the end of the day, statistics do not tell the offending behaviour of different races, but rather they measure the actions of the entity engaging in profiling. (OHRC 2003: 16)

CRIMINOLOGISTS WEIGH IN

University of Ottawa criminologist Ron Melchers (2003) expressed problems with the *Star*'s methodology. One factor that Melchers singled out was the use of Census data as a benchmark for determining the existence of the police's racial profiling of Black drivers. The assumption of the *Star* analysis was that the proportion of drivers stopped by police should be identical to proportions in the general population. Melchers pointed out that while the proportion of drivers stopped by police is a measure of *incidence*, population statistics are a measure of *prevalence*. To compare the two is to commit a "base error." As well, the impact of repeat offenders on aggregate crime counts needs to be considered. "Aggregate errors" are also committed when incidence statistics are used to infer prevalence. Not taking into account multiple or repeat offences by the same individuals "can result in a small but very active group having an inordinate impact on how a more diverse larger group encompassing them is perceived" (Melchers 2003: 351).

Melchers also took issue with the way in which race was operationalized in the *Star* analysis. He suggested that the Census definition (which relies on racial identity) and the police data (which rely on skin colour) are "essentially unrelated" (2003: 353). As well, he noted that police stops are not random but governed by a number of legally relevant factors that the CIPS data do not include (such as the age and condition of a vehicle, the day and time, the location, and driving behaviours).

With regard to the *Star*'s analysis of drug possession charges, Melchers noted that what the articles provided were single-variable descriptive statistics, and that "to determine whether and how much of the difference in treatment between Black and white suspects might or might not be explained by a single factor" would require multivariate analysis (Melchers

2003: 357). He did note, however, that Michael Friendly presented such an analysis to the Toronto Police Service on behalf of the *Star*. Friendly presented two models, one examining the likelihood of release at the scene and the other examining the decision to hold a suspect for a bail hearing by five independent factors (gender, employment status, citizenship, age, and across years). When factors were controlled for, the likelihood of Blacks being taken to the station was still between 1.3 and 1.7 times greater than that of whites, and Blacks were between 1.3 and 1.9 times more likely than whites to be held for a bail hearing (Melchers 2003: 358). But Melchers reserved judgment on these findings.

Similar to Gold (2003), Melchers took issue with the assertion that police departments have adopted racial profiling as an official policy and practice, pointing to the lack of any scientific merit to the practice of profiling offenders. He also stated:

> So much of what explains the over-representation of some groups in the criminal justice system is so systematically and seemingly intractably integrated into the functioning of all social institutions and behaviours: poverty, deprivation, isolation from broader social values, lack of community social cohesion, and so on. At least some groups of Canadians — for example those of Aboriginal or African ancestry — have experienced and continue to experience discrimination in so many ways that it would be unreasonable for the consequences not to show up in virtually every aspect of Canadian society. (Melchers 2003: 362)

What Melchers seems to be saying, then, is that systemic racism is such a pervasive aspect of Canadian society that we should not be surprised to find it has invaded the practice of policing.

While Gold (2003) and Melchers (2003) offered critiques of the *Star*'s analysis, Scot Wortley and Julian Tanner (2003) defended the newspaper's position by responding to the re-examination of the *Star* data conducted by sociologist Edward Harvey for the Toronto Police Service. They argued, "Many of the findings produced by Harvey are completely consistent with the racial-profiling argument" (2003: 369).

Wortley and Tanner criticized several aspects of the Harvey re-examination. For one, Harvey argued, "As a database, CIPS was designed as an administrative tool to assist TPS officers in the conduct of their duties. It is not and was never intended to be a research database" (Harvey 2003: 10).

Wortley and Tanner pointed out that social scientists — including crimi-nologists — undertake a great deal of research based on administrative or archival data not originally intended for research purposes. Moreover, while Harvey said the CIPS data were only a sample, Wortley and Tanner thought otherwise because, they said, the data set "was designed to represent the total population of criminal charges (and certain traffic charges) that were laid by the Toronto police during the study period" (2003: 374).

They also called Harvey to task for his decision to exclude cases involv-ing multiple offenders in his re-analysis. As Wortley and Tanner noted, if Black people were subject to racial profiling, then one would expect them to be more likely to be subject to arrest on multiple occasions. Harvey also eliminated multiple-charge cases. Previous research suggested that Black people were more likely to face multiple charges (overcharging) than whites. Eliminating multiple-charge cases would therefore reduce the likelihood of finding evidence of racial profiling. As well, Harvey also divided the data into division levels and included only those police divisions that had a Black population greater than 6 percent. This decision, according to Wortley and Tanner, ignored research that supported the "out-of-place" hypothesis, that is, that minorities are treated more harshly by police when they are found in predominantly white neighbourhoods.

Furthermore, in his analysis of arrests statistics Harvey added two more offences not considered by the *Star*: prostitution and impaired driving. His analysis found that while Blacks were overrepresented in charges for simple drug possession, cocaine possession, and out-of-sight traffic offences, whites were overrepresented in charges for prostitution and impaired driving (Harvey 2003: 39), which he took as proof that racial profiling did not exist. Wortley and Tanner (2003) noted, however, that the overrepresentation of Blacks for out-of-sight driving, cocaine possession, and simple drug posses-sion was far greater than the overrepresentation of whites for prostitution and impaired driving charges. By including 52 Division in their re-analysis, they also showed that Blacks in this district were overrepresented in all five offence categories (including prostitution and impaired driving). The overrepresentation of Blacks in the district was even greater than in ones where Blacks made up a larger proportion of the population, suggesting that Blacks are "treated more harshly by the police when they venture into predominantly white areas" (2003: 380). Finally, in terms of the issue of treatment after arrest, Wortley and Tanner (2003) pointed out that Harvey did not actually replicate the *Star*'s analysis of release and bail decisions for those charged with drug and cocaine possession. For these reasons, they cast his report as being "plagued with both methodological issues and problems of interpretation" (2003: 384)

The debate among criminologists continued, with Thomas Gabor (2004) responding to the claims put forward by Wortley and Tanner. For one, Gabor took issue with their definition of "racial profiling." Wortley and Tanner (2003: 369–70) had stated that it occurred:

> when the members of certain racial or ethnic groups become subject to greater levels of criminal justice surveillance than others. Racial profiling, therefore, is typically defined as a racial disparity in police stop and search practices, racial differences in customs searches at airports and border-crossings, increased police patrols in racial minority neighbourhoods and undercover activities, or sting operations that selectively target particular ethnic groups.... Racial profiling, therefore, is associated with racial bias in police investigation — not racial bias in arrest decisions or racial bias in police treatment after arrest.

In Gabor's view, this definition failed to distinguish between police actions based on bigotry and those that derived from "legitimate" police work:

> It is legitimate for a police service to deploy additional personnel in neighbourhoods experiencing high levels of illegal activity, regardless of whether or not the residents tend to be members of visible minority groups. In fact, members of besieged minority communities, including Toronto neighbourhoods beset by gang warfare, have been known to demand more rather than less attention from their local police service. (Gabor 2004: 458)

Gabor's point is similar to one made by Gold (2003) in making a distinction between reactive and proactive police work, especially when residents are demanding a greater police presence in their community. In this regard, research conducted in Winnipeg's inner-city communities (Comack and Silver 2006, 2008) confirmed that residents were certainly in favour of a greater police presence in their communities to combat the pressing problems of drugs, gangs, and violence. Nevertheless, what they did *not* want to see was an aggressive, incident-driven form of policing that pits the police against the community. In other words, inner-city residents envisioned a very particular role for the police — not as an external force that reacts to crime but as one part of a wider effort of community mobilization in which the police work *with* the community to implement community-driven solutions for the problems that engender crime and violence.

As Gabor rightly noted, police are often placed in a difficult situation: "If they fail to respond to the concerns of residents in these areas, they may be accused of insensitivity toward the relevant minority group. If they take aggressive measures, however, they may face accusations of profiling and of over-policing minority neighbourhoods" (2004: 460). Clearly, the operative word here is "aggressive." While police departments may intensify their presence in particular communities — often at the behest of residents — the form that such policing takes can become a matter of concern.

EXPERIENCES OF RACIAL PROFILING

In the midst of the firestorm of controversy created by the *Toronto Star* articles, the Ontario Human Rights Commission (OHRC) announced in December 2002 that it would conduct an inquiry into racial profiling. While much of the focus of the debate to that point had been on whether or not racial profiling by police did occur, the OHRC took a different approach. Rather than focusing on whether there was evidence to either prove or disprove the existence of racial profiling (in all manner of institutions, not just in the form of police stops), the OHRC concentrated on the impact of racial profiling on those who have experienced it: "The Commission has consistently stated that the purpose of its racial profiling inquiry is not to prove or disprove the existence of racial profiling. It is the Commission's view that previous inquiries have considered this and have found that it does occur" (OHRC 2003: 9). The main objective of the inquiry, therefore, was "to give those who have experienced profiling a voice to express how it has impacted them and to provide an analysis of how profiling affects more than just those communities most likely to experience it" (OHRC 2003: 4).

The terms of reference for the inquiry were announced in February 2003 and the project was widely advertised in community newspapers and organizations. Over four hundred submissions were received by mail and through an online questionnaire on the Commission's website. The definition adopted by the inquiry specified racial profiling to be "*any action* undertaken for reasons of *safety, security or public protection* that relies on *stereotypes* about race, colour, ethnicity, ancestry, religion, or place of origin rather than on reasonable suspicion, to single out an individual for greater scrutiny or different treatment" (OHRC 2003: 6). The Commission also noted that age and/or gender can influence the experience, and that racial profiling needs to be distinguished from criminal profiling, which "isn't based on stereotypes but rather relies on actual behaviour or on information about suspected activity by someone who meets the description of a specific individual. In other words, criminal profiling is not the same as racial profiling since the former is based on objective evidence of wrongful behaviour while racial profiling is based on stereotypical assumptions" (OHRC 2003: 6).

The Commission deemed racial profiling to primarily be a "mindset" that involves stereotyping people based on preconceived ideas about their individual characters. Similar to the Commission on Systemic Racism in the Ontario Criminal Justice System (Ontario 1995), the point was made that this stereotyping may be conscious or overt, or it may be subtle and unconscious; "in many cases the person engaging in it may not even realize that it has occurred" (OHRC 2003: 6). The Commission also provided a clarification:

> Discussing a concern with profiling is not the same as saying that every member of an organization profiles, that profiling is an intentional policy of the organization or even that it is an intentional act of those who engage in it. While profiling can be intentional, it can also be inadvertent. Therefore, saying that profiling occurs should not necessarily be interpreted as an accusation that those who engage in it are racist. (OHRC 2003: 7)

While the Commission's inquiry covered all forms of racial profiling, the institution that was most commonly identified by respondents was the police. The Commission found:

> Some of the words that were used to describe the effects on relationships with police included: suspicion, distrust, anger, antagonism, hostility and fear. Many described fearing for their own safety when interacting with police officers and some said that, rather than feeling that the police were there to protect them from crime, they felt the need to be protected from police. (OHRC 2003: 24)

One consistent outcome reported to the inquiry was the "disempowering impact of profiling. Several participants used the words 'impotent,' 'powerless,' 'helpless' and 'emasculated' to describe how they felt as a result of one or more incidents of profiling" (OHRC 2003: 35). Participants reported feelings of profound embarrassment and shame at an incident of racial profiling that occurred in public or in front of family and friends. The Commission cited, for example, the case of "an African Canadian man who teaches in an elementary school and was pulled over and searched by police during the day in the neighbourhood where he teaches" (OHRC 2003: 43).

Experiences of racial profiling had an impact on people's behaviour and activities. Several respondents reported that they changed their driving habits — perhaps no longer driving a particular type of vehicle so they would not attract police attention, or making sure to have their documentation such as driver's licence and proof of registration before they left home, or checking their licence plate for visibility, and ensuring that there were no other issues with the appearance or function of the car (OHRC 2003: 38). Others reported that they self-imposed a curfew to avoid being on the streets after dark. As the Commission (2003: 38) noted, "While all of these measures to ensure that the law is being followed should be taken by all citizens, the reality is that those who do not experience profiling often take these things for granted." Indeed, for some racialized individuals, the experience of racial profiling has come to be normalized; it is an accepted or expected part of their lives that they believe they cannot do anything about (OHRC 2003: 41).

In the days following the release of the OHRC report, *Paying the Price: The Human Cost of Racial Profiling,* senior police officials responded with denials. Chief Fantino, for instance, deemed the report to be "totally divorced from the reality of today." Responding to a recommendation of the Commission that police services should install cameras in police cruisers so that interactions between the police and the public could be monitored, the police chief remarked, "I don't believe our police are so corrupt, so dishonest, so racist, that we need to have body packs on them, cameras on their back and watchdogs at everything they do" (cited in Tanovich 2003–4: 909). The chief also filed a Freedom of Information request to obtain the full names of people who had complained to the Commission (Sewell 2010: 77).

MERE "ANECDOTES"?

Law enforcement and public officials were not the only ones to express criticism of the OHRC's report. Criminologist Gabor (2004) deemed the data on which the Commission based its conclusion about the pervasiveness of racial profiling in the province to be mere "anecdotes." In Gabor's view, the Commission was treating "purported (rather than documented) bias displayed by individuals interchangeably with 'profiling,' a term that suggests a systemic bias practiced in a widespread manner by members of a profession or organization against an entire group. It is quite a leap from the first scenario to the second" (Gabor 2004: 462).

Gabor's critique was also directed at a study conducted by Wortley and Tanner (2003, 2005) involving a survey of 3,400 Toronto high-school students about their experiences with police. More than 50 percent of the Black students (474) surveyed reported being stopped by police two or more times over a two-year period. Of the almost 1,300 white students interviewed, 22.7 percent said they were stopped by police over the same period. Similarly, over 40 percent of Black students claimed that they had been physically searched by police in the previous two years, compared to 17 percent of their white counterparts.

In taking into account criminal activity, drug use, gang memberships, and leisure activities, the statistical relationship between race and police stop and search practices actually got stronger, suggesting that good behaviour does not shield minority youth from unwanted police attention. According to Wortley and Tanner (2003: 372):

> Multivariate analysis revealed that racial differences in police stop and search practices were actually greatest among students with low levels of criminal behaviour. For example, 34% of the black students who had not engaged in any type of criminal activity still reported that they had been stopped by the police on two or more occasions in the previous two years, compared to only 4% of white students in the same behavioural category. Similarly 23% of black students with no deviant behaviour reported that they had been searched by the police, compared to only 5% of whites who reported no deviance.

These researchers interpreted their findings to mean that racial profiling does indeed exist in Toronto. Their conclusions went even further to suggest that racial profiling led to an increased likelihood of Black people being caught breaking the law as compared to white people carrying out similar forms of criminal activity. As an example, they found that 65 percent of the Black drug dealers in their high-school study reported being arrested "at some time in their lives," compared to only 35 percent of the white drug dealers (2003: 373).

Like Gabor, Gold (2003: 391) was similarly critical of the use of "anecdotes," arguing that this kind of evidence relates more to "beliefs" than it does to "facts." In Gold's view, even the Wortley and Tanner study was faulty in this regard: "Such surveys simply measure opinions and claims, not facts. They are anecdotes in bulk" (2003: 397). As Gabor (2004: 463) maintained:

> Ethnic or racial "profiling" must be documented empirically, rather than through anecdotes. The evidence must show that a dispro-portionate emphasis on minorities or minority communities, in a particular context, is unwarranted; that is, that it is not supported by the official crime or survey data available. Also, such evidence should include recruitment data, training materials, interviews with police personnel, internal documents, and other organizational sources.

One of the difficulties with this position is the problem of gaining access to the kinds of data that Gabor identified. Police departments, like other sectors of the criminal justice system, are notoriously reluctant to give access to such information. To carry out its analysis, for instance, the *Star* had to make a Freedom of Information application to gain access to the CIPS. More significantly, Gabor's position suggests that people's experiences of everyday racism — cast as mere "anecdotes" — are not pertinent to an understanding of the issue. In other words, his position privileges the "truth" of the criminal justice system and its personnel and disparages the standpoints of those who are subject to unwarranted police actions. While Gabor (2004: 463) suggested that "external studies" were also required because "studies that rely exclusively on police data to show that minori-ties are over-represented in certain crimes are vulnerable to the criticism that these data reflect biased practices in the first place," he did not indicate what data those "external studies" could draw upon (given that "anecdotal evidence" was so roundly dismissed).

As the Commission on Systemic Racism noted, quantitative studies are often seen as "more objective and reliable than other ways of establishing systemic racism" (Ontario 1995: 58). Nevertheless, these methods also have their limits. As Marian Fitzgerald warns, an overreliance on quantitative methods may lead people to think too narrowly about racism:

> Once we try to reduce [racism] to a set of discrete, measurable components we have already lost its essence. What is racial ... is not only multifaceted, it arises and manifests itself differently in differ-ent places at different times for different groups. ... It is not a "thing" of itself but is produced variously by a wide range of interactions between combinations of factors .... What produces a racial result

for one group in one situation at one time may comprise none of the elements which produce a racial result for another group in a different situation at another time or in a different place. (Fitzgerald cited in Ontario 1995: 58)

Similarly, Simon Holdaway (1997) notes that regression analysis has become one of the primary means of determining the extent to which racialized factors are part of an explanation of offending and victimization rates amongst different racialized groups. Like other research methods, regression analysis makes certain assumptions about the social phenomena being studied. With regard to race, the assumption is made that it is "an object that can be studied" (1997: 385); race is conceptualized "as a discrete variable, an object arrested in time and space that can be disconnected from other apparent, objective 'non-racial' explanators" (1997: 385). Rather, "interrelated factors frame relationships between groups defined by racialized criteria. They constitute and sustain the structure of racialized relations" (1997: 386). As such, Holdaway argues, "Race cannot therefore be straightforwardly isolated as a discrete, statistical variable." The tendency of much criminological research to objectify race and regard it as a separate variable within the criminal justice system "fails to take adequate account of the historical and continuing social structural, cultural and other constraints that sustain racialized relations.... Furthermore, the use of regression analysis fails to place race within the world of mundane social relationships, extracting it from the everyday to the reified world of criminological positivism" (1997: 387).

THE KINGSTON STUDY

At the same time as concerns about racial profiling became prominent in Toronto, an incident in Kingston, Ontario, in March 2001 drew the attention of the media. It involved two Black youths, brothers aged seventeen and twelve, who were sitting in a Mercedes-Benz with a white teenage girl. The car, rented by the boys' father, was parked outside an apartment complex while the father was inside making a brief visit with a friend. A woman living in the complex spotted the car and its occupants. The woman had been assaulted by a Black man and left for dead and was now in a witness protection program. Thinking that the man who attacked her was in the vehicle, she phoned 911.

Responding to the operator's questions about the suspects and their identity, the woman acknowledged that she could not positively identify the individuals. Still, she said, "You know, I'm sure there's not a lot of black people running around in Mercedes in Kingston … who dress like, like the hip-hop style, driving a $60,000 car." The Kingston police responded quickly, surrounding the car with their guns drawn. As law professor David Tanovich puts it in his account, "One by one, the occupants were ordered out, told to get on their knees, handcuffed, and placed in the police cruiser" (2006: 78).

After intervention by the boys' frantic father, the youth were released at the scene. Police offered no apology to the traumatized youth or to their families. Both families of the youth lodged a formal complaint with the Kingston Police Department. They questioned the degree of force used and whether the race of the boys was a factor in the incident. An independent investigation cleared the officers of charges that they had used excessive force in the takedown. There was also a finding of no basis for the claim that race and racism had played a role in the officers' response. While Kingston Police Chief William Closs concurred that the incident was dealt with according to police protocol, he did concede that the officers involved should have extended an apology at the scene.

In the spring of 2003, the older brother, now nineteen years old, was again confronted by Kingston police as he was walking home from an evening basketball game with a friend (who was also Black). As Stephanie Simpson (2010: 5) tells it:

> A Kingston police officer, responding to an anonymous report of suspicious persons wearing dark clothes and looking into car windows, stopped the two youth and demanded to speak to them. When the youth refused to co-operate with the officer by not removing their hands from their pockets, the officer drew his weapon and called for back-up. Once again, both young men were found innocent of any wrongdoing and released at the scene.

These two incidents — in combination with the public attention on racial profiling following the *Star*'s series — prompted Police Chief Closs to take action. He became the first police chief in Canada to ban racial profiling (Tanovich 2006). In addition, the Police Chief retained the services of criminologist Scot Wortley to initiate a data collection project to "test the hypothesis that police officers treat people equally as they exercise wide margins of individual, operational discretion by initiating non-casual contacts with citizens" (Closs and McKenna 2006: 145).

From October 1, 2003, to September 30, 2004, Kingston police officers were instructed to complete a contact card whenever they stopped a civilian and questioned them in a non-casual manner. They were to record the race, age, and sex of the person stopped, and the location, reasons for the stop, and final disposition. The project (see Closs and McKenna 2006) was driven by three main questions. Are police more likely to stop racial minority citizens than stop white citizens? Are racial minority citizens stopped for different reasons than white people are? Are the outcomes of minority stops different from the outcomes of stops involving white citizens? The resulting data set consisted of 10,114 cases. About two-thirds of the stops were of pedestrians; one-third of the people were in vehicles. Using Census data as a benchmark, Wortley's analysis found:

- Black male residents of Kingston between the ages of 15 and 24 were three times more likely to be stopped and questioned by the Kingston police than people from other racial backgrounds;
- Black over-representation is greater for pedestrian stops than for vehicle stops;
- While Aboriginal people were over-represented in pedestrian stops but under-represented in vehicle stops, their over-representation is eliminated once controls for individuals who are stopped on multiple occasions are introduced;
- Males and young people, regardless of race, are more likely to be stopped by police than women and older people;
- There were no major racial differences in the reasons for police stops or in case dispositions;
- Black people were over-represented in all reasons for stops and case-outcome categories. (Closs and McKenna 2006: 150-51)

In contrast to the negative response of Toronto's Police Chief Fantino to the *Star* analysis, Kingston Police Chief Closs responded to these findings by issuing an apology: "Especially to the black community and the aboriginal community where there's disparities, we apologize. I apologize." The Police Chief went on to say, "What we're doing wrong if we're doing anything wrong is systemic and that's my problem. So I apologize to the black community, the aboriginal community and we'll do better" (CTV News 2005). Closs became an advocate for "bias-free policing," that is, where decisions are "based on reasonable suspicion or probable grounds rather than stereotypes about race, religion, ethnicity, gender or other prohibited grounds" (Closs and McKenna 2006: 146).

As Simpson (2010: 7–8) notes, while the findings from the Kingston data collection project probably offered some validation to the problem of racial bias that the Black youth and his family had been complaining about for years, the report had little impact on his everyday life. Several months after the report's release in May 2005, this same youth was surrounded by police cruisers outside of his home and charged with an "out-of-sight" traffic violation.

THE *TORONTO STAR* REDUX

In February 2010 the *Toronto Star* published a second series of articles on race and crime using police data from the period 2003 to 2008 (Rankin 2010a, 2010b, 2010c; Bruser 2010). The newspaper had submitted a request to the Toronto Police Service Board in May 2003 asking for data on police stops so that it could update its 2002 report. The Board refused to release the information. The *Star* took the matter to arbitration, where it won the right to obtain the data, but the Board appealed the decision to the courts, where it was victorious, and the *Star* appealed. The matter was finally heard by the Ontario appeal court, which ordered the police to release the data in January 2009.

In addition to the CIPS, the *Star* gained access to the Master Names Index (MANIX), a database of records gathered from contact cards filled out by police officers in mostly non-criminal encounters with the public. The cards include details on the appearance, age, sex, location, mode of transportation, and skin colour of the person stopped, as well as information on the person's associates. The police use these cards to link people and find witnesses and suspects in later crimes. Between 2003 and 2007 Toronto police filled out 1.5 million contact cards detailing encounters with 1.1 million individuals. In 2008 the Field Information Reports (FIRs) replaced MANIX as the repository for contact card data. While using the same details from the contact cards as the MANIX, the FIRs now also include data on reasons for stop (for example, general investigation, loitering, or traffic stop). From late 2007 to the end of 2008, the police filled out 315,000 contact cards covering 242,000 individuals (*Toronto Star* 2010a).

The *Star*'s analysis of the CIPS data found that the patterns described in its 2002 analysis remained. As in the earlier analysis, the paper used Census data of the Toronto population as a baseline for making comparisons between racialized groups. The analysts acknowledged, "Making benchmark comparisons with the general population can be problematic, but it is the only available framework" (*Toronto Star* 2010a: 3). As in 2002, the analysis of the 2003–8 CIPS data found that Black drivers were much more likely to be ticketed for out-of-sight traffic offences than whites were, and Black people were still more likely to be held for bail when facing a simple drug possession charge. Blacks were charged for criminal and drug offences and ticketed for certain traffic offences at an overall rate of three times their baseline population in Census data. They were also more likely to have been arrested or ticketed more than once (*Toronto Star* 2010a: 4).

The contact card data, which had never before been analyzed, added a new dimension to the investigation of racial profiling. The *Star's* analysis found that in relation to their proportion in the Toronto population (8.4 percent), Black people were three times more likely to be carded by police, whereas the percentage of white people carded was about the same as their percentage in the population (53.1 percent). Young males of every skin colour were disproportionately documented, but Black males between the ages of fifteen and twenty-four were carded at a rate 2.5 times higher than were white males of the same age. Significantly, four out of five people carded by police in 2008 had not been arrested and charged in the previous five years. As well, the areas of the city that had a higher percentage of whites in the population were also the ones in which Black people were most likely to be overrepresented, suggesting that police were more likely to be suspicious of Black people when they were "out of place" (*Toronto Star* 2010a).

In contrast to the police response to the 2002 *Star* articles — which involved vehement denials that racial profiling was occurring — Toronto Police Chief Bill Blair, who had taken over from Julian Fantino in 2005, was more willing to acknowledge the existence of racial profiling:

> I'm not suggesting for a moment that bias can't be a factor here. We're only human beings. Bias can affect any of our decision making, and we've just got to be aware. You have to know that that's a possibility.... We're not trying to make any excuses for this. We recognize that bias in police decision making is a big, big issue for us, and so we're working really hard on it. (*Toronto Star* 2010b)

Still, Blair was more reticent when it came to the matter of the police practice of completing contact cards on people who were not involved in criminal activity. Contact cards, he maintained, were merely a way for police officers to "get to know" a neighbourhood (Rankin 2010a) and to gather information that might be useful when criminal events do happen to occur. Blair admitted, "We don't fill out those cards for everybody," and noted that police targeted racialized neighbourhoods on the basis that those were the areas with the highest level of victimization (*Toronto Star* 2010b). Although mindful that racialized youth were likely to perceive carding as a form of harassment, the Police Chief defended this practice of "intelligence gathering":

> If there's 10 kids on the corner, the first time you go into that neighbourhood, or a first time a car pulls into that neighbourhood, and you talk to those 10 kids, you fill out the contact cards, nine of those kids are great, fine, they're not a problem, they might be pissed at us, quite frankly, because they think they've been stopped and been treated unfairly…. We understand the perception of those young people: the police are asking me this because they think I'm a bad guy. And we've got to be sensitive to that, and I understand that thinking entirely, and so we've got to explain ourselves, what we're actually doing there. (*Toronto Star* 2010b)

The police practice of keeping contact cards has come to the attention of the judiciary. In a 2004 Ontario court case, Justice Harry Laforme referred to the practice:

> Although I do not dispute that [contact] cards might well be a useful and proper investigative tool for the police, in my view the manner in which the police currently use them make them somewhat menacing…. This kind of daily tracking of the whereabouts of persons — including many innocent law-abiding persons — has an aspect to it that reminds me of former government regimes that I am certain all of us would prefer not to replicate. (Cited in Sewell 2010: 79–80)

Police may well be inclined to justify carding as "good police work" because it provides a basis for finding potential witnesses and suspects when crime breaks out. But that rationale is most likely cold comfort for people living in racialized neighbourhoods — people forced to abide by the practice on a daily basis.

FROM RACIAL PROFILING TO RACIALIZED POLICING

Encounters between racialized groups and the police in Ontario, then, have often been framed within the context of racial profiling. Moreover, much of the focus of the racial profiling debate has concentrated on the "driving while Black" practice — on the police decision to stop and search racialized individuals.

The issue of "driving while Black" has been raised in other provinces. On June 4, 2008, Robert Wilson, a thirty-five-year-old African-Canadian minister and rapper known as "Fresh I.E.," was in his Chrysler 300 with a passenger — a Black youth protégé he mentors — and used a Starbucks drive-through to get a coffee. Apparently he forgot part of this order and returned for a second time. That was when an officer, spotting him, became suspicious and decided to run a licence plate check. Either the wrong licence plate was entered or the results from the check were misinterpreted; the result was that the vehicle was reported as stolen.

Several police cruisers converged on Wilson's car, boxing it in at a red-light intersection. Approaching the vehicle with weapons drawn, police removed Wilson and his passenger from the car. The officers forced Wilson to the ground, emptied his pockets, handcuffed him, and placed him in the back of a police cruiser. Meanwhile Wilson was telling them that he owned the vehicle. The officers apparently laughed at him when he told them he was a minister. Some fifteen minutes elapsed before the officers checked Wilson's identification and found that he was, in fact, the registered owner of the vehicle. Wilson and his young passenger were released and the officers offered an apology.

Feeling humiliated and wronged by the incident, Wilson reported it to the media. The following day, in response, Winnipeg Police Chief Keith McCaskill issued a statement admitting that his officers had made a mistake. Still, the Police Chief was adamant that the incident was not a case of racial profiling, but rather of "human error." Although Wilson accepted the apology he maintained that racism was the underlying issue. This was not the first time that he had been targeted by police. In the previous year he had been stopped by police officers five times. Wilson said he was making his story public in an attempt to "let the public know that this is happening" and "to be a voice for people who regularly experience racial stereotyping" (cbc News 2008a).

The decision by police to define an expensive vehicle with two Black occupants as "suspicious" raises concerns about the police practice of profiling. Nevertheless, the practice is only part of the puzzle of racialized groups' encounters with police. While some writers have maintained that racial profiling is "another word for racism or racialization" (Tator and Henry 2006: 8) and "a manifestation of systemic racism" (Tanovich 2003–4), the use of the term has a decidedly individualized focus; specifically, on the exercise of discretion by individual police officers. What is missing is the need to set the issue within the broader dynamics involved in the encounters between racialized groups and the police as an institution. "Racialized policing" implicates that broader context.

Policing and police work do not occur in a social vacuum. Given that race and racialization — defined earlier as the production of difference, the process of constructing racial categories, identities, and meanings — exist in the wider society, it is unreasonable to presume that the practice of policing will be an exception. We need to uncover, therefore, the ways in which race and racialization are implicated in what Holdaway (1997: 384) calls the "mundane processes and related ideas that are part of organizational life." To do so involves situating policing within its broader societal context.

Drawing upon the work of Richard Ericson (1982), I argue that a primary purpose of policing is the "reproduction of order." Moreover, given the existing dynamics of race and racialization, the "order" that the police are charged with reproducing is decidedly "raced" (as well as gendered and classed). It is in the process of surveilling the social spaces that they are assigned to govern that race and racialization are put into everyday policing practices as officers bring to bear the cultural frames of reference or stocks of knowledge that inform their work.

Policing and the Reproduction of Order

In both the public imagination and official discourse, the images of police as "crime fighters" and "law enforcers" dominate. Media portrayals (such as the popular television shows *Cops* and *Law and Order*) regularly feature these images. Police departments use them to justify more personnel, more equipment, and more enabling legislation. In the minds of most police officers, "real" police work is crime work, a view that is also endorsed by their organizations. In commenting on police culture, Eugene Paoline (2003: 202) states, "Traditionally, police training, the creation of specialized divisions, the focus on crime statistics, and most importantly, performance evaluation and promotion, all reinforce the law enforcement orientation."

Of the different positions within a modern police department, patrol work is "by far the biggest assignment in policing" (Bayley 2005: 141).

Police officers, working alone or in pairs, and either in cruisers or on foot (and sometimes bicycles), patrol the various districts of an urban area. In his survey of twenty-eight police forces in five different countries, David Bayley found that 65 percent of officers in the United States are assigned to patrol work, with 64 percent in Canada, 56 percent in England and Wales, 54 percent in Australia, and 40 percent in Japan. Much of this work is in response to calls from the public because "over 90 per cent of the work of patrol officers is generated by dispatch" (Bayley 2005: 141, 142). While patrol work makes up the bulk of policing assignments, other tasks include criminal investigation, regulation of motor vehicle traffic, and administration. Among the modern police departments that Bayley studied, "About 60 per cent of police personnel patrol and respond to requests for service, 15 per cent investigate crime, 9 per cent regulate traffic and 9 per cent administer" (2005: 148).

Although police officers may view fighting crime as their main purpose, research reveals that very little of the work of patrol officers has to do with crime. In Britain and the United States, as Bayley (2005: 142) shows, only a small percentage of calls to the police — somewhere between 15 and 20 percent — are about crime; and often police who respond to initial reports of crime do not find that a crime has been committed. As Bayley concludes, "The real proportion of requests to the police that involve crime" may be somewhere in the range of 7 to 10 percent. Patrol officers spend little time on making arrests, and most of the crime that they deal with is minor in nature. As John Sewell (2010: 10) notes, "The average Canadian police officer can expect to make seven or eight criminal arrests a year, or one arrest every six or seven weeks. The majority of these crimes involve property, not violence to a person."

Nevertheless, Egon Bittner (2005) maintains that arrest statistics are a poor indicator of the nature of police work. He also takes issue with the view that police officers are simply engaged in the rote application of law. Police, according to Bittner, are not mere "functionaries of the law." They do not simply "walk around, respond to service demands, or intervene in situations, with the provisions of the penal code in mind, matching what they see with some title or another, and deciding whether any particular apparent infraction is serious enough to warrant being referred for further process." While police on occasion do simply apply the appropriate law to a situation, "in their routine work," Bittner says, they are usually using the provisions of the law "as a means for attaining other objectives" (2005: 158). In a similar vein, Ericson suggests that police use the law according to the other forms of social control that are available and can be used effectively.

> For the patrol police, this is particularly the case in interpersonal disputes and problems of public order and decorum. When all else fails or is deemed likely to fail, the officer decides he must remove one party in the conflict from the situation, and consequently he arrests someone. A specific infraction with a clearly applicable law does not determine the arrest, but rather *the law is used to make the arrest to handle the situation*. (Ericson 1982: 14; emphasis added)

If, as research has shown, very little of the activity of police patrol work involves fighting crime, and if police are not simply law enforcers or mere "functionaries of the law" in the work they undertake, then what *is* their main purpose?

Given that police regularly make house calls and are available around the clock, they are called upon to attend to all manner of social problems and issues. Research findings suggest that police are more likely to be engaged in "social work" than in crime-fighting or law enforcement activities; these findings have been taken as evidence that the nature of police work needs to be re-envisioned to better reflect the reality of the police role in contemporary societies. Bittner (2005: 165) argues that equating the work of police officers with that of other social service providers is a mistake because "the service they perform involves the exercise of a unique competence they do not share with anyone else in society." As Bittner notes, police are typically attuned to respond to circumstances that involve "something-that-ought-not-to-be-happening-and-about-which-someone-had-better-do-something-now!" In particular, what separates the police from other service providers is that their work "consists of coping with problems in which force *may have to be used*" (2005: 165). Indeed, as Philip Stenning and his colleagues (2009: 98) remind us, "Police organizations are not commonly called 'police *forces*' for no reason." While police departments may vary in the styles of policing they adopt — including the more recent turn to a community policing model (see, for example, Fielding 1995, 2005; Rosenbaum 1994; and Chaco and Nancoo 1993) — what ultimately distinguishes the police as an organization is the authority to use force.

But to what end is this authority to use force directed? In his now classic study, Ericson develops the argument that "patrol police are essentially a vehicle in the 'reproduction of order.'" Their mandate is "to transform troublesome, fragile situations back into a normal or efficient state whereby the ranks in society are preserved." But as Ericson clarifies, "It is not the mandate of the police to produce a 'new' order." Rather, "their sense of order and the order they seek to reproduce are that of the status quo." As well, Ericson specifies: "The term 'reproduction' implies that order is not simply transmitted in an unproblematic manner but is worked at through processes of conflict, negotiation, and subjection" (1982: 7).

Ericson's formulation has relevance for situating policing within the context of race and racialization, that is, as racialized policing. While the order that police are assigned to reproduce will differ in certain historical periods and between societies, it will nonetheless be an order *of a particular kind*. In other words, the very order that police are consigned to reproduce can be a racialized one. Drawing on Omni and Winant's (1994) notion of racial formation, with its focus on how racial projects work to produce race at the level of cultural representation (that is, as a descriptor of group or individual identity, social issues, and experience) and on how particular institutional arrangements are organized along racial lines, racialized policing can be said to constitute one of the projects through which race is interpreted and given meaning and the means by which the racialized order of a society is reproduced.

But this notion of racialized policing requires more texture. How is race interpreted and given meaning in the everyday, routine practices of policing? Stated differently, what are the cultural frames of reference or stocks of knowledge that police draw upon in the reproduction of a racialized order?

The Culture of Policing

Within the vast literature on policing, the most common way of analyzing police work has been through the lens of "police culture." In this view police work is typically seen as an occupation that, like other occupational groups, has developed a cultural repertoire of formal and informal rules and shared beliefs about how the work of the organization is to be done. It is through the process of socialization into this occupational culture that new recruits are said to learn the elements of the job. As Paoline (2003: 199) notes, however, "If one were to ask about the nature of police culture, one would find that there are many different definitions and interpretations." Paul Manning (1989: 360), for instance, defines police culture as the "accepted practices, rules, and principles of conduct that are situationally applied, and generalized rationales and beliefs." Robert Reiner (1992) equates police culture with the values, norms, perspectives and craft rules that inform police conduct. Despite these variations, the emphasis is on how the work environment of policing produces the distinctive world view of the police officer.

In his classic book *Justice without Trial*, Jerome Skolnick (1975) referred to this world view as the "policeman's working personality." Skolnick (1975: 42) suggested, "The police, as a result of combined features of their social situation, tend to develop ways of looking at the world distinctive to themselves." He saw the police officer's working personality as contoured by two elements associated with the job: danger and authority. While the element of danger makes an officer especially attentive to signs indicating a potential for violence and law-breaking, the element of authority separates the officer from the civilian world. Together, these elements create social isolation, and a corresponding social solidarity among officers.

While police work may involve a distinctive world view, police culture is not "monolithic, universal nor unchanging" (Reiner 1992: 109). Given the hierarchical structure of police organizations, differences will exist — for example, between "street cop" culture and "management cop" culture. As well, officers are not simply "passive or manipulated learners" of police culture (Chan 1996: 111). In attending to these issues, Clifford Shearing and Richard Ericson argue that rather than simply being socialized into and guided by the rules of the police culture, officers are active participants in the construction of the culture in their everyday practices through the constant telling of police stories.

> In their street talk police officers use stories to represent to each other the way things are, not as statements of fact but as cognitive devices used to gain practical insight into how to do the job of policing. For them the appropriate criteria for evaluating stories is not their truth value in a scientific sense but rather whether the knowledge they capture "works." Such stories, be they told in words or in action or via spectacles, capture the sedimented residue of generations of police experience and convey it in a form that police officers can capture and use to construct their actions on an ongoing basis. (Shearing and Ericson 1991: 491–92)

For Shearing and Ericson, then, police culture is more akin to a storybook than a rule book, "a tool kit used in the production of order." These stories enable police officers to make decisions "on a moment-to-moment basis, often without a moment's reflection." They provide a way of seeing by constructing a "vocabulary of precedents" that officers use in their daily work. "Like biblical parables and legends police stories provide directions for being a police officer, guidance as to how officers should experience the world if they are to act as police officers within it" (1991: 485, 487, 490, 491).

Holdaway (1997) notes that while race is not a discrete category in the culture of policing, mundane features of the rank-and-file occupational culture operate to sustain processes of racialization. In this respect, one way in which race invades the culture of policing is in relation to the ever-present concern with danger. While much of police work may be mind-numbingly monotonous, as police spend considerable time waiting around for "something-that-ought-not-to-be-happening" to occur, the *potential* for danger or for violence to break out is always present. As Bittner (2005) notes, in determining whether a situation is, in fact, one where "someone-had-better-do-something," police officers draw upon their stock of knowledge — their storybook — about particular persons, places, and past events. Skolnick (1975: 45) suggests that police officers develop "a perpetual shorthand to identify certain kinds of people as symbolic assailants, that is, as persons who use gesture, language, and attire that the policeman has come to recognize as a prelude to violence." Because of the ever-present threat of danger, then, police officers develop a heightened sensitivity towards those individuals whom they consider to be the "usual suspects," opening the way to form judgments about, say, particular racialized groups. Skolnick (1975), for instance, found that police officers in the U.S. city he studied came to identify the Black man with danger.

In the same way that racialization enters into constructions of "usual suspects," however, it also informs constructions about particular places and spaces.

Racialized Spaces

Sherene Razack (2002) and her colleagues have explored how "place becomes race," that is, "how the constitution of spaces reproduces racial hierarchies" (Razack 2007: 74). Contrary to familiar, everyday notions, spaces do not simply "evolve, are filled up with things, and exist either prior to or separate from the subjects who imagine and use them" (2007: 76). Rather, spaces are abidingly *social*. They have not only a materiality in that they connect to the social relations that produce and use them but also a symbolic meaning attached to them. Spaces can variously come to represent places of home, work, or leisure, sites of comfort and the familiar, or places of danger and disorder. Together, the material and the symbolic "work through each other to constitute a space" (2007: 77). From this standpoint, racialization processes can be directly experienced as spatial:

> When police drop Aboriginal people outside the city limits leaving them to freeze to death, or stop young Black men on the streets or in malls, when the eyes of shop clerks follow bodies of colour, presuming them to be illicit, when workplaces remain relentlessly white in the better paid jobs and fully "coloured" at the lower levels, when affluent areas of the city are all white and poorer areas are mostly of colour, we experience the spatiality of the racial order in which we live. (Razack 2007: 75–76)

As such, it is through everyday routines and experiences that space "comes to perform something in the social order, permitting certain actions and prohibiting others. Spatial practices organize social life in specific ways" (2007: 77).

In reporting on his study of the encounters between Black youth and police in six Ontario cities, Carl James commented on the importance of "the street" as a social space for marginalized youth:

> The streets serve many purposes. For the car owner or drivers, the street may be the "public" asphalted path used to drive from one place to another and/or a place to park one's vehicle. For pedestrians, particularly those with no alternatives, the street, or more specifically, the sidewalk, is much more. It is a public path to move about, get from one place to another, and a social space; probably the most available, accessible and relatively non-restrictive social space in which to meet, "hang out," and converse. For some "street users," particularly young, working-class apartment dwellers, because of their limited access and opportunities to alternative leisure and recreational spaces, the sidewalk, the street, the street corner and the mall become an integral part of daily living and a part of cultural life. (James 1998: 162)

Nevertheless, while "the street" constitutes a meaningful part of everyday life for many marginalized youth, their presence and visibility in that space make them ready targets for heightened police surveillance and intervention. From a police perspective, youth who congregate on the streets are considered to be "doing nothing" or "up to no good." As a result they are regularly stopped and questioned. Many of the Black youth that James interviewed reported that these regular stops emanated from the notion that "all Blacks look alike" (1998: 167). According to James, "In policing Black youth — stopping, questioning and harassing them, and placing the onus on them to prove that they are not the 'suspects' that police seek — law enforcement agents engage in a process of othering which in turn contributes to their criminalization of the youth" (1998: 172).

In reproducing order, then, police work involves not just the policing of individuals but the policing of spaces. Over time, certain spaces come to be identified as places in which crime and violence are most likely to occur. For instance, inner-city communities populated by impoverished Aboriginal people and new immigrants are more likely to be seen as "disordered" and "dangerous" places, whereas suburban white middle-class neighbourhoods — with their tree-lined streets, manicured lawns, and spacious homes — become spaces of "civility" and "respectability." In carrying out their task as reproducers of order, then, police concentrate their attention and activity on the former and not on the latter racialized spaces. In the process, they help to constitute and normalize particular spaces — and the people found within them — as "disorderly" and "dangerous."

MOVING FORWARD

Racial profiling has been a contentious issue in Ontario over the past two decades. While attention to the phenomenon does expose some of the ways in which race and racialization enter into the encounters between racialized individuals and police officers, we need to broaden our focus beyond the interpersonal level to include the ways in which race and racism play out in institutional practices and systemic processes. The notion of racialized policing does that. It offers the potential to move us away from arguments that rest on simplistic claims that "police are racist bigots" or the problem is one of "a few bad apples" and enables a better appreciation of the complexity of the matter of encounters between racialized groups and the police.

The debates, government inquiries, and criminological research on the issue of racial profiling have focused mainly on the experiences of African Canadians. One notable exception, however, is the report of the Ontario Human Rights Commission (2003), which did include a special section on the impact of racial profiling on the Aboriginal community. As the Commission acknowledged, "Aboriginal peoples in Canada occupy different political, historical and individual realities from other Canadians" (2003: 55). Aboriginal people are not just another "minority group" or "ethnic group," and characterizing them that way fails to take into account the special place they occupy in the nation's history as the original peoples of the land. The historical treatment of Aboriginal people, including their encounters with police, is also unique and has played an important role in the colonial project that is Canada.

Chapter Three

COLONIALISM PAST AND PRESENT

Colonialism is not simply a historical artifact that has no bearing on contemporary events. As Patricia Monture (2007: 207) advises, it is "a living phenomenon…. The past impacts on the present, and today's place of Aboriginal peoples in Canadian society cannot be understood without a well-developed historical understanding of colonialism and the present-day trajectories of those old relationships." Encounters with the police call for this same understanding, this same deep need for context. Nevertheless, as the Commissioners for the Royal Commission on Aboriginal Peoples (RCAP 1996: vol. 1 chap. 3) noted, "most Canadians are simply unaware of the history of the Aboriginal presence in what is now Canada." Many Canadians, the commissioners pointed out, have "little understanding of the origins and evolution of the relationship between Aboriginal and non-Aboriginal people that have led us to the present moment."

Yet it is not so much the case that Canadians have *no* national memory of their history. Rather, as Amanda Nettelbeck and Russell Smandych (2010) point out, colonial societies such as Canada and Australia have developed particular "foundational narratives" about their histories of European settlement, including the role of frontier police forces in managing and containing the Aboriginal populations. One distinct feature of our collective imaginary — our sense of who we are as a nation — is that Canada is one of the few countries in the world to claim a police force as a national symbol. You need only visit a local tourist shop to find iconic images of the "Scarlet Riders" on everything from postcards to coffee mugs. As Peter C. Newman once proclaimed, "In Canada's case, the Mountie symbolizes not merely law and order but Canada itself" (cited in Brown and Brown 1978: 127). The officers of the Royal Canadian Mounted Police (RCMP) are so identified with the national interest that criticism of the force is akin to an unpatriotic act.

The precursor to the RCMP, the North West Mounted Police, has also been part of this national memory, especially in terms of its origins and purpose in relation to the Aboriginal people who populated the land that became known as the Northwest Territories. According to this foundational narrative, the NWMP was established in 1873 by a benevolent federal government to protect the Aboriginal population of the Northwest from whiskey traders and other outlaws and "to ensure that all the people of the Canadian North West — Indians and Métis, settlers and traders — might have the opportunity of living under a system of law impartially enforced and guaranteeing equal rights to all" (Brown and Brown 1978: 2). This Canadian experience of a benign and peaceful stance towards Aboriginal people is often contrasted to the Wild West of the U.S. experience, where the "Indians" were nearly wiped out and the law of the fast gun and lynch mob prevailed. As Nettelbeck and Smandych observe, historical sites across Western Canada keep the foundational story of the NWMP as a mediating and peacekeeping force alive. "In regional museums, monuments and murals," they say, a constant refrain is repeated: "that the NWMP provided protection to Indigenous peoples and brought law and order to the west" (2010: 369).

Apart from visiting museums and historical sites, most Canadians get their understanding of their nation's history — and of Aboriginal people — from movies and television and what they learned in school. In my own experience, early lessons about Aboriginal people came from watching Saturday-afternoon horse-opera movies and television shows featuring cowboys and Indians of the American Wild West. In this racialized narrative the cowboys were invariably the heroic "good guys" who always won out in the end against the "savage" Indians.

Other lessons came from my formal schooling. *Pages from Canada's Story* (Dickie and Palk 1957) was the text used for many years to teach countless numbers of Canadian students about our colonial past. The text presents the story of white settlement in unproblematic terms — and never mentions colonialism. When the book covers the settling of the Canadian West and the treaty process, for instance, it matter-of-factly informs students: "White settlers soon made their way in such numbers to the North-West Territories that the Indian could no longer claim the great prairie as his hunting-ground. Treaties were made with various tribes for the surrender of the land to the Government" 1957: 374). At the time the lieutenant governor of the territories was David Laird, and, as the text would have it, "Mr. Laird dealt so fairly with the Indians, and explained the treaties to them in such an understanding way, that very little trouble resulted" (1957: 374).

Pages from Canada's Story also introduces students to the role of the NWMP in the settling of the West. The officers were "messengers of law and order" (Dickie and Palk 1957: 371) known as "Red Coats." As the text explains, "The matter of uniforms was given special consideration. Someone who knew of the Indian's love of colour must have had a voice in the choice of the bright scarlet coat which later became known as the 'Queen's red,' and stood, in the eyes of the Indians, for order and justice" (1957: 370). The book emphasizes the ostensibly benevolent and paternalistic role played by this paramilitary force. Commenting on the arrival of a NWMP detachment at Fort Whoop-Up in 1874, the text quotes none other than Chief Crowfoot, leader of the Blackfoot tribe, as saying that the Redcoats "have protected us as the feathers protect the birds from the frosts of winter" (1957: 372). But it goes on: "The Indians early learned to respect the men who faced danger unafraid and whose word was never broken. 'Before you came,' said old Chief Crowfoot [who was actually only forty years old at the time] to Colonel Macleod, 'the Indian crept along. Now he is not afraid to walk erect'" (1957: 372–73). Clearly, the impression left on young minds by this history lesson was that if it were not for the arrival of the white man and his police force, Aboriginal people would have simply disappeared into the annals of time.

While we would like to think that things have changed since I received my formative schooling so many decades ago, Aboriginal scholar Susan Dion (2005) suggests otherwise. Her work with elementary school teachers and students has led her to conclude that the Canadian educational system continues to reproduce a discourse that positions Aboriginal people as a "romantic, mythical and frequently inferior Other."

> The study of Aboriginal people by Canadian school children continues to focus on how we lived prior to European contact. When attention is given to Aboriginal people in the post-contact period, it is without serious consideration of events that led to current conditions. The perspective taken suggests that the Europeans were stronger, more advanced and therefore progressed, while Aboriginal people were victims of that progress. The Europeans are not shown to be in any way responsible for the impacts on Aboriginal people. (Dion 2005: 40)

To contextualize the contemporary situation of Aboriginal people and their encounters with police, then, we first need to clarify the historical record.

Sherene Razack (2007: 74) notes, "The national mythologies of white settler societies are deeply racialized stories." For instance, one of the enduring components of Canada's foundational narrative is that explorers and settlers arrived from Europe to a *terra nullius,* an "empty land," that could be claimed and used for their own purposes. In this decidedly Eurocentric account, the original inhabitants of the land were depicted as "savages" in need of the civilizing influences of the European newcomers. Missing from this account is any recognition of the sophisticated trading and commercial exchanges, and customs and traditions practised by the various tribes that populated the space now known as Canada. Also missing is a recognition of the forms of governance that prevailed. As AJI commissioners Alvin Hamilton and Murray Sinclair (1991a: 54) note, "Before the arrival of the Europeans, Aboriginal peoples had their own laws and customary practices for maintaining peace and stability within their communities — including the use of force and ostracism to enforce social norms and the role of elders in administering those norms."

What transpired after that European arrival — which can best be described as colonialism — was, in the words of John McLeod, at its core "a lucrative commercial operation, bringing wealth and riches to Western nations through the economic exploitation of others." Developing especially through the late seventeenth and early eighteenth centuries, the seizing of "foreign" lands for settlement was in part motivated by the desire to create and control markets abroad for Western goods, as well as securing the natural resources and labour power of different lands and people at the lowest possible cost. As McLeod puts it, colonialism "was pursued for economic profit, reward and riches. Hence colonialism and capitalism share a mutually supportive relationship with each other" (2000: 7). A key characteristic of colonialism is the effort to govern the indigenous inhabitants of the occupied lands. At its heart, therefore, is the construction of unequal relations of power between the colonizers and the colonized.

Colonialism is not just the work of capitalists or the state. Joyce Green (2006) points out that the primary motivation of those immigrating to the new lands was the prospect of economic opportunities and advancements (including cheap or free land) that were not available to them in their homeland. To this extent, *all* newcomers are complicit in the colonial project: "To different degrees every colonizer is privileged, at least comparatively so, ultimately to the detriment of the colonized" (Green 2006: 512).

COLONIALISM PAST

The project of colonizing the indigenous population and constructing a white settler society began in Canada in the seventeenth century. While Aboriginal people were initially valued for their skills and knowledge, as these were indispensable to the survival of the newcomers, this power balance began to shift as more and more Europeans arrived. "By the early 19th century, Eurocanadians had made Aboriginal people a minority in their own lands," Celia Haig-Brown states. "Acting through the power of organized religion and colonial governments, Canadians insisted that Aboriginal peoples should abandon their ways, languages, spiritual and economic systems, seasonal movement to hunting and gathering places and most importantly their lands" (cited in Dion 2005: 36).

This colonial project involved a number of strategies, one of which was signing treaties that transferred large tracts of land over to the government. As the Royal Commission on Aboriginal Peoples (1996: vol. 1 chap. 8) notes, "Treaties and other agreements were, by and large, not covenants of trust and obligation but devices of statecraft, less expensive and more acceptable than armed conflict." Another colonial strategy was the passage of the Indian Act in 1876 —legislation that consolidated previous rulings and provided a national foundation "based unashamedly on the notion that Indian cultures and societies were clearly inferior to settler society" (RCAP 1996: vol. 1 chap. 8). The 1876 annual report of the Department of the Interior expressed the assimilationist and paternalistic philosophy that prevailed at the time. Indians were to be treated as "children of the state":

> Our Indian legislation generally rests on the principle, that the aborigines are to be kept in a condition of tutelage and treated as wards or children of the State.... The true interests of the aborigines and of the State alike require that every effort should be made to aid the Red man in lifting himself out of his condition of tutelage and dependence, and that is clearly our wisdom and our duty, through education and every other means, to prepare him for a higher civilization by encouraging him to assume the privileges and responsibilities of full citizenship. (Cited in RCAP 1996: vol. 1 chap. 8)

The Indian Act defined in law who was an "Indian" and specified how someone could lose status as an Indian. An Indian was legally defined as "any male person of Indian blood reputed to belong to a particular band, and any child of such person and any woman who is lawfully married to such a person" (Gibbins and Ponting 1986: 21). Under this definition, an Indian woman who married a non-Indian man ceased to be an Indian in legal terms, and both she and her children lost all claims associated with that status (for example, residence on a reserve, use of reserve property, and participation in band affairs). In contrast, a non-Indian woman who married an Indian man would gain legal status as an Indian, as would the children from that union. This provision in the Indian Act remained in effect until it was abrogated in 1985. Aboriginal people were also denied basic political rights; they did not have a legal right to vote in provincial elections in British Columbia and Newfoundland until 1949, in Quebec until 1969, and in federal elections until 1960.

In addition to replacing traditional systems of governance by a restricted form of democracy in which only men had a voice and vote, the Indian Act gave considerable power to the Indian agents, who represented the Department of Indian Affairs. Hamilton and Sinclair state:

> Each agent had full authority to conduct trials anywhere in the country involving Indians charged with violating the *Indian Act* or with certain crimes under the *Criminal Code*. As a result, the Indian agent could direct the police to prosecute "troublemakers" and then sit in judgment. The agents effectively had power over all aspects of daily life. (1991a: 64–65)

Aboriginal people also experienced considerable restrictions on their mobility. With the relinquishing of their land to the government under the treaty process, most tribes were relegated to smaller tracts of land as part of the reservation system. A pass system was imposed as early as 1885 under which Aboriginal people were prohibited from leaving their reserve without first securing written permission from the local Indian agent. While the pass system had no legislative basis and therefore could not be legally enforced, Indian agents could withhold rations for those who refused to comply, and those found off the reserve without a pass could be prosecuted for trespass under the Indian Act or for vagrancy under the Criminal Code (Hamilton and Sinclair 1991a; RCAP 1996).

To further this colonial project the government also created a number of status offences that applied only to Aboriginal peoples. An 1884 amendment to the Indian Act outlawed the Potlatch (ceremonial gift-giving) and Tamanawas (medicine or healing ceremony) and imposed sanctions of two to six months' imprisonment for those found in violation. In 1885 another amendment outlawed Sun Dances, providing for imprisonment of two to six months for violators. As Andrea McCalla and Vic Satzewich (2002) note, missionaries — tasked with the "civilizing mission" of the colonial project — saw the persistence of these cultural practices as "devil worship." One Anglican missionary wrote to the Department of Indian Affairs about his first encounter with the Blackfoot people whom he was sent to convert:

> I arrived in July when that great heathen festival, the Sun Dance, was in full swing. … The fantastic costume, of the people, the paint and feathers, the then to me foreign tongue, made my heart sink within me, and if I ever felt the hopelessness of a task set me to do it was then. (Cited in Pettipas 1995: 97)

The giveaways associated with these cultural practices were inimical to the capitalist ethic — respect for private property and pursuit of individual accumulation — that the government was endeavouring to instill in Aboriginal people. As well, the hours taken to prepare for the ceremonies were considered to be time that could be better spent engaging in more "legitimate" economic pursuits. Yet Aboriginal people were not passive bystanders to these efforts to outlaw their culture (McCalla and Satzewich 2002). Resistance took the form of holding ceremonies in secret and altering the practices to make them seem more "acceptable" to European eyes.

One plank of the colonial project that was more difficult to resist was the residential school system, which was initiated in the 1880s with the specific objective of assimilating Aboriginal people into mainstream Canadian society. Aboriginal children were forcibly removed from their homes and transported — often some distance away — to attend these large, racially segregated industrial schools. Attendance was compulsory. Indian agents were empowered to commit children under sixteen to the schools and to keep them there until they were eighteen. By way of contrast, non-Aboriginal children were not subject to compulsory schooling. Manitoba, for instance, did not introduce compulsory schooling until 1916. In addition, federal legislation passed in 1894 allowed for the arrest and conveyance to school of truant Aboriginal children, and for fines or jail terms for parents who resisted (Hamilton and Sinclair 1991a).

The government delegated this civilizing project of the residential school system to religious organizations and churches, which were given the task of transforming the children from "savages" into "citizens" by inculcating the values of Christianity and industry so that the youngsters could take up positions as "functioning" members of the emerging capitalist society. As the 1889 Annual Report of the Department of Indian Affairs explained:

> The boarding school dissociates the Indian child from the deleteri-

ous home influences to which he would otherwise be subjected. It reclaims him from the uncivilized state in which he has been brought up. It brings him into contact day to day with all that tends to effect a change in his views and habits of life. By precept and example he is taught to endeavour to excel in what will be most useful to him. (Cited in Hamilton and Sinclair 1991a: 68)

By the 1930s eighty residential schools were spread across the country, with children registered from every Aboriginal culture (RCAP 1996: vol. 1 chap. 2). Eventually, a total of 139 residential schools were in operation in Canada. Some 150,000 First Nation, Inuit, and Métis children were forced to attend the schools.

Much has been written in recent times about the residential school system, especially in the wake of revelations by survivors about the harsh treatment received at the schools (see, for example, York 1990; Hamilton and Sinclair 1991; RCAP 1996; Milloy 1999; Knockwood 2001). What we now know from this work is that conditions at the schools were abysmal; they were built with the cheapest materials, employed untrained staff, and were overcrowded due to the government's financial inducements to increase enrolments (Blackstone and Trocmé 2004). The expressed goal was to produce educated graduates, but few of the children completed the full course of study. In 1945, for example, no students were enrolled beyond Grade 8 in any of the schools (RCAP 1996: vol. 1 chap. 2). Children were poorly fed and clothed; so many of them died from preventable diseases (such as malnutrition, smallpox, and tuberculosis) that several of the schools even had their own graveyards. Physical punishment was the norm. Children were beaten for speaking their indigenous languages; those who tried to run away were shackled to their beds. Suicide attempts by the children were common. Not only were physical abuse and neglect rampant, but so too was sexual abuse — something that was never cited in all of the major reports on the residential school system and only became public knowledge once survivors began to break the silence and tell their stories (RCAP 1996: vol. 1 chap. 2).

While the effort by the European colonizers to take control over the lives of Aboriginal people involved a number of strategies, including the signing of treaties, the Indian Act, and the residential school system, the North West Mounted Police played an instrumental role in carrying out this colonial project or "civilizing mission."

The North West Mounted Police

The primary role of the NWMP — like that of other frontier police forces — was "to ensure the submission of Indigenous peoples to colonial rule" (Nettelbeck and Smandych 2010: 357). While the foundational narrative of the NWMP posits that the force was brought into being in response to the Cypress Hills Massacre in May 1873, when U.S. whiskey traders murdered several Assiniboine peoples, Lorne and Caroline Brown (1978: 10) have a different view: "This is true only in the sense that the massacre hastened the organization of the Force. The establishment of the Force had been planned and officially authorized prior to this, and the primary reason for establishing it was to control the Indian and Métis population of the North West." Prime Minister John A. Macdonald had been making plans for the policing of the Northwest since 1869. His main concern was to keep peace between Aboriginal people and settlers in order to encourage economic development.

The plans for the NWMP were approved by an order-in-council on April 6, 1870. The force was to march west with the Canadian military in 1870, but this plan was shelved with the passage of the Manitoba Act, which left the administration of justice in the hands of the new province. Plans continued, however, for controlling that part of the Northwest outside of Manitoba, particularly because government officials worried that the Métis of Manitoba would ally themselves with Aboriginal tribes farther west and take a stand against the federal government. There were also concerns that any unrest would interfere with the progress on the building of the Canadian Pacific Railway and limit plans to settle the area with immigrants. A military presence was therefore increasingly seen as necessary.

Officially established by an act of Parliament in the spring of 1873, the NWMP was "to be a semi-military body directly controlled from Ottawa, and not by the local government officials in the North West" (Brown and Brown 1978: 13). While an earlier proposal had called for the inclusion of Aboriginal people on the force (similar to what had transpired under British colonial rule in India), the Act made no special provisions for this condition. The events of the Red River "Rebellion" and the unrest following it had "convinced the authorities that the native peoples were not likely to become loyal servants of their colonial masters" (1978: 13).

While the force was not intended to be put into effect until 1874, the Cypress Hills Massacre caused the government to speed up its plans. The government's fear was that "the outrage in the Cypress Hills and other atrocities of this nature might provoke the Indians into open warfare against the whites" (Brown and Brown 1978: 13). Also of concern was the unrest generated by the prosecution of some of the activists in the Manitoba provisional government of 1869–70, with fears raised about the whereabouts and activities of Louis Riel and "the fanaticism of the French Canadian Half-breeds" (cited in Brown and Brown 1978: 14).

The first years of the NWMP were not without controversy. Members of the force encountered severe hardships — poor food, deplorable living conditions, delays in receiving wages, and bullying by officers — which led to a high rate of desertion. Concerns were raised about alcoholism and a high percentage of personnel suffering from venereal disease. In 1880 a member of Parliament from Manitoba reported on the sexual exploitation of Aboriginal women. Prostitution was apparently rampant in the vicinity of NWMP posts, and the police were spreading venereal disease among the Aboriginal population (Brown and Brown 1978: 16).

As Sarah Carter (1999: 129) notes, the NWMP "had powers that were unprecedented in the history of police forces." In addition to the power to arrest, the NWMP were granted magisterial powers: they were able to prosecute, judge, and jail an accused. The force was also charged with implementing the government's policies towards Aboriginal people. As AJI Commissioners Hamilton and Sinclair (1991a: 592) note:

> Whenever an Indian agent felt the need for assistance in enforcing government policy regarding Indian people, he called upon the Mounted Police. Indian children who ran away from residential schools were sought and returned by NWMP officers. Indian adults who left their reserves without a pass from the Indian agent were apprehended by the Mounted Police.

Given that the historical record was written largely by the white colonizers, the standpoint of Aboriginal people during this period of history remains in the shadows — and especially because Aboriginal people use oral as opposed to written narratives to communicate and learn from their own past (see RCAP 1996: vol. 1 chap. 3). Nevertheless, we do know that factors such as the virtual extinction of the buffalo, the arrival of increasing numbers of settlers, the impact of the infectious diseases that newcomers brought with them, the negative effects of the whiskey trade, and the threat of starvation all took their toll on the Aboriginal population. Due to these conditions, some of the people may well have welcomed the presence of the NWMP. Yet, as Brown and Brown (1978: 20) note, "a state of constant tension between the police and the Indian nations" was the norm, given that "the Force represented the interests who were rapidly destroying the Indian economy and way of life and was frequently called upon to protect those same interests."

This tension became even more pronounced during and after the Saskatchewan Rebellion of 1885. While the NWMP was not the cause of the rebellion (and repeatedly warned the government that unrest was likely to occur), the force participated along with regular military forces in suppressing it. The NWMP was also instrumental in apprehending and meting out punishment to the rebels, including sentences of imprisonment and the execution of Métis leader Louis Riel and eight others. Brown and Brown (1978: 22) write:

> The authorities punished Métis and Indians suspected of having supported the rebellion regardless of whether they had been tried for specific offences. They virtually wiped out the Métis as a distinct national and political group. They burned and looted their homes and destroyed their property. They withheld annuities from those Indian bands that had participated in the rebellion and confiscated their horses and arms. From that time on they made greater efforts to restrict Indians to the reserves and strictly regulated the sale of ammunition to them. Most of these punitive measures were carried out by the Mounted Police.

As Carter (1999: 161) notes, after 1885 a significant shift occurred in Euro-Canadian attitudes towards Aboriginal people: "If there was a shred of tolerance before, or the possibility of working towards a progressive partnership, it was shattered in 1885, as thereafter Aboriginal people were viewed as a threat to the property and safety of the white settlers." After 1885 government policies aimed at controlling and monitoring the lives of Aboriginal people were "pursued with great vigour" (1999: 162). During this period the pass system was implemented (accompanying the outlawing of practices and ceremonies such as the Potlatch and Sun Dance). The number of NWMP officers was greatly increased to enhance the effort to monitor and control Aboriginal people.

A tradition of active, armed violence was missing from the Canadian experience, which was notably different from that of the United States. Between 1866 and 1885 the U.S. West saw 943 military engagements

(Ennab 2010: 161). By comparison, the Canadian Northwest saw only six or seven comparable clashes, most of them taking place in the two years prior to the Métis resistance of 1885. As Ennab (2010: 186) argues, overt physical violence was replaced with compulsion and coercion:

> It was through intimidation and broken promises along with the larger colonial disciplinary system that was shaping the rationalities of the inhabitants that a few red-coated Mounties were able to coerce Aboriginal people to stay on reserves. If it was not for this, the NWMP would have needed more investment in the ongoing, armed engagements, which they could not afford, thus jeopardizing the entire colonial enterprise. Most Aboriginal people recognized that even if the NWMP were not able to "destroy" them, they were able to push them on the side to starve.

Historians have uncovered many instances in which members of the NWMP acted with fairness and concern towards Aboriginal people. But as Brown and Brown (1978: 19) argue:

> That certain individuals in the Force sympathized with the plight of the Indians and attempted to carry out a disagreeable task in as humane a manner as possible does not alter the nature of the Force and their work. Most police officials knew whose interests they served and knew that to be 'too soft on Indians' endangered their career in the Force.

As such, even though the conquest of the Canadian West was not nearly so bloody an affair as it was in the Western United States, and violence by the frontier police against the Aboriginal population was not as rife as it was in Australia (Nettelbeck and Smandych 2010), the NWMP did play a crucial role in implementing the Canadian colonial project. The NWMP, according to Brown and Brown, was "a crucial part of a conscious scheme by which powerful economic and political interests destroyed the economy and way of life of entire peoples and wrested a vast territory from its inhabitants for a pittance." Moreover, these authors argue, "Anyone who describes the role of the NWMP during this period as constituting the 'glorious foundations of a great tradition' must surely be either hopelessly naïve or lacking in moral sensitivity" (1978: 23).

The name of the North West Mounted Police was changed to the Royal North West Mounted Police (RNWMP) in 1904 in recognition of the force's service to the Empire. As settlement of the West continued, with Saskatchewan and Alberta gaining provincial status in 1905, the RNWMP acted in the capacity of a provincial police force. The modern version of the force — the Royal Canadian Mounted Police — came into being in 1920 when the RNWMP was amalgamated with the Dominion Police. During the Great Depression of the 1930s, the RCMP expanded its scope. Some of the provinces and many smaller municipalities facing financial troubles disbanded their police forces and contracted the RCMP instead. This contractual relationship continues to the present day.

This history of the NWMP, then, has a direct connection to contemporary relations between Aboriginal people and the police. As AJI commissioners Hamilton and Sinclair note, memories of the treatment at the hands of the force "linger in many communities." The history of the relationship has "coloured the perceptions Aboriginal people hold of other police forces in the province. The impact of past wrongs has been reinforced by the negative experiences of today" (1991a: 593).

Just as significant, the strategies of the colonial project laid down in the earlier period of Canadian history would have had profound and long-lasting impacts. The Indian Act of 1876 — with its decidedly paternalistic and assimilationist bent — continues to inform the lives of Aboriginal peoples. Although the Act has been repeatedly amended, its fundamental provisions have remained intact. It "still holds a symbolic but powerful grip on the thinking of Canadians" towards Aboriginal people (RCAP 1996: vol. 1 chap. 8). Similarly, residential schools had a profound and long-lasting impact. Although their phasing out began in the late 1940s, it was not until 1996 that the last federally run residential school was shut down (DIAND 2003). The generations of children who attended the schools were cut off from their families, their communities, and their cultural and spiritual teachings. Survivors were confronted with the difficult challenge of healing from years of abuse and neglect. Being deprived of healthy parenting role models also left them with diminished capacities as adults to raise and care for their own children. In the words of the AJI commissioners, "These policies have caused a wound to fester in Aboriginal communities that has left them diminished to this day" (Hamilton and Sinclair 1991a: 505).

COLONIALISM PRESENT

Colonialism has not disappeared; it has just taken on new forms in contemporary times. One of the ways in which colonialism is perpetuated is through racialized discourse. While past discourses cast Aboriginal people as "savage," "inferior," and "child-like" (and therefore in need of a civilizing influence and the benevolent paternalism of the state), more contemporary discourses include the notions of the "welfare recipient," the "drunken Indian," and the "criminal Other" (and therefore in need of heightened surveillance and control). As with discourses generally, these racialized constructions have their basis in material conditions. In contemporary times, social exclusion, poverty, violence, and alcohol use have dominated the lives of many Aboriginal people, and their overrepresentation in the criminal justice system has become a problem of large proportions.

Social Exclusion and Poverty

Social exclusion, as Grace-Edward Galabuzi (2009) notes, "is used to broadly describe the structures and the dynamic processes of inequality among groups in society, which, over time, structure access to critical resources that determine the quality of membership in society." These conditions define "the inability of certain subgroups to participate fully in Canadian life." The access to critical resources — whether social, economic, political, or cultural — arises "out of the often intersecting experiences of oppression relating to race, class, gender, disability, sexual orientation, immigrant status, and the like." Social exclusion is "also characterized by processes of group or individual isolation within and from Canadian societal institutions such as the school system, criminal justice system, health care system, as well as spatial isolation or neighbourhood segregation" (2009: 253–54).

Poverty is both a product and a cause of social exclusion, and it is also a racialized phenomenon in Canada. Being born Aboriginal means an increased likelihood of living in poverty. Almost 1.2 million people reported Aboriginal identity in the 2006 census, representing 3.8 percent of the total Canadian population (Statistics Canada 2008). In 2005 18.7 percent of Aboriginal families and 42.8 percent of unattached individuals who identified as Aboriginal experienced low income, compared to 8.4 percent of families and 28 percent of unattached individuals who were non-Aboriginal (Collin and Jensen 2009). Children and youth account for just under half (48 percent) of the Aboriginal population, and some 35 percent of Aboriginal children live with a lone parent, which means that Aboriginal adults will often be on their own, providing for a larger group of dependants than is the case for non-Aboriginal adults (Smylie 2006: 291). The poverty gap is most pronounced in the Prairie provinces. In Saskatchewan, for instance, where Aboriginal people make up 15 percent of the population, an Aboriginal person is about three and a half times more likely to be poor than is a non-Aboriginal resident (Noël 2009: 8). While conditions vary by region, if we apply the United Nations Human Development index to Aboriginal communities in Canada, they would rank 68 out of 174 nations. By comparison, Canada as a nation ranks in the eighth position (Graydon 2008).

Living conditions on many reserves have been defined as a matter of crisis proportions. Substandard and overcrowded housing is one pressing issue. In 2006, 28 percent of First Nations people were living in a home in need of major repairs, compared with just 7 percent of the non-Aboriginal population; First Nations people were five times more likely than non-Aboriginal people to live in crowded homes (Statistics Canada 2008). Access to potable water, adequate sanitation, and waste disposal services are resources that many Canadians take for granted. Yet in November 2010, 117 First Nation communities were under drinking water advisories (Campaign 2000 2010). Many reserve communities still do not have running water or sewer lines. These living conditions undermine the health of a community. Aboriginal people have shorter life expectancies and a higher risk of suffering from infectious diseases such as tuberculosis and chronic illnesses such as diabetes. The Royal Commission (RCAP 1996; vol. 3 chap. 3) found that rates of tuberculosis infection were forty-three times higher among registered Indians than among non-Aboriginal Canadians born in this country, and the incidence rate for diabetes was at least two to three times higher among Aboriginal than among non-Aboriginal people. These impoverished conditions generate a sense of hopelessness and despair. While the suicide rates vary widely among First Nations communities, the youth suicide rate in these communities is still between three and seven times greater than in Canada overall (Campaign 2000 2010).

Deteriorating social and economic conditions in many First Nations communities have prompted increased migration between First Nations communities and urban centres. As John Loxley notes, remarkably few Aboriginal people were living in urban centres such as Winnipeg up to the 1950s — perhaps "less than a dozen Indians" in 1901 "and only about 700 Métis in the city of 42,340." By 1921, 69 Indians lived in Winnipeg, and by 1951 only 210, in a city with a population of 354,000. "The Métis were invisible" (Loxley 2010: 151). As of 2006, however, over half (54 percent) of the Aboriginal population of Canada now live in urban centres (Statistics Canada 2008).

Conditions for Aboriginal people living in these urban settings are no better than on reserves. Aboriginal residents of urban areas are more than twice as likely to live in poverty as are non-Aboriginal residents. In 2000, for instance, 55.6 percent of urban Aboriginal people lived below the poverty line compared to 24.5 percent of non-Aboriginal urban residents (NCCAH 2009–10). In 2006 almost half (49 percent) of First Nations children living off-reserve and nearly one-third (32 percent) of Métis children were members of low-income families (Collin and Jensen 2009: 19). The highest concentration of urban Aboriginal people is in the inner-city communities of major cities in the Western provinces. Winnipeg has the highest concentration of Aboriginal people in Canada (Statistics Canada 2008), and most of them live in the inner city. While Aboriginal people make up 10 percent of Winnipeg's population, they constitute 25 percent of those living in poverty (MacKinnon 2009: 30). Unemployment explains some of this disparity. As RCAP (1996) notes: "Aboriginal people living in urban centers fare somewhat better than reserve residents in gaining employment, but their unemployment rate is still two and a half times the unemployment rate of non-Aboriginal people, and their total annual income from all sources lags behind by 33 per cent."

Jim Silver (2006a: 17) observes that "the spatial distribution of Aboriginal people in cities... parallels their spatial distribution outside urban centres." That is, just as they have historically been confined to rural reserves, now in cities they are being set apart from mainstream Canadian life. Their "move to the city is too often a move from one marginalized community to another." Nevertheless, much like the assimilationist policies of an earlier era, the difficulties encountered by Aboriginal people who have migrated to urban centres are often interpreted as being not the result of their social exclusion but of their own failure to successfully integrate into mainstream capitalist society.

Colonialism has produced the social and economic marginalization of Aboriginal people in contemporary Canadian society — something that even the Supreme Court of Canada acknowledges: "Many aboriginal people are victims of systemic and direct discrimination, many suffer the legacy of dislocation, and many are substantially affected by poor social and economic conditions" (R. v. Gladue 1999: 20).

Violence and Alcohol Use

For Aboriginal communities one of the legacies of colonialism is inordinately high levels of violence. While many Canadians, especially women and children, encounter violence in their lives (Statistics Canada 2011; Johnson 1996), in the lives of Aboriginal people it is an even more pressing social issue. In interviews with 621 Aboriginal people living in four Canadian inner cities, Carol La Prairie (1994) found that 70 percent of the males and 75 percent of the females reported family violence in childhood. A study by the Ontario Native Women's Association (1989) found that eight out of ten Aboriginal women had experienced violence, many of them as young children. In the 2009 General Social Survey, 15 percent of Aboriginal women (compared with 6 percent of non-Aboriginal women) who had a spouse or common-law partner in the previous five years reported being a victim of intimate partner violence. Aboriginal victims of this violence were also nearly twice as likely than non-Aboriginal victims (60 percent versus 33 percent) to report the most serious forms of domestic incidents (being hit with an object, beaten, strangled, threatened or assaulted with a firearm or a knife, or forced to engage in an unwanted sexual act), and twice as many Aboriginal as non-Aboriginal victims (57 percent versus 29 percent) said they were injured as a result (Perreault 2011; see also Bopp, Bopp, and Lane 2003; Brownridge 2003; Canadian Panel on Violence Against Women 1993; Moyer 1992).

While studies that report on the incidence of particular types of abuse are useful in documenting the nature and extent of the violence encountered by Aboriginal people, several writers have noted that separating out and focusing on specific forms of abuse is highly problematic. Sharon McIvor and Teressa Nahanee (1998: 63) state: "Compartmentalizing 'types' of violence within Aboriginal communities into distinct categories of investigation is counter-productive. Sexual, physical, and emotional attacks are inter-related and inter-generational in our communities. Treating these acts as discrete events serves only to obscure our everyday lives." Similarly, Patricia Monture-Angus (1995: 171) tells us that "focusing on a moment in time or incidents of violence, abuse or racism, counting them—disguises the utter totality of the experience of violence in Aboriginal women's lives." Indeed, the violence experienced by Aboriginal people is systemic; it "has invaded whole communities and cannot be considered a problem of a particular couple or an individual household" (RCAP 1996: vol. 3 chap. 2).

One explanation often offered to account for the high levels of violence in Aboriginal communities is the use of alcohol. Sharon Moyer (1992), for instance, found that 70 percent of the homicide incidents involving Aboriginal people between 1962 and 1984 involved the use of alcohol. The General Social Survey found that violent crimes involving an Aboriginal victim were more likely (67 percent) than incidents with a non-Aboriginal victim (52 percent) to involve alcohol or illegal drug use of the perpetrator (Perrault 2011). Accordingly, alcohol use is often taken as a sign of "cultural difference" that marks Aboriginal people off from the rest of Canadian society. According to this view, excessive drinking has become commonplace in Aboriginal communities to the point at which it is now an accepted cultural practice that leads to "drinking parties" where violence is likely to break out (see Comack and Balfour 2004).

However, explaining violence in Aboriginal communities by pointing to the use of alcohol and, more generally, to the notion of "cultural difference" contains a number of problems. Many of the Aboriginal women interviewed for *Women in Trouble* (Comack 1996) indicated that they turned to alcohol and other drugs as a way of escaping their difficult pasts (see also McEvoy and Daniluk 1995). In this regard, these women are no different than many other Canadians who regularly turn to alcohol as a means of coping with distress in their lives. In the view of the Royal Commission (RCAP 1996), alcohol abuse is not a cause of violence but a parallel means of dealing with deep distress. In a similar fashion, AJI commissioners Hamilton and Sinclair (1991a: 498) state: "Ultimately, it must be recognized that the presence and influence of alcohol and substance abuse in Aboriginal communities and among Aboriginal people are a direct reflection of the nature and level of despair which permeates that population."

Moreover, to say that violence in Aboriginal communities is the result of cultural differences raises another question: different from what? More often than not, it is the standards of the dominant white culture that are used as the measuring rod by which Aboriginal people are transformed into the deviant Other. Such an approach only works to reproduce the racism that prevails in the mainstream society. In this regard, centring explanations for violence in Aboriginal communities on the use of alcohol can align too easily with racist stereotypes, including the two most invidious of these, the "squaw" and the "drunken Indian" (see Sangster 2001; Larocque 2000). As Donna Sears put it so powerfully to the Royal Commission, "The portrayal of the squaw is one of the most degrading, most despised and most dehumanizing anywhere in the world. The squaw is the female counterpart of the Indian male savage and, as such, she has no human face. She is lustful, immoral, unfeeling and dirty." Sears draws a direct connection between "this grotesque dehumanization" and the constant vulnerability of Aboriginal girls and women to serious physical, psychological, and sexual abuse: "I believe there is a direct relationship between these horrible racist, sexist stereotypes and violence against Native women and girls" (cited in RCAP 1996 vol. 3 chap. 2).

The racist stereotype of the "drunken Indian" works in a similar fashion. Bolstered by a dominant, regularly reinforced discourse that is content to explain private troubles as being rooted in individual circumstances (as opposed to systemic processes), the common view is to see Aboriginal people as being intoxicated and "out of control." Such representations merely function to objectify and devalue Aboriginal people. Ignored are the historical processes by which alcohol was introduced into Aboriginal life and the social conditions that have fostered its continued use, as well as the general use of alcohol as a socially sanctioned resource in contemporary society.

Explanations that rest on cultural difference to account for the prevalence of violence in Aboriginal communities, then, are highly suspect. Rather than cultural difference, the prevalence of violence and alcohol use in Aboriginal communities is more accurately located as a contemporary manifestation of colonialism. As the Canadian Panel on Violence against Women (1993: 173) argues, poverty is a key factor in the perpetuation of this violence: "The impact of poverty on the Aboriginal family and community is immeasurable. Poverty, in its severest form, is a fact of life for many Aboriginal people.... It is the daily stress, financial hardship and chronic despair inflicted by poverty that contribute to the widespread abuse of Aboriginal women and children."

Overrepresentation in the Criminal Justice System
The volatile mixture of poverty, violence, and alcohol use that colonialism has perpetrated on Aboriginal individuals and communities also figures into the overrepresentation of Aboriginal people in the criminal justice system. The statistics are telling.

- Although Aboriginal people made up just 3 percent of the Canadian population in 2007–8, they accounted for 18 percent of admissions to provincial and territorial jails and 18 percent of admissions to federal prisons. This overrepresentation is most acute in the Prairie provinces. In Saskatchewan, Aboriginal people made up 11 percent of the population and a whopping 81 percent of provincial sentenced custody admissions in 2007–8. In Manitoba, Aboriginal people made up only 15 percent of the population yet represented 69 percent of provincially sentenced custody admissions (Perrault 2009).

- The overrepresentation of Aboriginal women is even more acute than it is for Aboriginal men. In 2007–8 Aboriginal women accounted for 24 percent of the female inmate population in provincial and territorial jails, while Aboriginal men accounted for 17 percent of the male inmate population (Perrault 2009).
- The number of Aboriginal people held in custody has been steadily increasing. Between 2001 and 2007 Aboriginal people admitted on remand increased by 23 percent, compared to a 14 percent increase for the general population. Aboriginal people are incarcerated at a rate of 1,024 per 100,000 population in comparison to 117 per 100,000 for the general population (Sapers 2007: 11–12).
- According to a one-day snapshot conducted in 2003, the Aboriginal youth incarceration rate was 64.5 per 10,000 population compared to 8.2 per 10,000 population for non-Aboriginal youth. Aboriginal youth were almost eight times more likely to be in custody than their non-Aboriginal counterparts. Aboriginal youth in Saskatchewan were thirty times more likely to be incarcerated than their non-Aboriginal counterparts. In Manitoba, Aboriginal youth were sixteen times more likely to be incarcerated than were non-Aboriginal youth (Latimer and Foss 2004).

La Prairie (2002) found that Aboriginal people's overrepresentation in the criminal justice system was not a uniform phenomenon. For one, studies showed that only a small proportion of incarcerated Aboriginal people committed their offences while on a reserve; most were living in an urban area at the time the offence was committed. For example, a one-day snapshot of Aboriginal youth in custody in Canada revealed that more than half (58 percent) of the Aboriginal youth were in a city when they committed or allegedly committed the offence for which they were currently being held (Bittle et al. 2002: 10–11). While offences by First Nations youth were mainly committed on-reserve in the Eastern provinces, they were mainly committed off-reserve in the Western provinces. For example, 67 percent of Aboriginal youth in Manitoba and 65 percent of those in Saskatchewan committed or allegedly committed the offence for their current admission in a city (Bittle et al. 2002: 85, 104).

For another, while urban areas contribute to the majority of incarcerated Aboriginal offenders, there are regional variations. La Prairie found that these variations could be accounted for by the degrees of disadvantage experienced by Aboriginal people. More specifically, Winnipeg, Saskatoon, Regina, and Thunder Bay contribute the most to Aboriginal overrepresentation. These are also cities with the largest percentage of Aboriginal people living in extremely poor neighbourhoods. According to La Prairie (2002: 202), therefore, the concentration of poor, single-parent, and poorly educated Aboriginal people living in the inner core of these cities explains their greater likelihood of involvement with the criminal justice system.

More recently, Samuel Perrault examined factors that contribute to the overrepresentation of Aboriginal people in the criminal justice system. According to the 2006 Census, 38 percent of Aboriginal people aged twenty years and over had not completed high school, compared to 19 percent of Aboriginal people. As well, the unemployment rate among Aboriginal people was 14 percent compared to 6 percent among non-Aboriginal people (2009: 12). Nevertheless, Perrault found that while the level of education and employment status help to explain some of the overrepresentation of Aboriginal adults in custody, "the incarceration rates for Aboriginal adults aged 20 to 34 still remain higher than for their non-Aboriginal counterparts even when high school graduation and employment are considered." As such, Perrault concludes, "Other factors beyond education and employment, therefore, may also contribute to the representation of Aboriginal adults in custody" (2009: 14).

What are those other factors? Clearly, race and racialization come into play here. An inescapable connection exists between the historical forces of colonialism that have shaped contemporary Aboriginal communities and the overincarceration of Aboriginal people. Poverty, social exclusion, violence, and alcohol use have become all too regular features in the lives of Aboriginal people, and prison — with all of its negative effects (see Comack 2008) — has become for many young Aboriginal people the contemporary equivalent of what the Indian residential school represented for their parents (Jackson 1989: 216). Still, explaining the disproportionate incarceration rates of Aboriginal people on crime-producing conditions in their families and communities tells only part of the story. Left out of the equation is the role of the criminal justice system in the production of crime.

THE PRODUCTION OF "CRIME"

While La Prairie directs our attention to the impoverished living conditions of Aboriginal people, she also suggests another possible factor to account for Aboriginal people's overrepresentation in the criminal justice system: "that the majority of offences (of incarcerated Abriginal offenders) were committed off-reserve may be explained by the potential for the criminal justice system to *respond differently* to offenders on and off-reserve" (LaPrairie 2002: 189; emphasis added). In other words, we need to acknowledge the role that the police — as the first point of contact with the criminal justice system — perform in the criminalization of Aboriginal people.

Despite the ways in which it is represented in public discourse and official statistics, "crime" is not an obvious or straightforward category. Like the idea of race, crime is a social construction that varies over time and place. As Wendy Chan and Kiran Mirchandani (2002: 14) note, "Definitions of crime and categories of criminality are neither fixed nor natural." Stuart Hall and his colleagues (1978: 188) make a similar point in saying that crime cannot be treated as a "given, self-evident, ahistorical, and unproblematic category." At the same time that crime cannot be separated from the social context in which it occurs, it is also "differently *defined* (in both official and lay ideologies) at different periods; and this reflects not only changing attitudes amongst different sectors of the populations to crime, as well as real historical changes in the social organization of criminal activity, but also the shifting *application* of the category itself" (Hall et al. 1978: 189).

Like the process of racialization, the process of criminalization involves the exercise of a particular form of power; in this case, the "power to criminalize" or "to turn a person into a criminal" (Comack and Balfour 2004: 9). In the same way that racialization involves a "representational process of defining an Other" (Miles 1989: 75), criminalization involves establishing a binary between "the criminal" and "the law-abiding." This dualism reinforces the view that those who are deemed to be criminal are not like "the rest of Us" — not only in terms of what they have done, but also who they are and the social spaces in which they move. The net result is that the criminal justice system and policing reproduce "a very particular kind of order" (Comack and Balfour 2004: 9).

At its core the goal of criminalization is "to target those activities of groups that authorities deem it necessary to control, thus making the process inherently political" (Chan and Mirchandani 2002: 15). For instance, criminologists have long noted that the criminal justice system devotes far more resources to the policing of the poor and marginalized in society than it does to controlling the harmful activities of the wealthy and their corporations (Snider 2006; Reiman and Leighton 2010). Crimes that are promulgated "in the suites" of large corporations (price-fixing, tax evasion, environmental pollution, and workplace health and safety) have been documented as producing great harm in lives lost and financial costs incurred. Yet these actions receive far less attention in the criminal justice system than those that occur "in the streets" (assaults, robbery, and theft). One result of this focus of criminal justice intervention is that measures taken to control and contain the threat posed by "crime" have resulted in the construction of particular racialized groups as troublesome "problem populations." Hence, the policing of Aboriginal people becomes racialized.

Similar to the role played by the NWMP in the colonial project of creating the white settler society, contemporary police forces in Canadian society have been assigned a central role in the management and containment of "problem populations." This is especially the case in the urban centres of the Prairie provinces. It falls to the police as "reproducers of order" to devote their considerable resources to the realization of that objective. In doing their surveillance of the racialized spaces of the inner city, police come to define Aboriginal people as "troublesome" and therefore in need of control. The result can be deadly.

Chapter Four

THE SHOOTING OF J.J. HARPER

At about 2:30 a.m. on the morning of March 9, 1988, John Joseph Harper — a member of the Wasagamack First Nation, father of three, and executive director of the Island Lake Tribal Council — was walking home along Logan Avenue in Winnipeg's inner city when he was approached by a police officer, Constable Robert Cross. Knowing that he had no legal obligation to talk to him, Harper at first ignored the officer. The constable asked Harper to show some identification. Harper refused, saying "I don't have to show you any." The constable repeated the demand, but Harper again refused and attempted to walk past him. Cross grabbed Harper's arm and spun him around. In a matter of seconds J.J. Harper lay dying on the ground with a police bullet in his chest.

Controversy still surrounds what exactly happened in those few minutes when the two men met on a darkened Winnipeg street. Only Cross survived the encounter, and his recollection of how his gun came to be unholstered and then fired was inconsistent. Cross was adamant that his gun was not drawn when he approached Harper. He initially reported that Harper was the aggressor, that Harper pushed him to the ground and reached out for his gun. Cross later indicated that he had pulled Harper down on top of him as he fell to the ground. There was a struggle, and the constable's finger somehow ended up on the trigger of his gun. The gun went off, and Harper was shot.

In the days following Harper's death a deep divide emerged. On one side of that divide stood the Winnipeg Police Department and its supporters, including justice officials, the mayor, and many members of the general public who were incredulous that their police force could be accused of any wrongdoing in Harper's death. On the other side stood the leaders and members of the Aboriginal community, the lawyers who represented the Harper family, and more sceptical members of the general public — including judges and journalists who were intent on uncovering the "truth" of the matter.

How are we to make sense of the death of J.J. Harper? Was it, as the Winnipeg police chief and other officials claimed, an unfortunate accident brought on by Harper himself? Or was Harper's death a manifestation of racialized policing practices? What makes the case all the more troubling are the events that transpired in the immediate aftermath of the shooting, including a less than adequate police investigation, a speedy exoneration of the officer, and a discrediting of the Aboriginal witnesses who were present that night. Competing versions played out as the case unfolded, and in the process one question figured prominently in the controversy: what role did race and racism play in Harper's demise?

THE SEQUENCE OF EVENTS

On the early morning of March 9, 1988, Winnipeg police officers were on the lookout for a recently stolen vehicle. Constable Cross and his partner, Constable Kathryn Hodgins, spotted the stolen car when they were driving around the Weston area, part of Winnipeg's inner city. They phoned in the licence plate number and began to pursue the car and its two male occupants. The car ended up skidding into a snow bank, and its young occupants — one turned out to be nineteen years old, the other, thirteen — took off running. The thirteen-year-old stopped when Cross yelled for him to do so, but the nineteen-year-old kept on going. After asking the thirteen-year-old to describe his accomplice, Constable Hodgins relayed a description of the suspect as "male, native, black jacket, blue jeans" and "apparently approximately twenty-two years old" over the police radio. Soon six other police officers arrived to search for the suspect. Constable Cross left the thirteen-year-old in the back of the police cruiser, with his partner to mind him, and joined in the search on foot. Soon after, Cross heard over his radio that the second suspect was in custody. Only a minute later he encountered J.J. Harper walking down the street.

Constable Cross knew, then, that a young Aboriginal suspect had already been taken into custody after running hard to elude police. Constable Hodgins had initially described the suspect over the police radio as "approximately twenty-two years old." One of the officers engaged in the pursuit had subsequently broadcast a description of the suspect as "native male, 5' 9", slim build, wearing a grey jacket and jeans." Harper was thirty-seven years old. He was wearing a black cloth jacket and blue jeans. He was walking in the direction of where the stolen vehicle had landed in the snowbank, and it seems that he did not show any signs that he had been running. Harper was also considerably heavier than the young suspect, and much stockier. Nevertheless, Cross made the decision to approach Harper. Cross later testified during the inquest into Harper's death that he thought Harper fit the description of the suspect better than the young man in custody. As it turned out, Cross was wrong — none of the other police officers involved had any doubt that they already had the right person in custody.

Soon after the shooting occurred, several more police officers arrived at the scene to begin their investigation into what had transpired. That initial investigation was fraught with difficulties. The police made no attempt to separate Cross from the other officers present. The acting sergeant took Cross's gun (but not its holster), but put it in his own holster (contrary to established protocols for the treatment of such an exhibit). The police did no thorough canvassing of neighbourhood homes, and questioned neither of the two civilian witnesses (the car theft suspects) as to what they might have seen or heard. Officers conducted only a token search of the scene of the shooting, during which they failed to notice Harper's broken glasses lying on the ground (a newspaper reporter later found them). The scene was hosed down before daybreak, making any further investigation impossible. While the police conducted standard ballistics tests on Cross's gun, they made no effort to obtain fingerprints from it.

As per police protocol when an officer's gun has been discharged, the Winnipeg Police Department's Firearms Board of Enquiry submitted a report to the chief of police the morning of March 10. The report concluded, "There was no negligence on the part of Constable Cross. His conduct in this matter appears to be above reproach" (cited in Hamilton and Sinclair 1991b: 66). Only thirty-six hours after the shooting, Police Chief Herb Stephen issued a press release saying that Harper's death was "precipitated by the assault on the officer by Harper" and there was "no negligence on the part of the officer" (cited in Hamilton and Sinclair 1991b: 68). The officer (who was not mentioned by name) was therefore cleared of any wrongdoing.

Members of the Aboriginal community expressed their dissatisfaction with the findings of the police investigation by holding vigils and demonstrations. Framing Harper's death as racially motivated and symbolic of deeper problems with the justice system, they made demands for a public inquiry. But like the police chief, other city officials were more content to define Harper's death as an accident. Winnipeg mayor Bill Norrie told reporters: "This is not a racial incident. It was just timing, circumstances, and events. The Native community's demand for an inquiry will be satisfied by the inquest" (cited in Sinclair 1999: 56–57).

THE INQUEST

The inquest into the events surrounding Harper's death was held over twelve days in April, 1988. Judge John Enns heard testimony from fifty-four witnesses, including the two Aboriginal youth who had been taken into custody that night and three Aboriginal people who had been driving by in a car. During the inquest two distinct and conflicting versions of the events surrounding Harper's death emerged: the account of the police officers versus the account of the Aboriginal witnesses. These versions differed dramatically on two key points: whether police officers had their guns drawn; and whether officers made racial slurs against the two Aboriginal youth.

Competing Truth Claims

Both of the car theft suspects testified that they saw officers draw their guns at various times that night. Alan, the thirteen-year-old, said he saw Constable Hodgins draw her revolver when she left the cruiser he was in to look for her partner, Constable Cross, after hearing the gun shot. Melvin Pruden, the nineteen-year-old, testified that during his attempt to evade police he encountered another officer (Constable Randy Hampton) in a back lane and that the officer pointed a gun at him and said, "Stop or I'll shoot." Three Aboriginal witnesses who were passing by in a car testified that as they were driving down Logan Avenue a police officer (who turned out to be Constable Hampton) ran in front of their car. All three witnesses said that the officer was holding what looked like a gun in his right hand and grasping his right wrist with his left hand. During the inquest proceedings, all of the officers at the scene — including constables Hodgins and Hampton — maintained that their guns were never drawn that night, and that maybe what the witnesses saw was their hand-held radios.

Pruden testified that on his capture he said to the officers, "Took you a while to catch me, eh?" — which he thought annoyed them. He also said that an officer slammed him against the hood of the police cruiser a couple of times, hitting his head, and called him "a fucking Indian." His companion Alan was in the back of the cruiser when Constable Hodgins pulled it up close to the scene where the body lay on the sidewalk. He thought it was his cousin, Pruden. Alan reported that Constable Hodgins turned to him at one point and said, "You little thief, if you hadn't stolen the car none of this would have happened." Alan also said that Hodgins called him "a blue-eyed fucking Indian." For their part, the officers denied using force in arresting Pruden, and they denied calling him "a fucking Indian." Constable Hodgins also denied making a racist comment to Alan.

Constructing the Key Players

As these competing truth claims played out during the inquest, the character of the two key players — Robert Cross and J.J. Harper — also took on particular proportions. During the inquest proceedings, Constable Cross faded into the ranks of uniformed officers. As journalist Don Gillmor (1988: 51) described the scene in an article he wrote for *Saturday Night* magazine, "It was not an individual who had encountered Harper, it was the police force." In contrast, Harper's character — and its flaws — played out more prominently. The autopsy revealed that Harper had a blood alcohol level of .22 milligrams (almost three times the level of legal impairment for drivers). Crown Attorney William Morton queried the chief medical examiner: "That usually means somebody who is belligerent." To which the doctor agreed. "May verbally, and even physically attack people?" the Crown attorney asked. "Yes, sir," replied the doctor (Sinclair 1999: 69–70). A letter found in Harper's pocket from his wife was leaked to the media. In the letter his wife warned that Harper's drinking was driving them apart and that she needed a home where she could feel safe. Harper had spent the evening at the St. Regis Hotel drinking a mixture of coffee and brandy, and then moved on with his friends to the Westbrook Hotel on Keewatin Street. He apparently consumed a few beers there before heading home down Logan Avenue. It was then that he met up with Cross — who in his statement also described Harper as "belligerent."

In addition to Harper's character, the character of the civilian witnesses was also at issue. With charges pending for their role in the car theft, both Pruden and Alan were already painted with the brush of the "criminal Other." Pruden reinforced this label when he failed to appear in court to provide testimony on several occasions, and a charge of failure to appear was eventually laid. Alan was reluctant to give a statement to police about what he saw and heard that night. Already in trouble with the law, he was afraid of getting into more trouble. According to Gillmor's account, "His mother phoned their legal-aid lawyer and asked her what to do. 'Just tell the truth,' was the lawyer's advice." Linda Morissette was one of the Aboriginal witnesses who had driven down Logan Avenue at the time the police were in pursuit of Pruden near Stanley Knowles Park. As Gillmor reported, "Though she had not been drinking when she and her friends drove by the park that night, she was worried that they would all be perceived simply as 'drunken Indians'" (1988: 52, 51).

THE INQUEST REPORT

The inquest report was released on May 26, 1988. In his report, Judge Enns observed that Winnipeg's Aboriginal community had an "utter distrust" of the police and he agreed that Constable Cross's decision to question Harper "could easily be perceived as yet another instance of police harassment" (cited in York 1990: 151). While the judge recommended that the police department "vigorously pursue a program of recruiting natives" to ease this tension, journalist Geoffrey York noted that the judge's description of the sense of harassment as merely a "perception" by Aboriginal people implied that it had no basis in reality. In contrast, Aboriginal leaders were convinced "that there would not be such a widespread feeling of harassment unless there were facts and personal experiences to support it" (1990: 151).

Judge Enns concluded, "Both the allegations of racial slurs and the allegations of drawn revolvers are not credible" (cited in Hamilton and Sinclair 1991b: 79). Newspaper columnist Gordon Sinclair (1999: 133) summarized the judge's conclusions in one sentence: "All the police told the truth and none of the Native witnesses were credible." In writing about the inquest results, Gillmor noted that Judge Enns's ruling on the conflicting testimony followed a certain line of logic: "Allegations of racial slurs and allegations of drawn revolvers were not credible because the native witnesses were not credible. The natives were not credible because natives have an inherent mistrust of the police." Gillmor pointed out that the judge did not consider the corollary: "If racial slurs *were* made and guns *were* drawn, it would be indicative of the police's deep mistrust of the Aboriginal community." As it stood, "The wholesale rejection of native testimony was certainly indicative of the court's mistrust" (Gillmor 1988: 51).

Judge Enns's main conclusion was that "despite certain shortcomings in the area of police investigation, it is my view that the shooting occurred as a result of the deceased pushing down the officer and then attempting to take his revolver. The officer's attempt to keep control of his gun is justified and the ensuing shooting I find to be accidental. I therefore exonerate Constable Cross" (cited in Hamilton and Sinclair 1991b: 78). In addition to setting up a program to recruit Aboriginal people to the police force, the judge recommended a study seminar for provincial court judges to consider inquest procedures and a continued expansion of training for ambulance operators.

Aboriginal leaders were not satisfied with the results of the inquest. Ovide Mercredi, for one, stated: "The inquest didn't bolster the confidence of the native chiefs. If there had been a better investigation, even if Cross was still exonerated, they would have accepted it. But the inquest didn't reveal what happened. It is unresolved, and there are no guarantees that it will not happen again" (cited in Gillmor, 1988: 51). With concerns mounting over the state of Aboriginal-police relations, calls for a public investigation into the issue became louder.

THE ABORIGINAL JUSTICE INQUIRY

On April 13, 1988, while the inquest into Harper's death was still in progress, the NDP government passed an order-in-council creating the Aboriginal Justice Inquiry of Manitoba. One of the mandates of the inquiry was to investigate all aspects of Harper's death, including "whether there exists any evidence of racial prejudice with respect to any of the events which led to the death of J.J. Harper or the investigation of his death" (Hamilton and Sinclair 1991b: 2). To realize their mandate, the commissioners drew upon all of the evidence of the inquest. In addition, they heard testimony from forty-one witnesses (including Constable Robert Cross) over twenty-six days of hearings that began in August 1989; and they examined a dozen pieces of evidence that were either not considered or not considered in the same depth at the inquest.

The AJI's conclusions were in sharp contrast to those of the inquest. While Judge Enns had found all of the police witnesses and none of the Aboriginal witnesses to be credible, Commissioners Hamilton and Sinclair took an opposing view.

The Encounter
As the commissioners noted, "It is difficult to piece together the facts of the fateful encounter between J.J. Harper and Const. Robert Cross. Only Cross survived that encounter and we have only his account of the struggle which culminated in the death of Harper" (Hamilton and Sinclair 1991b: 29). According to the account of Constable Cross, he confronted Harper within a minute of hearing of Pruden's arrest. In his statement to police Cross said he had approached Harper, asking for identification. Harper had declined to provide it. The constable said he "could smell liquor on his breath and he seemed belligerent." Cross said that he then advised Harper, "You match the description of a suspect I'm looking for, for the theft of auto and I would like to see some identification." According to Cross, Harper replied that he didn't have to show him anything and walked away (Hamilton and Sinclair 1991b: 30).

Harper's decision not to produce his identification is supported by Canadian jurisprudence. As the commissioners note, while the duties of a police officer are broad in scope, the power of an officer is not unlimited. Police are not authorized to stop people on the street at random. Under common law, "Police officers conducting an investigation have the right to ask questions of citizens and to request they identify themselves. Officers do not, however, have the power to force citizens to comply" (Hamilton and Sinclair 1991b: 33).

Under section 7 of the Canadian Charter of Rights and Freedoms, "Everyone has the right to life, liberty and security of the person and the right not to be deprived thereof except in accordance with the principles of fundamental justice." Section 9 of the Charter states, "Everyone has the right not to be arbitrarily detained or imprisoned." Section 495 (1) of the Criminal Code specifies the powers of arrest:

A peace officer may arrest without warrant:
a) a person who has committed an indictable offence or who, on *reasonable grounds*, he believes has committed or is about to commit an indictable offence,
b) a person whom he finds committing a criminal offence, or
c) a person in respect of whom he has *reasonable grounds* to believe that a warrant of arrest or committal in any form set out in Part XXVI-II in relation thereto, is in force within the territorial jurisdiction in which the person is found. (Cited in Hamilton and Sinclair 1991b: 33–34; emphasis added)

It is at the moment of arrest — defined by the Supreme Court of Canada as the "seizure or touching of a person's body with a view to [his or her] detention" (cited in Hamilton and Sinclair 1991b: 35)—that an individual loses his or her right to refuse to answer a police officer's questions.

The commissioners also point out that under section 25 of the Criminal Code a police officer is authorized and justified in using as much force as necessary in enforcing and upholding the law:

Every one who is required or authorized by law to do anything in the administration or enforcement of the law
(b) as a peace officer or public officer, is, if he acts on *reasonable grounds*, justified in doing what he is required or authorized to do and in using as much force as is necessary for that purpose. (Cited in Hamilton and Sinclair 1991b: 34; emphasis added)

As such, if an officer intends to arrest a citizen that officer has the authority to use however much force is necessary to accomplish that action, and the citizen loses his or her right to resist. Nevertheless, "If an officer does not place the citizen under arrest, or if the officer is not making a lawful detention and has no intention of doing so, the officer exceeds his or her authority by grabbing and detaining the citizen forcibly" (Hamilton and Sinclair 1991b: 33).

One of the key criteria specified in the Criminal Code regarding the powers of arrest and use of force by police officers is that there are "reasonable grounds" to support such actions. Constable Cross, however, testified before the inquiry that while he had some "slight suspicion" that Harper could have been the car thief, he had no reasonable and probable grounds to arrest him. As such, the commissioners held that "since Cross had neither reasonable nor probable grounds to believe that Harper had committed an offence, Cross' detention of Harper was inappropriate" (Hamilton and Sinclair 1991b: 38).

The Shooting

While Cross initially claimed that Harper had jumped him or hit him and knocked him to the ground, his later testimony indicated that it was Cross who had grabbed hold of Harper. The commissioners noted, "Even if we cannot say exactly what happened, we can say, with some assurance, that the confrontation did not occur in the manner which was accepted as fact by the Firearms Board of Enquiry, the police chief and Judge Enns at the inquest" (Hamilton and Sinclair 1991b: 38). They go on to elaborate:

> Cross acknowledged having had his finger on the trigger and having pulled it. We also know that Cross had hold of the revolver during the entire scuffle. It would be reasonable to conclude that if Harper did have any control over the revolver at such a close range, he would not have allowed it to be pointed at him, let alone be fired. We conclude that Harper never had any significant degree of control over Cross' revolver. (Hamilton and Sinclair 1991b: 39)

The commissioners also stated that the effort to protect Cross and to shift the blame to Harper took precedence in the police investigation: "We have been left with the impression that an 'official version' of what happened was developed. We are satisfied that version is inaccurate" (Hamilton and Sinclair 1991b: 39).

The Issue of Witness Credibility

One of the inconsistencies in this "official version" emerged from a comparison of police officers' notes with the transcripts of police radio broadcasts describing the car theft suspect. The commissioners suggested, "It appears that other officers may have attempted to bolster the credibility of Cross' account by making their notes on the suspect's description correspond with his." In one instance, it was revealed during the inquiry that Constable Bill Isaac (the officer who apprehended Pruden) had rewritten his notes. When the inquiry requested copies of all police officers' notebooks, the constable had turned over the revised version. One of the changes that Isaac had made was with regard to the colour of Pruden's jacket — from grey to black — such that the altered version conformed to the description of the jacket that Constable Hodgins had initially broadcast over the police radio (as opposed to the description that had been broadcast shortly afterward). The commissioners concluded, "In both their note-taking and their testimony at the inquest and at this Inquiry, several officers were less than truthful. This is a disturbing finding but it is one which we feel compelled to make" (Hamilton and Sinclair 1991b: 20).

Another inconsistency pertained to whether officers had their guns drawn that night. While several civilian witnesses testified that they saw police officers with their guns drawn, all of the officers pointedly denied that any gun — with the exception of Cross's gun — had been taken out of its holster. On this matter the commissioners noted, "From time to time police officers have cause to draw their weapons. The public understands it may be necessary when an officer is in danger or when potentially violent persons are being arrested or approached. There may have been such a situation on March 9, 1988 when Melvin Pruden was being flushed from hiding" (Hamilton and Sinclair 1991b: 20).

On the specific matter of whether Constable Hodgins had drawn her gun that night, as the thirteen-year-old Alan had said, the commissioners maintained that under the circumstances — hearing a shot fired, being on her own with an accused in custody, entering a dark alley to determine what was happening — one would *assume* or *expect* a police officer to have her gun drawn. "We would not criticize her for doing so. We believe she did have her gun drawn" (Hamilton and Sinclair 1991b: 21). With regard to the credibility of Alan, who had been involved in the car theft, the commissioners commented:

We are well aware of the dangers inherent in accepting the testimony of persons involved in the commission of offences when they are called upon to testify as to the circumstances surrounding those offences. Generally, one might expect that such witnesses would be tempted to shade their testimony in order to put themselves in the best possible light and to shift the responsibility for illegal activity onto others. Having considered those caveats about accepting such evidence, we nonetheless feel we can accept the evidence of Allan on this issue. We can conclude only that Hodgins denied having her gun drawn to support the contention of other officers, including Cross, that they did not have their guns drawn. (Hamilton and Sinclair 1991b: 21)

The commissioners also found Linda Morissette, one of the three people in the car that passed by at the same time as an officer was crossing the street, to be an "honest witness." They deemed her statement that she saw an officer with his gun drawn to be "essentially true" (Hamilton and Sinclair 1991b: 22).

The Investigation
On the matter of the police investigation, the commissioners stated:

Cross was accorded special consideration by fellow officers at every stage of the investigation. We can only conclude that this investigation was handled as though everything had occurred as Cross stated, and that the shooting "investigation" was done merely to corroborate and reinforce Cross' story. Both at the scene of the shooting and during the subsequent interrogation, much more attention was given to protecting Cross than was devoted to uncovering the facts of the case. (Hamilton and Sinclair 1991b: 63–64)

The commissioners were also critical of the Firearms Board of Inquiry, which exonerated Constable Cross even though many important pieces of information were missing: there were no statements from the two car-theft suspects about what they might have observed at the scene; no comprehensive canvassing of neighbouring houses had been conducted; the autopsy report was not yet available; and there were no reports on the analysis of physical evidence such as the weapon or the clothing of either Cross or Harper. Police Chief Stephen also came under criticism for distributing a press release before an investigation had been completed: "By prejudging the innocence of Cross and the wrongdoing of Harper, Stephen effectively foreclosed the possibility of a proper, independent and complete investigation. In effect, he sent a message to his department that the case was closed" (Hamilton and Sinclair 1991b: 69).

As well, the commissioners took issue with the findings of the inquest, stating that Judge Enns "reached conclusions to which we are unable to agree." In part, they explained these problematic conclusions by the judge's decision to limit cross-examination during the inquest. In particular, the commissioners maintained that if counsel for the Harper family, lawyer Harvey Pollock, had been permitted to question police witnesses more fully and freely, "It is possible that Judge Enns might have had a different appreciation of their credibility." As it stood, "the manner in which the evidence at the inquest was presented favoured the police version of events — a version we deem highly questionable and which, at our hearings, did not stand up well to close scrutiny" (Hamilton and Sinclair 1991b: 74).

Finally, the commissioners also directed criticism at the Crown attorney, William Morton, pointing to the close relationship between the Crown and the police department during the inquest and to Morton's failure to disclose evidence to the counsel for the Harper family.

The commissioners summarized their position on the investigation of the Harper shooting:

> It is our conclusion that the City of Winnipeg Police Department did not search actively or aggressively for the truth about the death of J.J. Harper. Their investigation was, at best, inadequate. At worst, its primary objective seems to have been to exonerate Const. Robert Cross and to vindicate the Winnipeg Police Department. We believe that evidence was mishandled and facts were obscured by police attempts to construct a version of events which would, in effect, blame J.J. Harper for his own death. (Hamilton and Sinclair 1991b: 113)

When the AJI's two volume report was released in August 1991, two other legal actions were still pending. Harper's half-brother, Harry Wood, had filed a complaint with the Law Enforcement Review Agency (LERA) regarding Constable Cross's conduct on the night that Harper was shot. LERA rendered its decision in the fall of 1992, finding Cross guilty of using excessive force and of abusing his authority (Sinclair 1999: 363). Citing mitigating factors — that Harper's death was an isolated incident, Cross's declining mental health, his previously clear record, and the undue economic hardship that an outright dismissal would bring — the LERA board refrained from dismissing Constable Cross from his position and instead imposed the penalty of reducing his rank to a fourth-class constable. The second legal action involved a civil suit launched by the Harper family against Constable Cross, Police Chief Herb Stephen, and the City of Winnipeg. A settlement was reached in January 1993 in the amount of $450,000 ($150,000 of which went to the Harper family's lawyers).

THE BLUE WALL

In line with Jerome Skolnick's (1975) observation that policing is an occupation that exhibits a considerable degree of social solidarity, writers have utilized the notion of the "blue wall" to refer to the police (see, for example, Talbot, Jaywardene, and Juliani 1983; Stroud 1983). The blue wall is a term that has two meanings: the physical barrier that police officers — dressed in blue uniforms — represents in protecting the public from harm; and the social barrier erected between a police force and the general public. Accordingly, when things go wrong, the police will unite in solidarity to protect their own. The social meaning of the blue wall was clearly in operation during the investigation into Harper's death. One of the significant findings of the AJI was that police officers "were determined to portray the department, and Cross in particular, in the best possible light" (Hamilton and Sinclair 1991b: 27).

In *The Blue Wall*, Cartsen Stroud (1983: 231) notes:

> Cut off from the public, isolated from department solidarity by the rigid hierarchy of the force, and subjected to the relentless assault of crime, violence, and despair generated by the street, the street cop is sooner or later reduced to a handful of certainties in an uncertain and frequently fatal world. They call these certainties The Line.

First and foremost of these certainties is "stand by your partner." According to Stroud (1983: 231), "A man could fail his wife, his children, his parents, and himself, but the loyalty to the police partner was perhaps the strongest social bond I've ever seen." As four of the Winnipeg police officers who testified at the inquest and inquiry had, at one time or another, been partnered with Constable Cross, "stand by your partner" could well have been in operation among the members of the force. Several other indicators, however, suggest that the blue wall or line was in evidence during the events that followed Harper's death.

Police officers — and the union that represents them — engaged in a number of tactics designed to protect their interests and to promote their version of events, including: efforts to scuttle the inquiry; the rewriting of police notebooks; intimidation of civilian witnesses; constructing retroactive police reports about Harper; and tipping off media sources with information that would disparage both Harper and the lawyer representing his family.

Setting up legal roadblocks. Soon after the government first announced the AJI, the Winnipeg Police Association (under the Manitoba Evidence Act) questioned the legal authority of the inquiry to examine the Harper matter, which suspended the proceedings until the case could be heard. The Manitoba Court of Appeal decided that the orders-in-council establishing the AJI were invalid because they were passed only in English (and not also in French). An act to re-establish the inquiry was then passed by the government in June 1989. That same month the Police Association challenged the authority of the inquiry to have access to police notebooks. The Court of Appeal ruled in July that while the AJI could not order the production of the notebooks, it could order that photocopies of portions of police notebooks relating to the Harper matter be produced (Hamilton and Sinclair 1991b: 3–4).

"Revising" a police notebook. Constable Bill Isaac testified at both the inquest and the inquiry. He was the officer who arrested Pruden. During his testimony at the AJI, Isaac revealed that he had two sets of notes: one made at the time and one made some time afterward. Isaac had rewritten his notes on the shooting, ostensibly to make minor corrections and add detail. When the inquiry requested copies of all police officers' notebooks, Isaac had turned over the revised version. As it turned out, Pruden had altered his notes to make them conform to the colour of the jacket that had been broadcast over the police radio. While an investigation into Isaac's conduct was undertaken by the police department, no perjury charges were laid. Instead, Isaac was transferred back to uniform, put on general patrol, and given a $4,000 pay cut (Sinclair 1999: 173).

Intimidation of witnesses. One of the regular observers at the inquest wrote a letter to the editor of the *Winnipeg Free Press*, relaying what he had witnessed in the hallway of the courthouse shortly after Linda Morissette and her two friends had testified: "Mr. Yaworek, Miss Morissette and Mr.

Houston were quietly sitting on a bench while representatives of the police force were badgering and laughing at them. 'You couldn't see anything, you were so drunk. You could see a gun but not whether the officer was male or female'" (cited in Sinclair 1999: 122). The bystander also reported watching two uniformed police officers arrest Larry Yaworek for having $99 in outstanding parking tickets. As he wrote: "The police had chosen to enforce the law, right at that time, in the courthouse. This can only be perceived as an intimidation tactic. It was a childish display of power" (cited in Sinclair 1999: 123).

Harper's police record. Two police reports were constructed about encounters with Harper in relation to the Intoxicated Persons Detention Act; one occurred at the end of 1986 and the other in August 1987. The police reports were not written up until March 31, 1988 — twenty-two days after Harper died. Both reports were prepared at the request of Sergeant Rex Keatinge. Both incidents were related to the domestic relationship between Harper and his wife. One report stated that Harper's wife had called police, and they had found him drunk and yelling obscenities. "According to the report, the police had tussled with Harper, at one point hitting him with a baton before handcuffing him" (Sinclair 1999: 194). The second report indicated that Harper had broken into the family home and fought with police before being subdued. The report specifically noted that the police officer had drawn his gun, but Harper had kept advancing toward him. Judge Enns had refused to have these reports entered as evidence at the inquest. While the inquiry was initially asked to accept the retroactively written reports as exhibits, lawyers for the police association withdrew the request. None of the four officers involved had written any of this information in their police notebooks.

Release of the letter Lois Harper wrote to her husband. A letter that Lois Harper had written to J.J., which was found in Harper's possession the night he died, spoke to how his drinking had been driving the couple apart and how she needed a home where she could feel safe. The Crown attorney for the inquest, William Morton, and the Harper family's lawyer, Harvey Pollock, had agreed that the letter was personal and would not be entered as evidence during the inquest. Police officers thought otherwise because the letter supported the claim that Harper was a "belligerent drunk." During an inquest recess, a CTV cameraman began filming the exhibits, including the letter. Its contents were featured on the evening newscast. It was later revealed that a CTV reporter had been tipped off by a police officer that the letter was included in the exhibits (Sinclair 1999: 95).

"Payback." In the fall of 1990 Pollock was arrested by Winnipeg police on a sexual assault charge. For some observers, his arrest (and especially the negative publicity it garnered) was interpreted as "payback" by members of the Winnipeg Police Department for Pollock's role in the Harper inquiry. The charge emerged when an Aboriginal woman who had called the police to assist in dealing with her teenage son told them, "You wouldn't believe what my lawyer Harvey Pollock did" (Sinclair 1999: 277). The officers wanted to hear more. The woman was upset that Pollock had lectured her about drinking when she had appeared in his office under the influence (Pollock's son had been killed by a drunk driver a few years previously). Enquiring about the injuries she had incurred and was seeking insurance compensation for, Pollock was reported to have put his hand on the woman's back, just above her buttocks. The officers — one of whom just happened to be Constable Kathryn Hodgins — provided the woman with information on how to contact the police department about laying charges of sexual assault. Police officers later appeared at Pollock's law office to take him into custody. On leaving the building on a "perp walk," he was photographed by a *Winnipeg Free Press* reporter — who, as it turned out, had been tipped off by a police officer about the impending charge. While the case received considerable media attention, the charges were later stayed by the Crown prosecutor.

The effort to place Constable Cross and the police department "in the best possible light" was most starkly exemplified in an exchange that occurred during the inquiry. One of the issues that the commissioners pursued was the circumstances under which police officers draw their guns. Constable Glen Spryszak, a former partner of Constable Cross and the acting supervisor who had initially taken charge of the scene of the shooting, was asked during his testimony whether he had ever run down a city street with his gun drawn. He answered "No." When asked again to reconsider his answer, the officer again said, without hesitation, "No." A television videotape was then played of an unrelated incident that occurred in April 1988, clearly showing Constable Spryszak running down a city street with his gun drawn. When asked to explain his previous denial, Spryszak shrugged his shoulders and suggested that he wasn't "running," only "jogging" (Hamilton and Sinclair 1991b: 27). In commenting on this incident, the AJI Commissioners noted that perhaps the officer simply had no recollection of having drawn his gun in that fashion. But given that Constable Spryszak was an officer with fifteen years of experience on the force, they questioned that explanation. "Undoubtedly, he was aware as well that having a gun drawn had become an issue at both the inquest and the Inquiry" (Hamilton and Sinclair 1991b: 27).

The "stand by your partner" certainty has been documented in other cases. In a book on policing in Canada, John Sewell comments on how police solidarity can lead officers "to report exactly the same take on events in which they participated, even if it appears clear that the police version is inaccurate." He cites a 2003 Toronto case involving a teenager charged with assaulting a police officer in an Etobicoke mall parking lot. Two other officers were present and recorded the same account as the charging officer in their notebooks. At the conclusion of the trial, the teenager's lawyer showed the court a videotape taken by a bystander that evening in the parking lot. The tape clearly showed the police officer making an unprovoked assault on the teenager. The judge dismissed the case and charged the officer with assault. The officer was subsequently convicted and sentenced to a brief period in jail. The fate of the two officers who obviously lied in both their notebooks and in their sworn testimony in court was never revealed (Sewell 2010: 69, 70).

The popularity of video and cell-phone cameras has inadvertently led to more cases of police misconduct coming to light. One of the earliest examples was the 1991 beating of a Black man named Rodney King by members of the Los Angeles Police Department (LAPD). King had been spotted speeding down a highway by two California Highway Patrol officers. A high-speed chase ensued, which ended when King's car was eventually cornered by LAPD officers. King and his two passengers were ordered from the car. When King failed to comply with officers' directives he was twice Tasered. Lying on the ground, King was hit over fifty times with police batons. He was kicked, and his head was stomped. Officers then proceeded to handcuff him and drag his body to the side of the road to wait for an ambulance to arrive. King suffered a fractured skull, a broken ankle, kidney damage, and numerous bruises and lacerations as a result of the beating. The police beating of Rodney King was captured on a video camera by a resident in a nearby apartment block. The video was shown by news outlets worldwide — to the degree that, as one CNN spokesperson put it, "television used the tape like wallpaper" (Linder 2001).

While King was subsequently released without charges, four of the officers involved were charged with excessive use of force. In April 1992 a jury decided that there was insufficient evidence to convict the officers.

News of this decision sparked rioting in Los Angeles, during which time fifty-four people died, hundreds were injured, seven thousand were arrested, and a billion dollars worth of property was damaged. Following the riot, the U.S. government brought federal charges against the four officers accused in the King case. In August 1993 the jury returned a guilty verdict on two of the accused. They were subsequently sentenced to serve thirty months in federal correctional camps (Linder 2001).

A more recent Canadian example of a civilian recording police miscon-duct on video emerged in the 2007 Tasering death of Robert Dziekanski — a case that also raised the issue of officers' complicity in fabricating their story of what transpired.

THE TASERING DEATH OF ROBERT DZIEKANSKI

Robert Dziekanski was a forty-year-old Polish immigrant who had em-barked on his first airplane ride, landing at the Vancouver airport on the afternoon of October 13, 2007. Although his mother had arrived at the airport from the B.C. interior to meet him, she eventually left in frustration when authorities told her that her son could not be found. Dziekanski, who was unable to speak English, remained in the Customs Hall area of the airport for six hours. While he did eventually manage to proceed through Secondary Immigration and was granted immigrant status, he ended up in the semi-secure International Reception Lounge shortly after midnight. As Dziekanski was becoming increasingly exhausted, confused, and agitated, RCMP officers were called. Because of the language barrier, communication between Dziekanski and the officers was limited. At one point, Dziekanski shouted in Polish, "Leave me alone. Leave me alone. Did you become stu-pid? Have you gone insane? Why?" Within twelve minutes of the officers' arrival, Dziekanski was Tasered five times. Suffering a heart attack, he died a few minutes later.

Footage of the incident was recorded on a digital camera by a young Canadian traveller, Paul Pritchard, who had been at the airport waiting for an early-morning connecting flight. Pritchard handed the camera over to police, who told him it would be returned within forty-eight hours. When it was returned, the camera had a new memory stick. The police had cho-sen to retain the stick containing the recording of the incident until their investigation was completed. When the original stick was finally returned one month later, Pritchard released it to the media. The video showing Dziekanski being Tasered was quickly circulated on the Internet. Within a matter of weeks, it had been viewed online by at least fifteen million people worldwide (Langton 2007).

After the incident was investigated by the RCMP Integrated Homicide Team, the Crown made the decision, on reviewing the evidence, that there was no basis for laying criminal charges in Dziekanski's death. However, in 2008 retired appeal court justice Thomas Braidwood was appointed to conduct a Commission of Inquiry into Robert Dziekanski's death. The Commission's mandate was divided into two phases: one focused on the police use of conducted energy weapons (Tasers); the other focused on the circumstances of Dziekanski's death.

In his report, Judge Braidwood concluded that the RCMP officers were not justified in using a Taser against Dziekanski. The four RCMP officers failed to properly assess and respond to the circumstances in which they found the man. They repeatedly deployed the Taser without justification and separately failed to adequately reassess the situation before further deploying it. "Despite their training, the officers approached the incident as though responding to a barroom brawl and failed to shift gears when they realized that they were dealing with an obviously distraught traveler" (Braidwood 2010: 11). Moreover, similar to the Harper case, the RCMP made an effort to construct an official version of the events that would put the force "in the best possible light." Dziekanski, like Harper, was constructed as combative and violent; in essence, as the master of his own fate. As with the police who testified before the AJI, the RCMP officers involved in the Dziekanski case were found to have deliberately misrepresented their actions in their notes and statements in order to justify their actions. The Braidwood Commission also uncovered a number of factual inaccuracies that had been circulated in the RCMP's media response to Dziekanski's death:

> That Mr. Dziekanski was combative and violent, that chairs were flying, that violence was escalating, that the conducted energy weapon was deployed against him only twice, and that he continued to be combative, kicking and screaming after being handcuffed. Based on what the investigation subsequently determined, these descriptions were inaccurate and without question they portrayed Mr. Dziekanski's behaviours as more threatening and dangerous than we now know them to have been. (Braidwood 2010: 360)

As in the Rodney King case, a bystander's video was all-important. If it had not been for the Pritchard video, the details of what had actually transpired in the death of Robert Dziekanski would never have come to light. In May 2011 British Columbia's attorney general announced that the four RCMP officers involved in the death of Dziekanski would face perjury charges for their testimony at the public inquiry. No charges were to be laid against the officers relating to Dziekanski's death (*Winnipeg Free Press* 2011).

While the notion of the blue wall helps to explain why police departments might be motivated to construct an official version of events aimed at placing their actions in "the best possible light," the question of interest here is: what role did race and racism play in J.J. Harper's demise?

RACE AND RACISM IN THE HARPER CASE

The denial of racism constituted a central element in the official version of the events in the Harper case. Several of the key players maintained that race and racism had no role to play in Harper's death. Police Chief Stephen testified before the inquiry that he did not condone racism and that "If something is brought to my attention, I would do something about it" (Hamilton and Sinclair 1991b: 97). The police chief also indicated that he had never disciplined or cautioned officers with regard to racism in the department. Likewise, other members of the Winnipeg Police Department were adamant that race and racism played no part in their work.

Frances Henry and Carol Tator (2000, 2002, 2006) argue that this "discourse of denial" — the failure to acknowledge that cultural, structural, and systemic racism exists — is a central part of a broader discourse of "democratic racism" that prevails in Canadian society. Founded on an ideological commitment to democratic liberalism (as reflected, for example, in the Canadian Charter of Rights and Freedoms and provincial human rights codes), Canada is, however, also a society in which racism continues to flourish both in everyday attitudes and behaviours and in institutional policies and practices. The concept of "democratic racism" is designed to capture the fundamental tension between these two features of the Canadian social fabric. According to Henry and Tator (2002: 23–24), democratic racism "is an ideology in which two conflicting sets of values are made congruent to each other. Commitments to democratic principles such as justice, equality, and fairness *conflict* with but also *coexist* with negative feelings about minority groups and discrimination against them."

When racism is acknowledged, it is more often than not understood as "isolated and individual discriminatory acts and expressions of racial bias" (Tator and Henry 2006: 124). On that score, evidence of racism in the

Harper case can be found in the use of racist language by the police officers involved. For instance, the AJI commissioners accepted the testimony of the two car theft suspects that racist comments had been made to them by police officers. One had been called "a blue-eyed fucking Indian" and the other "a fucking Indian." In their report the commissioners also referred to the Don Gillmor *Saturday Night* article. As part of his research, Gillmor had interviewed his boyhood acquaintance, Robert Cross, the day after the inquest report had been released. In his article, Gillmor quotes an unidentified officer (whom he later divulged to be Cross) as saying: "Harper was the author of his own demise. The natives drink and they get in trouble. Blaming the police for their troubles is like an alcoholic blaming the liquor store for being open late" (Gillmor 1988: 50). Similarly disparaging comments made by other officers at the scene were relayed to Gillmor by Cross: "That's right," one officer said, "bleed him dry." Another officer said, "If you're lucky, that fucker dies" (1988: 45). Nevertheless, all the officers who testified before the inquiry, including Cross, said that they did not make or hear any of the racist remarks quoted in Gillmor's article, with the exception of a racist joke that made the rounds of the Public Safety Building after the shooting.

Individual expressions of racial bias, then, are one way in which racism manifests itself in Aboriginal people's encounters with police. In that regard, the Harper shooting is not the only instance to have exposed such racist expressions. In September 1995 the Ontario Provincial Police (OPP) were involved in a standoff with Aboriginal people occupying Ipperwash Provincial Park. First Nations men, women, and children were in the park to protest the federal government's long-standing refusal to return the Stoney Point territory to them when an OPP officer shot and killed an unarmed protester named Dudley George. The Ontario government subsequently established an inquiry into the events leading to George's death. In his report Commissioner Sydney B. Linden noted that officers of the Ontario Provincial Police made racist comments concerning the Aboriginal people who were under surveillance at the time (Linden 2007). The most obvious instance, recorded on a videotape made by OPP officers who were posing as a television crew outside the park, occurred the day before the shooting. The tape was obtained by CBC News through a Freedom of Information request (Gray 2004). On a portion of the tape a voice responding to an inaudible question says, "No, there's no one down there. Just a big, fat, fuck Indian." Another voice warns, "The camera's rolling." But the only response is, "Yeah." Another voice then says, "We had this plan, you know. We thought if we could get five or six cases of Labatt's 50, we could bait them. And we would have this big net and a pit." People are heard laughing as the officer names his plan "creative thinking" and adds: "Works in the South with watermelons" (Gray 2004; Linden 2007: 29).

For Commissioner Linden, these racist comments were not an isolated incident. He cited a number of other tape-recorded conversations of various officers making derogatory remarks about Aboriginal people at the time of the occupation. The inquiry also learned of several inappropriate activities after the occupation, including the production and distribution of coffee mugs and T-shirts containing racist imagery to "commemorate" the OPP's actions at Ipperwash (Linden 2007: 30).

While race and racism can manifest themselves in such obvious ways, they are not confined to individual expressions of racial bias. As the AJI commissioners assert, Constable Cross had no reasonable and probable grounds to stop Harper. Why, then, did he make the decision to approach him? In the commissioners' view, race was the primary reason:

> Cross, we believe, got caught up in the excitement of the chase. We believe that he decided to stop and question Harper *simply because Harper was a male Aboriginal person in his path*. We are unable to find any other reasonable explanation for his being stopped. We do not accept Cross' explanation. It was clearly a retroactive attempt to justify stopping Harper. We believe that Cross had no basis to connect him to any crime in the area and that his refusal or unwillingness to permit Harper to pass freely was... *racially motivated*. (Hamilton and Sinclair 1991B: 32; emphasis added)

But the commissioners do not rest their conclusion that "racism exists within the Winnipeg Police Department" (1991b: 93) solely on the motivations of individual officers. They also direct attention to the policies and procedures of the Winnipeg Police Department that contributed to Harper's death.

In particular, the commissioners took issue with the use of race when issuing a description of a suspect. While the Department Procedures and Reporting Manual notes that "Caution must be exercised when releasing descriptions of suspects to the media, so as not to malign specific ethnic or racial groups," it also states that "Nothing in this policy is intended to prevent the use of specific facts which may assist in an investigation where the suspect has been positively identified as a member of a specific group" (cited in Hamilton and Sinclair 1991b: 93–94). One example provided in the manual is to refer to Aboriginal people as "Native in appearance."

The AJI commissioners maintained that "merely describing someone by reference to race appeals to stereotypes held about that group. Asking police to search for a 'native' calls upon officers to reach conclusions about how the person they are searching for looks, talks or behaves. There is no commonality among Aboriginal people in their appearance, manner of speaking or behaviour." In the commissioners' view, "To advise police officers that a suspect in an offence is a native is a license to commit racism. That should not be condoned" (Hamilton and Sinclair 1991b: 94). The commissioners go on to suggest:

> If officers were given proper descriptive details about such things as colouring, age, weight and hair length, they would avoid the kind of stereotyping that was at the root of the problem in this case. Cross, for one reason or another, ignored other particulars of the description of the suspect, seizing on the word "native." He stopped the first Aboriginal person he saw, even though that person was a poor match for the description in other respects and a suspect already had been caught. (Hamilton and Sinclair 1991b: 94)

While the practice of racial profiling by the department no doubt contributed to Harper's demise, the racism runs deeper. Writing about the death of Harper, Gillmor commented:

> The thing that made the incident possible, the thing that framed Harper's death, was racism. Not overt racism, perhaps, but a subtler, systemic brand — a set of prejudices that both Harper and Cross took into the situation. Harper was an educated man, aware of his rights, and intolerant of a police attitude he believed was biased and overbearing. Cross had grown up in a middle-class suburb six kilometers from the nearest native community. His early experience with Indians was as an alcoholic hurdle to be negotiated while buying beer in the North End. His police experience had simply reinforced that notion. That these two sets of ideas found one another on Logan Avenue at 2:30 in the morning was tragic but inevitable. (Gillmor 1988: 47)

Gillmor, in other words, was attuned to the realization that racialized spaces predominated in Winnipeg in the 1970s and 80s. As boyhood acquaintances, he and Robert Cross had grown up in a white, middle-class space. Together they had sojourned to the racialized space of the city's North End when they were underage youth to buy beer at a hotel vendor. As Gillmor (1988: 46) describes it, "The North End was another country, unmapped and hostile." This unmapped, hostile — and racialized — space was one that Cross regularly patrolled as a police officer. And it was in this space that Cross happened upon J.J. Harper on that fateful night.

To understand fully the ways in which race and racism played out in the Harper case, therefore, involves attending to the role of the police as reproducers of order. In carrying out their mandate of maintaining the status quo of a racially unequal social order, police come to define the spaces populated by Aboriginal people as disorderly and dangerous — and the Aboriginal people who inhabit those spaces as the "usual suspects" — with results that can be tragic for countless people.

COLLATERAL DAMAGE

The shooting of J.J. Harper and the ensuing events had a profound impact. First and foremost, both Harper's family and the Aboriginal community of which he was a member no doubt suffered greatly from his loss. But there were other forms of collateral damage.

Alan, the thirteen-year-old car theft suspect, was profoundly affected by what he witnessed that night. After the inquest, his mother reported to Gillmor that he had become withdrawn and wouldn't talk to anyone. She had taken him to a therapist to seek help for him, but Alan bolted from the waiting room. "Now he's wetting the bed," his mother said. "He's afraid to go out alone" (Gillmor 1988: 52). Alan had also testified before the inquiry that he had been having nightmares about the shooting during which he would cry out in his sleep, "Don't shoot me" (Sinclair 1999: 160).

Constable Kathryn Hodgins had been a member of the Winnipeg police force for nine years at the time of the shooting. The AJI Commissioners noted:

> It was apparent during the course of her testimony that the events of March 9 have affected Hodgins deeply. She testified to the fact, and spoke of the emotional and psychological devastation that followed that night. She had trouble performing her work and stated that what occurred at the inquest is beyond her recollection. Her doctor informed us in a letter that she has been diagnosed as suffering from post-traumatic stress disorder. (Hamilton and Sinclair 1991b: 21)

While he was placed on a reduced assignment for short periods after the shooting, Constable Robert Cross was never able to return to active duty. Suffering from anxiety and depression, he turned to alcohol to deal with the aftermath and was admitted to a psychiatric unit on at least one occasion. His doctors tried to delay his appearance at the AJI, on the ground that his testimony might lead to a "catastrophic," potentially life-threatening reaction (as he had suicidal ideation). Cross's marriage ended in 1992. He died in 1999. The official cause of death was "acute alcoholism" (Sinclair 1999: 159, 391).

On the morning he was scheduled to appear at the inquiry (September 20, 1989), Inspector Ken Dowson — the police officer in charge of the investigation into Harper's death — shot himself in the head in the basement of his home. In one of the suicide notes he left behind, Dowson expressed his regrets for some of the decisions he had made during the investigation (not fingerprinting the gun, not seeing Harper's glasses at the scene, not taking all the necessary photos). He wrote about how devastating the effect had been on all of the officers involved, "especially Cross and those young guys at the scene." Dowson also wrote, "I find it almost unbelievable that anyone could believe that the shooting of Harper was racially motivated." He commented on how the inquiry and the media had made the event into a circus. "They will never be satisfied until they have their pound of flesh, so I'll be the sacrifice. I was the one in charge and I was responsible" (Sinclair 1999: 214–15).

While Inspector Dowson was unable to conceive of how race and racism were implicated in Harper's death, the AJI report constituted a turning point in its formal acknowledgement of the troubled relations between Aboriginal people and the police in Manitoba. In addition to its investigation into Harper's death and the murder of Helen Betty Osborne (Hamilton and Sinclair 1991b), the inquiry heard testimony from Aboriginal people across the province about their experiences with police.

> We heard a litany of complaints and examples indicating that many, if not most, Aboriginal people are afraid of the police. They consider the police force to be a foreign presence and do not feel understood by it. They certainly do not feel that the police are in any sense 'their' force, that police operate on their behalf, or that the police are in any significant manner subject to a corresponding Aboriginal influence in their communities. (Hamilton and Sinclair 1991a: 597)

The AJI was not the only government-sponsored investigation into the treatment of Aboriginal people by the justice system at the close of the twentieth century. Another was the Royal Commission on the Donald Marshall, Jr. Prosecution (Nova Scotia 1989; see also Mannette 1992). Marshall, a member of the Mi'kmaq Nation, had spent eleven years in prison for an offence he did not commit. The Nova Scotia Royal Commission completely exonerated Marshall for any criminal liability in the killing of Sandy Seale, a seventeen-year-old Black Nova Scotian. The Commission determined:

> The criminal justice system failed Donald Marshall, Jr. at virtually every turn from his arrest and wrongful conviction for murder in 1971 up to, and even beyond, his acquittal by the Court of Appeal in 1983. The tragedy of the failure is compounded by evidence that this miscarriage of justice could – and should – have been prevented, or at least corrected quickly, if those involved in the system had carried out their duties in a professional and/or competent manner. That they did not is due, in part at least, to the fact that Donald Marshall, Jr. is a Native. (Nova Scotia 1989: 1)

In particular, the Marshall Commission (1989: 2) found that the initial response of police officers to a report of the stabbing was "entirely inadequate, incompetent and unprofessional." The Commission also determined that a subsequent investigation by the Sergeant of Detectives was inadequate, "partly because, in our view, he shared what we believe was a general sense in Sydney's White community at the time that Indians were not 'worth' as much as Whites" (1989: 3).

Government-sponsored investigations into Aboriginal-police relations continued into the twenty-first century with a Saskatchewan inquiry into the circumstances surrounding the death of Neil Stonechild, whose frozen body was discovered in a field on the outskirts of Saskatoon in 1990 (Wright 2004). That event — one of several — presented yet another twist on the phenomenon of racialized policing: Starlight Tours.

Chapter Five

STARLIGHT TOURS

On the morning of November 29, 1990, two construction workers discovered the frozen body of a young Aboriginal man, partially clad and wearing only one shoe, in a field on the outskirts of Saskatoon. The young man was later identified as Neil Stonechild. He had been last seen on the night of November 24, when the temperature had dropped to minus 28 degrees Celsius. Cuts and marks on his body suggested that he had been assaulted, but an autopsy concluded that he had died of hypothermia. The Stonechild family suspected that Neil Stonechild had been driven to the area and abandoned. A police investigation concluded that no foul play was involved in his death.

Some ten years later the frozen bodies of two more Aboriginal men were found on the outskirts of Saskatoon. The shirtless body of Rodney Nastius was discovered on January 29, 2000. He was last seen alive in the early morning hours of that same day in downtown Saskatoon. The frozen body of Lawrence Wegner was found five days later, February 3, 2000. He was wearing a T-shirt, blue jeans, and no shoes. Wegner was last seen alive on January 30, 2000. The day after his body was discovered Darrel Night and his uncle were talking to a police officer they happened to meet and told him about a similar experience. Night said he had been taken out of town by two Saskatoon police officers on January 28, 2000, and dropped off not far from where the bodies of Nastius and Wegner were found. Despite being dressed in only a jean jacket and summer shoes, Night managed to survive by attracting the attention of a worker at the nearby Queen Elizabeth Power Plant. The worker let him into the building to warm up and phone for a taxi.

The freezing deaths of Stonechild, Nastius, and Wegner and Night's revelation that police officers had dropped him off on a bitterly cold Saskatchewan night on the outskirts of the city generated a tidal wave of controversy over what came to be referred to as "Starlight Tours" — a seemingly benign term that connotes the police practice of detaining people, driving them to another location, and leaving them there to find their own way home. That all of these men were Aboriginal also raised the spectre of racism.

On learning of the deaths of Nastius and Wegner, members of the Aboriginal community in Saskatoon came together to share their grief and express their outrage. On February 17, students at the Saskatchewan Indian Federated College, which Wegner had attended, organized a public vigil and walk from the college to the police station (Adam 2000). On February 26, a solidarity walk of over five hundred people marched down 20th Street in Saskatoon to the police station (Kossick 2000). On March 25, 2000, a cleansing ceremony was held near the location where the bodies of Naistus and Wegner had been found. At the memorial service held after the ceremony, Bernelda Wheeler, an organizer of the Grandmothers Vigil for Justice, spoke about the phenomenon of Starlight Tours, telling how it was happening not just in Saskatchewan but everywhere across the country:

> It happens in Toronto, I know it happens in Halifax, I've seen it happen in Winnipeg, it is happening here in Saskatoon, it happens in Vancouver — all over the country everybody has known about it for many, many, years. We do not want that to happen anymore. I am a grandmother, I have grandsons out there, I hope one day to have great grandchildren. I want to know that these people are safe — that they can count on people like the police in every city, in every community, to be protected by them, rather than brutalized by them. (Cited in Kossick 2000)

As the news about the Saskatoon Starlight Tours spread, Aboriginal organizations reported receiving hundreds of phone calls about similar incidents across the province (Brass 2004; McNairn 2000). A reporter for the Saskatoon *StarPhoenix* was also receiving calls. He said that "everyone seemed to know someone who had been taken on a starlight tour, and now they were calling him" (Reber and Renaud 2005: 177). Demands for a public inquiry into the matter of Aboriginal-police relations in the province grew louder. Not confident in the criminal justice system's response, the Federation of Saskatchewan Indian Nations (which represents 74 First Nations in the province) hired its own investigator to look into allegations of police brutality against Aboriginal people.

Shortly after Night disclosed his experience to a Saskatoon police officer, Constables Dan Hatchen and Ken Munson were suspended from the Saskatoon Police Service (SPS) and an RCMP task force named Project Ferric was launched to investigate Night's allegations and the deaths of Nastius, Wegner, and Stonechild. In 2001 Hatchen and Munson were found guilty of unlawful confinement and sentenced to eight months' imprisonment. In February 2003 the Saskatchewan Justice Minister announced an inquiry into the death of Neil Stonechild and the investigations carried out by the SPS and the RCMP. Headed by the Honourable Mr. Justice David Wright, the Commission of Inquiry into Matters Relating to the Death of Neil Stonechild began sitting in September 2003. When the report of the inquiry was submitted in October 2004, Justice Wright made it clear that he was highly critical of the police investigation into Stonechild's death. He characterized it as "insufficient and totally inadequate" (Wright 2004: 212). Following the release of the report, Constables Larry Hartwig and Bradley Senger, the officers involved in the Stonechild case, were dismissed from the Saskatoon Police Service.

Much like the J.J. Harper case, the response to revelations of Starlight Tours was split into two opposing camps. Aboriginal activists and organizations declared the practice to be evidence of the racism rampant in the Saskatoon police force; police and their supporters said Starlight Tours were a myth perpetrated by special interest groups, and they denied the claims of racism and any wrongdoing on the part of the officers involved in the Night case and the deaths of the other Aboriginal men. But in the broader context of racialized policing these competing positions about Starlight Tours take on a different cast. William King and Thomas Dunn (2004: 341) suggest that the police practice of transporting troublesome persons to another location — otherwise known as "dumping" — is an informal policy that "is generally acknowledged by police practitioners." In Prairie cities such as Saskatoon, this racialized policing practice appears to have become one of the strategies that police utilize to reproduce order in their dealings with troubled and troublesome people.

DARREL NIGHT'S STARLIGHT TOUR

With only a Grade 11 education and no current job, thirty-four-year-old Darrel Night was typical of many Aboriginal people living in Saskatoon. Depending on various estimates, from one-third to almost one-half of Aboriginal adults in Saskatoon had less than a Grade 12 level of education. The unemployment rate for Aboriginal people in the city was about 22 percent, compared to 4.8 percent for the non-Aboriginal population (Anderson 2005: 36, 43). Also like many Aboriginal people, Night was in poor health. He regularly suffered from dizziness as a result of a bout with tuberculosis and meningitis. He coped with the imbalance it caused by keeping one eye closed. Also not uncommon, Night had a drinking problem and was no stranger to the police; he had received some twenty-two criminal convictions (Renaud and Reber 2005: 123). While the relationship between Darrel Night and the Saskatoon police was probably already strained, characterized by mistrust and suspicion on both sides, the events of January 28, 2000, brought the strain into bold relief.

On that night Night had been at a house party but left when a fight broke out in the early morning hours. He set off to walk the few blocks to his sister's home, where he was staying. After he left, the police were called to the house on a weapons disturbance because one of the men at the party had been threatening people with a knife. Constables Dan Hatchen and Ken Munson were two of the officers on patrol that night. Each of them had logged some sixteen years on the Saskatoon police force. They had been partners for six years. When they reached the house they were among the last of the police cars to arrive, and so they left the scene. It was then that they met up with Night, who was walking down the street.

As the patrol car slowed down alongside him, Night became belligerent, yelling at the officers: "About fucking time you guys showed up, get the fuck up and stop those fights. I have to tell you what to do?" He also gave them the finger (R. v. Munson and Hatchen 2003 at 6). As the vehicle went by, Night pounded on the side panel and the trunk. In return, the officers called Night a "drunken fucking Indian" (Zakreski 2000). Arresting Night for "causing a disturbance," they handcuffed him and put him in the back of their cruiser. Night assumed that he was being taken to the drunk tank. Instead, the officers drove him to the outskirts of the city, more than two kilometres from the Queen Elizabeth Power Plant. According to Night, they swore at him, "Get the fuck out of here, you fucking Indian" and removed the handcuffs. The cruiser then proceeded to drive away. When Night yelled, "I'm going to freeze out here," the officers stopped the car and yelled back, "That's your fucking problem" (Zakreski 2000). To that point the officers had not indicated on their car's mobile data terminal that they had left the scene of the house disturbance. It was only when they drove away from Night that they keyed "Available" into the terminal (Reber and Renaud 2005: 130). Contrary to police protocols, no record of their encounter with Night was made in their notebooks, and no report was filed with the Saskatoon Police Service. There was also no record of any attempt to check for outstanding warrants, criminal record, or other pertinent information about the man they had arrested (R. v. Munson and Hatchen 2003 at 4).

It took Darrel Night about twenty minutes to walk to the power plant from where the police officers had dropped him off in the minus-25-degree-Celsius weather. He hammered on the doors of the power plant in desperation, and it was another twenty minutes before he attracted the attention of a plant supervisor who was working the night shift. Despite his misgivings in seeing the poorly dressed man pounding on the door, the supervisor opened it to let him in. Night told him, "The police just dumped me out here" (Reber and Renaud 2005: 133). At Night's request, the supervisor called for a cab, which arrived shortly afterward to drive Night to his sister's place, less than one block from where he was arrested.

In addition to the plant supervisor and the cab driver, Night told his sister and other family members about what the police officers had done to him that night. But no official complaint was made. In Night's view, "Complaining was a waste of time" (Reber and Renaud 2005: 135). Some six days later, Night was driving with his uncle when they were stopped by a Saskatoon police officer for a seatbelt violation. While they were waiting for the officer to write up a ticket they heard the news over the radio that a frozen body had been discovered near the power station. Night's uncle ended up telling the police officer that the same thing had happened to his nephew. When the officer asked whether he talked to anyone about his experience, Night replied in the negative, saying "Nobody would listen to me anyway" (Reber and Renaud 2005: 155). The officer reported what he had learned to his superiors, and Night was brought to the police station to provide a statement.

In reporting on his experience, Night thought that the number of the cruiser was "57," mistaking the "2" for a "5." The officers in car 57 denied having anything to do with the incident, but they were relieved from duty anyway. News of the investigation spread throughout the police force. As journalists Susanne Reber and Robert Renaud (2005: 161) note, "Night's error forced Hatchen and Munson's hand. They admitted to [Deputy Chief Dan] Wiks that they were the ones who had taken Night out to the power plant, but maintained from the beginning that he'd asked to be let out of the car."

Saskatoon Police Chief Dave Scott immediately suspended Constables Hatchen and Munson. He also told reporters that the incident involving two of his unnamed officers "was in no way connected with the two other dead men" (Reber and Renaud 2005: 169). The bodies of Nastius and Wegner had been found only days earlier. Lawyer Donald E. Worme, however, was of a different mind. When Darrel Night came to his office in search of legal counsel, Worme immediately made the connection between his story and the deaths of the other two Aboriginal men.

While Police Chief Scott was intent on dealing with the issue in-house, Saskatchewan justice minister Chris Axworthy announced on February 16, 2000, that the RCMP would be put in charge of an investigation into the allegations made by Night and the freezing deaths of Nastius and Wegner. The RCMP task force would also investigate two other Aboriginal deaths that occurred around the same time as those of Nastius and Wegner. On January 19, 2000, fifty-three-year-old Lloyd Dustyhorn was found frozen to death outside his home three hours after he was released from police custody. Dustyhorn had spent eighteen hours in a police cell, suffering from hallucinations. When police left him on his doorstep it was minus 35 degrees Celsius and he was wearing only a shirt, pants, and shoes. On February 19, 2000, D'Arcy Dean Ironchild was found dead by members of his family. The thirty-three-year-old had been taken into custody by Saskatoon police for public intoxication on the previous evening. He was kept under observation in a holding cell and then released around midnight and sent home in a taxi (Canada 2002: 88).

THE FREEZING DEATHS OF RODNEY NASTIUS AND LAWRENCE WEGNER

Rodney Nastius was a twenty-five-year-old member of the Onion Lake First Nation. His frozen body was found in an area just north of the power plant the same morning that Darrel Night had been dropped off by police officers. Naistus was wearing only running shoes and a pair of black sweat pants; his jacket and T-shirt were found nearby (Renaud and Reber 2005: 136).

Naistus grew up on the Onion Lake reserve near Lloydminster, Saskatchewan. His parents separated when he was an infant and he spent time in foster and group homes on and off his reserve. As a youth Rodney got into trouble with the law, mostly for break and enters. The year before he died he was convicted of breaking and entering and sentenced to do time in an urban work camp. Naistus had just been released from the camp on January 27, and had spent the day before his body was found celebrating his freedom with his brother and cousin. He had left his cousin's house with an acquaintance around 9:30 in the evening with the intention of heading to a nightclub in downtown Saskatoon (McNairn 2004).

An inquest held in late 2001 identified the cause of death to be hypothermia but was unable to determine the circumstances of the death. While no police involvement was proven (Reber and Renaud 2005: 259), many people suspected otherwise. According to witness testimony at the inquest, Naistus was last seen walking outside a downtown bar with an open beer in his hand. The Naistus family's lawyer, Darren Winegarden, told reporters that an Aboriginal man wandering around downtown with open liquor would be "a prime target for pickup by police." A friend of Naistus also testified that he had offered him a place to stay that night. The friend happened to live on the same block where Night was picked up by constables Hatchen and Munson. The Saskatoon *StarPhoenix* had obtained information prior to the inquest that indicated both officers were on duty at the time of Naistus's disappearance and that "there were periods of time during their shift which are unaccounted for" (Coolican 2001a). Nevertheless, the RCMP investigators conducted a polygraph test on the two officers in which they denied having anything to do with Naistus that night. The Nastius family expressed their disappointment with the inquest's outcome. His uncle told a reporter, "There's too many unanswered questions left. ... The wounds are open more because we don't know any answers at all." The family pointed to the similarities with Night's story. "We're hoping that there's still somebody out there that knows something, that can come forward and make a closure of this" (Coolican 2001b).

Lawrence Wegner, the next man to be found, was a thirty-year-old Cree from the Saulteaux First Nation near North Battleford, Saskatchewan. The manager of the Saskatoon group home where Wegner had lived described him as a "gentle, sweet, good person." But Wegner could not handle tension. The group home manager was of the view that Wegner's bouts of panic and anxiety had led to problems with drug use and depression (Reber and Renaud 2005: 117). Wegner had enrolled in social work courses at the Saskatchewan Indian Federated College in 1999. He was reportedly a good student, but the stress associated with his schoolwork had led to more drug use.

On the evening of January 30 Wegner showed up at the home of his mother's cousin after smoking a large quantity of hash oil with his roommate. Despite the frigid weather he was wearing only a T-shirt and blue jeans and no shoes. Not recognizing him, the family kept the door closed. Nevertheless, out of concern for his condition, they phoned the police to report that a poorly dressed young man was heading up their street towards the hospital. One of Wegner's classmates and her friend happened to be driving in the neighbourhood that night. They later reported seeing him being put into the back of a police car. Another passerby also reported seeing a young Aboriginal man being put into the back of a police cruiser.

Some four days later railway workers discovered Wegner's frozen body a half a kilometre from the power station.

While the autopsy report noted a large bruise above Wegner's eye and hemorrhaging under his scalp, the pathologist concluded, "there is no external evidence of gross violence or trauma to the body" (Reber and Renaud 2005: 161). The cause of death was deemed to be hypothermia. Wegner's family was not convinced by this finding. As Brian Hutchinson wrote in *Saturday Night*:

> Saskatoon police told the Wegners that their son had probably walked from the hospital to the power station, a distance of six kilometres, in his stocking feet. Curiously, there were no holes in the socks he'd been wearing that night. Mary Wegner later saw her son's body in the city morgue. There were scratches on the back of his hand, she recalls, an ugly bruise on his forehead, and a "purple mark all around his face. [The police] say it was from exposure.... I think he was killed." (Hutchinson 2000)

RCMP investigators later told Wegner's parents that Saskatoon police officers had been called to a disturbance near the hospital that evening. But no report was filed and there was no record that Wegner had ever been apprehended (Hutchinson 2000). As part of the RCMP investigation, all forty of the SPS officers who were on duty the night that Wegner died were interviewed; all of the officers denied having had any contact with him (Coolican 2002). While witnesses said they had seen blood on Wegner's clothing, confirmation of that statement was not possible because the SPS had failed to confiscate his clothes as evidence.

An inquest into Lawrence Wegner's death was held in February 2002. The construction of the thirty-year-old as a "schizophrenic drug addict" predominated the proceedings, even though toxicology tests showed that he had only elevated levels of THC and therapeutic levels of the prescription drugs he was taking for depression (Reber and Renaud 2005: 267). While witnesses testified about seeing Wegner being put into a police car on the night he died, their credibility came into question because they had only come forward once the inquest was underway. The two Aboriginal women said they had been "too scared to speak up" (Reber and Renaud 2005: 268). One of the unexplained issues relating to the death pertained to how Wegner was found with no shoes on his feet but was wearing socks that were not soiled. An RCMP officer took off his shoes and tested the theory about walking along the railroad tracks that night to the place where his body was eventually found; the officer's socks became filthy and tattered (Reber and Renaud 2005: 270).

At the close of the inquest coroner Hugh Harradence instructed the jury that it could not assign blame for Wegner's death. He informed the jury members that they could consider three possibilities for how he met his demise: accident; non-culpable homicide; and undetermined. The coroner also warned the jury about dealing too heavily with the "broader issues of tension to police and the aboriginal community," which had been a subject of growing controversy. He further noted that the inquest had heard "no evidence of a dumping practice" by Saskatoon police (Coolican 2002). In the end, after deliberating for twelve hours, the jury rendered a verdict of "undetermined." Wegner's death was "too suspicious to be ruled accidental, but they were unwilling to declare it a homicide" (Reber and Renaud 2005: 271). While the Aboriginal community conducted round dances and sweats in support of the Wegner family, his parents were left with no explanation for their son's death. As Wegner's father commented, "We're still dealing with unanswered questions to what happened to this human being" (Hubbard 2004).

Several commentators suggested that if Darrel Night had not survived to tell about his experience, the phenomenon of Starlight Tours would never have come to public attention. As it was, despite being part of the "largest criminal investigation in the history of Saskatchewan" (Hutchinson 2000), the RCMP investigations into the deaths of Nastius and Wegner — and the freezing deaths of Lloyd Dustyhorn and D'Arcy Dean Ironchild shortly after they had been released from police custody — did not result in any criminal charges. Criminal charges were laid, however, in the Darrel Night case.

THE TRIAL OF CONSTABLES HATCHEN AND MUNSON

In March 2000 the RCMP task force concluded its investigation into Night's allegations of police misconduct. That April, based on the assessment of the Public Prosecutions Division of Saskatchewan Justice, Saskatoon police constables Dan Hatchen and Ken Munson were charged with forcible confinement and assault in the Night case. The RCMP investigation had eliminated the two officers from suspicion in the deaths of Wegner and Naistus after they had taken a polygraph test.

The trial of Hatchen and Munson began on September 11, 2001, in a packed Saskatoon courtroom before an all-white jury. During the nine-day trial Night's character and credibility came under heavy attack by the defence lawyers, who cast him as "a drunk, a liar and a racist" (Burton 2001). As newspaper columnist Randy Burton (2001) described it, "There were moments during the trial of policemen Ken Munson and Dan Hatchen when you could have sworn it was Night on trial, not the two cops."

In his police statement Munson said that Night had pleaded with the officers, saying "Come on, guys, you don't have to do this, let me go and I'll walk back from anywhere, just drop me off" (cited in Reber and Renaud 2005: 256). Night, for his part, was adamant that he had pleaded with the officers *not* to be left on the outskirts of Saskatoon. Neither officer disputed leaving Night near the power plant on the night in question. They said in their statements that "they'd felt Night could take care of himself, despite the cold, his light clothes and the fact that he'd been drinking" (Reber and Renaud 2005: 256). The officers apparently only began to worry about what happened to the man who was in their charge when news of Wegner's death became known. Because they had never asked Night his name they had no way of knowing whether the frozen body belonged to him. In the officers' view, what they did may have been an error in judgment, but it was not a crime.

The jury delivered its verdict on September 20, 2001, finding Hatchen and Munson guilty of forcible confinement but not guilty of assault. The Saskatoon Police Service immediately fired both officers. Prior to their sentencing hearing the two men surprised the court by requesting a traditional Aboriginal sentencing circle.

Sentencing circles were initiated by the criminal justice system to provide the Aboriginal community with an alternative to incarceration and promote a healing process for both victims and offenders. The criteria for when to hold a sentencing circle include: that the offender accepts responsibility and acknowledges the harm done to society and the victim; that the offender has "deep roots" in the community in which the circle is held and from which the participants are drawn; that the victim is a willing participant in the process; and that any disputed facts have been resolved in advance (Justice as Healing 1998; see also Woolford 2009: 63–67).

None of these criteria were met in the Hatchen and Munson case. For instance, the two officers had pleaded not guilty to the charges and testified that they were not legally responsible for what had happened to Night. They had also made known their intention of appealing their conviction on forcible confinement, and their lawyers conducted what Night's lawyer, Donald Worme, described as a "tough, aggressive, difficult defence" (Barnsley 2002).

While they expressed remorse for the negative impact that had been visited on the other members of the Saskatoon Police Service, the men were not as forthcoming in expressing remorse for their treatment of Night.

Lawyers for Hatchen and Munson argued that a sentencing circle would help to "heal the rift" between the Aboriginal and white communities (Burton 2001). Few in the Aboriginal community agreed with that position — including Darrel Night, who refused to participate in such a proceeding. In the end, Judge Eugene Scheibel rejected the request, saying that it "defies both reason and logic."

> The complainant has indicated he is not prepared to participate in a sentencing circle, given the attitude of the accused. Who could fault him for refusing to participate in what he sees as a sham, one lacking in sincerity, one lacking in true remorse and one where those who have inflicted the wrong accept no responsibility for their actions. In that situation what possible benefit could there be in holding a sentencing circle—there can be no healing, only the reopening of old wounds. (*R. v. Munson* 2001a at 22)

Sentencing took place on December 7, 2001. In keeping with Section 718.2 of the Criminal Code the judge took into account aggravating and mitigating factors that would give weight to his decision. He noted:

> There is no doubt there are strong suspicions that race played a part in this offence. However, suspicion is not evidence and since the Crown has failed to prove beyond a reasonable doubt that race played a role, I am unable to consider whether or not race was an aggravating circumstance.... Therefore under s. 718.2 the only aggravating circumstance that can be considered by the Court is "evidence that the offender in committing the offence, abused a position of trust or authority in relation to the victim." (*R. v. Munson* 2001b at 24 and 25)

The judge commented that the accused were "on duty police officers sworn to uphold the law," and that they had "a general obligation to protect the public and a specific obligation to ensure that no harm would come to the complainant and that he would be treated lawfully during the execution of their duties" (*R. v. Munson* 2001b at 26). By taking Night to the outskirts of the city and dropping him off on a bitter cold winter morning, "The accused demonstrated a flagrant disregard for the life, safety and well-being of the complainant" (2001b at 27). The judge therefore held that it was clear the officers had "abused their position of trust to a high degree." He added that "the actions of the accused are so reprehensible that the Court must denounce the unlawful conduct in the strongest terms" (2001b at 30).

As for mitigating factors, Judge Scheibel noted, "Both accused have already incurred significant punishment as a result of their actions" (2001b at 37). They had been dismissed from the Saskatoon Police Service and lost their pensions. They and their families had been publicly humiliated and were in financial ruin. Nevertheless, the judge also commented:

> The actions of the accused have had a tremendous impact on the community. They have seriously damaged race relations in the City of Saskatoon and surrounding area. In addition, their actions have unfairly affected all of the rest of the officers of the Police Department by leaving feelings of mistrust within the aboriginal community. (2001b at 39)

Noting that the sentence would have been higher "had the Crown proven beyond a reasonable doubt that the offence was motivated by race and absent the statements of remorse by the accused" (2001b at 44), the judge sentenced each of the men to a term of eight months of incarceration in a provincial correctional centre. Both men were released on bail pending an appeal.

THE HATCHEN AND MUNSON APPEAL

Hatchen and Munson appealed both their conviction and sentence. The appeal was based on eight grounds.

1. *That the trial judge had erred in not allowing a change in venue.* Early in the proceedings Munson and Hatchen had applied for a change of venue to either Swift Current or Estevan, Saskatchewan, arguing that the media publicity surrounding the case — including connections made to the deaths of Wegner and Nastius — precluded the possibility of a fair trial. The trial judge dismissed the application on the grounds that the publicity surrounding the case was province-wide and the relatively small populations of Estevan and Swift Current would hinder the jury selection process (*R. v. Munson* 2001c). The appeal court found no error of principle in the decision of the trial judge concerning venue. It deemed the trial judge's application of law to be correct and his decision not to allow the application a reasonable one (*R. v. Munson and Hatchen* 2003 at 26).

2. That the trial judge had erred by not allowing the accused to cross-examine the complainant on a statement of claim issued on his behalf. Night had launched a civil suit claiming $2 million in damages for the pain and suffering resulting from his experience. During the criminal trial Munson's lawyer endeavoured to cross-examine Night as to the injuries alleged in the suit. The defence counsel's intention was to question Night's credibility and establish an ulterior motive for his criminal complaint. The trial judge ruled that counsel was permitted to cross-examine Night as to whether he sustained the injuries alleged in the claim, which counsel did. In his charge to the jury, the trial judge mentioned the civil action, indicating that this evidence could be used to determine whether or not the lawsuit motivated Night to embellish his evidence. While the appellants argued that the trial judge had erred in restricting cross-examination, the appeal court held that the appellant's counsel was in fact allowed to do so sufficiently during the trial. The court also noted, "We cannot see how his failure to do so could have affected the result, since few facts are in dispute and the conviction rests not on the evidence of the complainant alone, but also on the evidence given by the appellants themselves" (*R. v. Munson and Hatchen* 2003 at 38). The court found no basis for appeal on this ground.

3. That the trial judge erred in refusing to allow into evidence a tape recording of a telephone call made by the complainant to the Saskatoon Police on a 911 line respecting a matter unrelated to the case. On February 1, 2000, Night had made several phone calls over a twenty-minute period to the 911 line. Calling from an outdoor phone booth, he was concerned about two white males who had threatened to run him down with their car. Increasingly impatient with the delay in arrival of police assistance, Night became angry and abusive towards the 911 operator and the police. When transcripts of the calls were introduced during the trial, Night admitted that he made the calls but also said he was drunk at the time and had no memory of the incident because he had "blacked out." The defence applied to have the 911 recording put into evidence because it would show Night's bias against the police and contradict his claim that he feared the police. The trial judge ruled that the tape "did not show bias on the part of Night; that the tape could not be used to attack Night's character, since he had not put his character in issue; that the subject of the calls had no relevance to the facts of this case; and that the prejudicial effect of the tape substantially outweighed any probative value" (*R. v. Munson and Hatchen* 2003 at 43). The appeal court agreed, noting that the tape "merely showed that the complainant, in a drunken state, was belligerent and disrespectful, feared for his safety, sought help from the police, and believed they were not taking him seriously. In these circumstances the tape, dealing with an incident that had nothing to do with the case, was properly ruled inadmissible" (*R. v. Munson and Hatchen* 2003 at 45).

4. *That the trial judge erred in failing to instruct the jury fully regarding the provisions of SS. 495(3), and 498(3) of the Criminal Code.* Sections 495, 496, and 497 of the Criminal Code elaborate on the police powers of arrest and detention with respect to summary conviction offences. In his charge to the jury the trial judge explained the relevant parts of ss. 495, 496, and 497. The appeal court quotes the judge as saying:

> What this means is that the police officers have power under Section 495(2) to arrest an accused person whom they find committing a summary conviction offence, if the arrest is necessary to establish the identity of the accused, to prevent the continuation or repetition of the offence or the commission of another offence or where the officers have reasonable grounds to believe the accused will fail to attend court.
>
> In this case, the police never asked the complainant what his name was. Therefore, his arrest was not necessary for purposes of identity. There is no suggestion that the complainant would fail to attend court, this appears to be of no concern to the accused because they made no effort to find out who he was. However, there is some evidence, if believed, that tends to show that the police believed on reasonable grounds, having regard to all the circumstances, that they needed to prevent the continuation or repetition of the offence of causing a disturbance by the complainant. If you accept that evidence, then there was no requirement on the part of the police to immediately release the accused, with the intention of compelling his appearance by way of a summons or appearance notice.
>
> If you do not accept that the police needed to prevent the continuation or repetition of the offence of causing a disturbance, then he should have been released forthwith with a summons or appearance notice, and a failure to do so would result in the unlawful detention of the complainant. (Cited in *R. v. Munson and Hatchen* 2003 at 53)

Hatchen and Munson were convicted on the offence of forcible confinement. Section 279.(2) of the Criminal Code defines the offence:

> 279.(2) **Forcible Confinement**—Every one who, without lawful authority, confines, imprisons or forcibly seizes another person is guilty of:
>
> > (a) an indictable offence and liable to imprisonment for a term not exceeding ten years or;
> > (b) an offence punishable on summary conviction and liable to imprisonment for a term not exceeding eighteen months.

The key element of their appeal was that the confinement must be "without lawful authority." In their joint factum they argued:

> 10. As a matter of law, the behaviour constituting an offence must be described in the *Criminal Code*. There is no offence of "failing to release a person who is arrested forthwith," and accordingly, it is not a criminal offence for a police officer to fail to release a person immediately, once a decision is made to release the person. Depending on the circumstances, there may be an arbitrary detention, and/or the police officer's actions may give rise to a civil claim of false imprisonment, but these are not criminal offences. ... The appellants are "peace officers" and afforded protection under the provisions of Section 495, Section 497 and 498. The appellants are deemed to be acting lawfully and in the execution of their duties even if the complainant was not immediately released from custody. (Cited in *R. v. Munson and Hatchen* 2003 at 55)

The appeal court found this argument to be without merit. The court noted that sections 495 to 498 of the Criminal Code do not apply in circumstances where police officers have decided not to charge a person. "These sections of the Code do not speak to such circumstances and have no application to them. They do not and cannot, if there is no intention to charge the person with an offence, provide authority to continue to detain the person, at least in the circumstances of this case. Nor do they provide any immunity from prosecution for criminal offences which may occur as a result of detention without lawful authority" (*R. v. Munson and Hatchen* 2003 at 57).

While the appeal court justices accepted that there is no offence of "failing to release immediately upon a decision not to charge," they point out that the offence of forcible confinement does exist. The only element of the offence with which the appellants took issue was whether they had the lawful authority to continue to detain Night after they decided not to charge him. The court noted:

> While one can conceive of arguments that continued detention may be necessary in certain circumstances for purposes such as the safety of the person detained, or the safety of others, even where no charges are contemplated, no such circumstances existed here. In this case the purpose of the police officers in continuing to detain Night was to convey him to a remote place from which he would be forced to walk home inadequately dressed for the winter weather. Any argument that the law allows this is unacceptable. (*R. v. Munson and Hatchen* 2003 at 60)

5. That the trial judge erred when he recharged the jury in answer to its questions regarding unlawful confinement. During its deliberations the jury had twice asked the judge for clarification on the offence of unlawful confinement (for instance, in terms of the legal responsibility of a police officer once a decision has been made not to lay a charge). The judge restated his original instruction to the jury on Section 279 of the Criminal Code. The appeal court found the judge's original instruction to have been correct, and deemed the judge to have made no error in this regard.

6. That the judge erred in failing to instruct the jury regarding an honest but mistaken belief in consent. The defence of "honest but mistaken belief" is more often put forward in sexual assault cases, where the defendant admits to the *actus reus* (sexual intercourse occurred) but maintains that *mens rea* (intent to commit sexual assault) is absent because the accused "honestly believed" that the complainant was consenting to the sexual activity in question (see, for example, *R. v. Park* 1995). In the Hansen and Munson case, the appellants had asked the judge to instruct the jury that if they honestly but mistakenly believed Darrel Night had consented to being detained and then released on the outskirts of Saskatoon, this would entitle them to an acquittal, as the actions of the officers would have been a mere "error in judgment." The judge held that there was nothing in evidence to support a defence of "honest but mistaken belief," and the appeal court concurred with this decision.

7. *That the judge erred in declining to use a sentencing circle when imposing sentence.* The appeal court noted that the decision to use a sentencing circle is largely at the discretion of the trial judge. In this case, the court found that the judge had taken into account all the relevant factors in deciding that a sentencing circle was inappropriate, including the lack of remorse, sincerity, and acceptance of responsibility on the part of Hanson and Munson and the unwillingness of Night and the Aboriginal community to participate in a sentencing circle. The court found no error in this decision.

8. *That the judge erred in sentencing the appellants to a term of eight months imprisonment, rather than imposing a conditional sentence to be served in the community, or a sentence of imprisonment to be served intermittently.* Noting that the trial judge had provided careful and detailed reasons for his decision (*R. v. Munson* 2001b), the appeal court found no basis for interfering with the sentence of eight months' imprisonment.

With the appeals against both the conviction and sentence dismissed by the court in March 2003, Hatchen and Munson were sent to the Saskatoon Correctional Centre to serve their sentence. They were both released from a halfway house in August 2003.

One year later, Conservative MP Maurice Vellacott requested that the RCMP investigation of the Darrel Night case be reopened on the basis that new evidence had emerged. The claim was being made that Night had asked the officers to drop him off near Clancy Village, an apartment complex where a relative of Night lived. The complex was 2.5 kilometres from where the police officers had left him. This information was said to support the argument that "the officers did not just drop Night off arbitrarily, 'in the middle of nowhere' but lends credence to the officer's testimony that what [Night] asked was, 'Drop me at the end of the road. I'll walk home, and I'll be calm'.... In summary, the two officers took pity on the man and, instead of charging him, dropped him off where he asked them to. Their decision was wrong, but it was not criminal. Internal discipline was warranted, but a criminal sentence was not" (Vellacott 2004).

After the RCMP produced a report on its investigation of the claim of new evidence, Saskatchewan justice minister Frank Quennell wrote to Vellacourt: "My officials advise me that the police investigation of your suggestion that Mr. Night had a relative living very close to where he was dropped off has conclusively shown that not to be the case.... Further, I am advised that even if it were the case, it makes no difference to the liability of the two former police officers.... I am satisfied that in this case the prosecution was properly undertaken and the correct result achieved" (cited in Nickel 2005).

THE FREEZING DEATH OF NEIL STONECHILD

Born in 1973, Neil Stonechild was just seventeen years old when he died. While his mother's family was from Waywaysecapo First Nation in Manitoba, the family had moved to Saskatoon when Neil was seven years old. In addition to being an army cadet, Stonechild had taken up wrestling at the age of fourteen, a sport for which he demonstrated considerable skill. As he got older, however, the lure of hanging out with friends, partying, and drinking alcohol brought him into trouble with the law. By the age of seventeen he had spent several stretches at a youth detention centre. At the time of his death he was supposed to be serving a six-month open custody sentence at a Saskatoon group home. But Stonechild went AWOL and the police, alerted to him being unlawfully at large, were on the lookout for him. On the Saturday evening of November 24, 1990, he had appeared at his mother's house. He promised his mother that he would return to the group home, but wanted to have just one last weekend of freedom before he did. He also phoned the manager of the group home that night to tell her that he was intending to turn himself in the next day.

Trading his leather gloves for a bottle of vodka, Stonechild and his friend, sixteen-year-old Jason Roy, walked to another friend's house, where they played cards and drank. Stonechild and Roy had been friends for three or four years, after meeting each other when they were residents at Kilburn Hall, a youth detention centre. Like Stonechild, Roy had a history of run-ins with the law and was in breach of a probation order at the time. After a few hours the two youths left the house to go in search of Stonechild's former girlfriend, who was babysitting at a Snowberry Downs apartment complex. On the way they stopped at a nearby 7–Eleven to warm up, but were told to leave when they caused a disturbance in the store. Not knowing the apartment number, the two began ringing the buzzers at random in the hopes that someone would let them in. Increasingly feeling the cold, Roy decided to leave his friend, who continued to search for the right apartment. Stonechild eventually found it, but his ex-girlfriend would not let the drunken young man in.

The police were called and a dispatch order that said "DRUNK TO BE REMOVED NEIL STONECHILD, 17 YEARS OLD" was broadcast at 11:51 p.m. Two officers, constables Larry Hartwig and Brad Senger, responded to the dispatch by punching "en route" into their mobile data terminal. They entered "at scene" at 11:56 (Wright 2004: 73). Hartwig had been on the force for three years. His usual partner, Constable Ken Munson, had been seconded to a project investigating break and enters in the city, and that was why Senger, newly graduated from the police academy and still in his probationary period, accompanied Hartwig on the ride (Renaud and Reber 2005: 32). According to the police dispatch log, the officers never found Neil Stonechild. They inputted "GOA" (gone on arrival) into their mobile terminal at 12:17 a.m.

Jason Roy, however, had a different recollection. Roy said he was walking down Confederation Drive when a police cruiser pulled out of a back lane and stopped him. Roy also said his friend Neil was in the back seat of the car. According to Roy, Stonechild was handcuffed, his face was bloody, and "he was freaking out. He was saying, 'Jay, help me. Help me. These guys are going to kill me'" (Wright 2004: 35). When the officers asked his name Roy offered the name of his cousin, Tracy Lee Horse, knowing that his cousin had no priors. He watched as they typed the name into their mobile terminal. The officers asked him, "Do you know this guy in the back?" (Wright 2004: 37). Being unlawfully at large and not wanting to join his friend in the backseat, Roy denied it. The officers then let him go on his way. The time of the CPIC query was 11:56 p.m. (Wright 2004: 74).

As the cruiser drove off, Roy noted, "Neil was looking out the back of the window, just staring at me. He looked — he just looked scared. He just looked really, really scared, and my thoughts at the time were, 'Well, he's just going to go back to Kilburn Hall, that will be it. I'll see him when he gets out'" (Wright 2004: 37). Some five days later, Neil Stonechild's frozen body was discovered lying face down in the snow. He was wearing a T-shirt, wool lumberjack jacket, leather-and-fabric baseball jacket, blue jeans, and only one running shoe. His trademark baseball cap was nowhere to be found. The temperature had dropped to minus 28 degrees Celsius that night. An autopsy indicated the cause of death to be hypothermia.

A three-day investigation led by Saskatoon Police Sergeant Keith Jarvis concluded that there was no evidence of foul play. Jarvis's theory was that Stonechild had wandered about in the north end of Saskatoon after drinking and had fallen down and died from the cold. He also surmised that the teenager might have been heading to the nearby adult correctional facility to turn himself in to the authorities (Wright 2004: 102).

Neil Stonechild's family and friends were not convinced there was no foul play. Because Stonechild had recently run into a conflict over some stolen guns, they initially thought that someone involved in that dispute had taken him outside the city and abandoned him. At the funeral the family was distressed to see cuts on his nose and scrapes on his wrists (Reber and Renaud 2005: 71). His mother and sister had made several attempts to express concern with the police about their investigation. As well, two police officers who knew the family — Constable Ernie Louttit and Sergeant Eli Tarasoff — had attempted to raise concerns about the case with their superiors. But with the police investigation formally closed, nothing more was likely to be done to discover how Stonechild had died.

In March 1991, a Saskatoon *StarPhoenix* reporter decided to do a follow-up on Stonechild's death. During an interview with the reporter his mother, Stella Bignell, pondered whether the police investigation would have been more thorough if her son had been white. Department media spokesperson Sergeant Dave Scott vehemently denied the allegation of racism, saying, "a tremendous amount of work went into that case" (Craig 1991). When the RCMP task force to investigate the deaths of Nastius and Wegner and the allegations of Night was announced in February 2000, an article published by the *StarPhoenix* on February 22 raised the matter of the suspicious circumstances surrounding Stonechild's death. In the article his mother was again quoted as expressing her frustration and distress about her son's death and the failure of the Saskatoon Police Service to follow up on its investigation. The article also made reference to the claim of Stonechild's friend, the last person to see him alive, noting that the unnamed friend had long maintained that he had seen Neil Stonechild in the back of a Saskatoon police car that night. The story also mentioned that, as the car drove away, his friend heard Neil say, "They're gonna kill me, they're gonna kill me" (Perreaux 2000). Soon after the *StarPhoenix* article was published, the Stonechild case was added to the RCMP task force's investigation.

THE RCMP INVESTIGATION INTO STONECHILD'S DEATH

While RCMP sergeant Ken Lyons was the lead investigator of Project Ferric, RCMP corporal Jack Warner was put in charge of the Stonechild file. One of the difficulties encountered by the RCMP investigators was the limited police record available on the matter. Warner had access to the coroner's report and to a file with photos from the autopsy and the scene where the body was found. There was also a copy of a 1993 report by SPS sergeant Bob Morton indicating that Stonechild's clothes had been destroyed (despite his mother's request to reclaim them). However, Warner's investigation was hampered by the fact that the police file on the Stonechild case had also been destroyed. When the Saskatoon police station was renovated in 1998 and 1999, Dave Scott — who had become Chief of Police — had approved the culling and destruction of files.

Over the next two and a half years, the RCMP interviewed some two hundred witnesses regarding Stonechild's death (Wright 2004: 138–39). One of the first people to be interviewed was Sergeant Keith Jarvis, who had led the SPS investigation. Jarvis's memory of the Stonechild case was hazy. He had retired from the force in 1993 and told the investigators he had destroyed his notebooks soon afterward (Reber and Renaud 2005: 205–06). The investigators also interviewed police officers who had been on duty the night Stonechild died, but most of them — with the exception of Sergeant Eli Tarasoff — seemed "to be suffering from almost total amnesia" (2005: 219).

Nevertheless, a breakthrough in the investigation came in March 2000. On interviewing Jason Roy, Corporal Warner discovered that Roy had given police the false name of "Tracy Lee Horse" on the night of November 24, 1990. On checking the record of the Canadian Police Information Centre (CPIC), Warner learned that Constable Brad Senger had been the officer to enter the name into the system. He also learned that Constable Larry Hartwig had queried the names of Neil Stonechild and Bruce Genaille on their mobile terminal that same night. Stonechild's name was entered at 11:59 p.m., and Genaille's at 12:04 a.m. Genaille happened to be Stonechild's older cousin, and the two looked a lot alike. Genaille told the investigators that he had been walking down Confederation Drive when two officers in a police car stopped and asked him if he was Neil Stonechild. When he asked why they were looking for Stonechild the officers said they were responding to a disturbance at the 7-Eleven. After Genaille produced his driver's licence the officers let him go on his way. Genaille said that he was so flustered he couldn't be sure whether the police had entered his name into their computer terminal at the time (Reber and Renaud 2005: 36).

When Constable Larry Hartwig was approached by RCMP sergeant Lyons in early May 2000, he volunteered that he had known Neil Stonechild. Hartwig had arrested Stonechild twice in April 1989 and once in October 1990 when he had stopped him for driving without a licence (Reber and Renaud 2005: 222). During a formal interview, Hartwig insisted that he had worked the night shift alone on November 24, 1990. He also commented, "I've never given anybody a screen test." When asked what that meant Hartwig replied, "You're driving down the street, you hit the brakes and the guy [in the back] hits the — the silent patrolman" (2005: 229). As Reber and Renaud (2005: 229) remark, "Hartwig had just been told he was a suspect in a criminal investigation, had insisted he had never abused a prisoner in any way and then proceeded to give an explicit description of how to smash a detainee into the metal barrier separating the back and front seats of a police cruiser."

Both Hartwig and Senger staunchly denied having Stonechild in their custody on the night of November 24, 1990. Nevertheless, both officers refused to undergo polygraph tests to confirm their denial. When Senger finally relented in December 2001, the polygraph expert concluded that his answers were "deceptive," meaning that he "was not responding truthfully to the three issue questions and did have Neil Stonechild in his custody on the night of November 24, 1990" (Reber and Renaud 2005: 266). A second polygraph taken a few years later came to the same conclusion (2005: 289).

One of the issues pursued in the RCMP investigation pertained to the marks on Stonechild's body that appeared in the autopsy pictures. Suspicious that the marks on his wrists had been made by handcuffs and that the cuts across his nose suggested he had been beaten, Warner consulted with Alberta's chief medical examiner, Dr. Graeme Dowling. Dowling's analysis of the autopsy pictures did not rule out the possibility that some of the injuries had been caused by the force of a blunt instrument (Reber and Renaud 2005: 215). Pursuing the issue further, Warner contacted a photogrammetry specialist, Gary Robertson, to calculate whether the injuries on Stonechild's nose could have been caused by handcuffs. In January 2001 Robertson reported his opinion: "The Peerless handcuffs matched the imprint as to dimension and orientation" (2005: 243). Stonechild's body was exhumed in April 2001, but the examination produced little.

Another breakthrough in the RCMP investigation came in July 2000, when Sergeant Jarvis's notebook was located in the police archives. The notes indicated that Jarvis knew at the time that Hartwig and Senger had attended to the call at Snowberry Downs. It also indicated that Jarvis had met with Jason Roy after Roy had phoned to tell him about being with Neil on the night of November 24 —though the notebook had no details about their meeting.

The original copy of the Saskatoon police investigation report into Stonechild's death was destroyed in the late 1990s, but a photocopy of the twenty-one-page report was turned over to the RCMP investigators by Constable Ernie Louttit in March 2001. One of the Saskatoon police officers who had attempted to raise questions about the police investigation at the time of Stonechild's death, Louttit had discovered a copy of the report among his files. The report included a signed statement by Jason Roy taken by Sergeant Jarvis. In the statement Roy made no mention of seeing Stonechild in the back of a police car on the night of November 24, 1990.

Corporal Jack Warren submitted his fifty-page report of the Stonechild investigation in July 2001. The cover letter, written to the executive director of public prosecutions of the Saskatchewan Justice Department, spelled out the main concerns that emerged from the investigation:

> There is compelling independent evidence through CPIC records to show that Constables Hartwig and Senger did have Neil Stonechild in their custody. There is compelling evidence to suggest that Neil Stonechild had been struck on the face with a set of handcuffs and that he had handcuffs on his wrists prior to his death. There is compelling evidence to show that the outstanding warrant for Neil Stonechild was on the CPIC system and that the system was working properly at the time he is believed to have been in custody. What we have not been able to determine is what transpired between the time that Csts Hartwig and Senger encountered Neil Stonechild and the date his body was discovered. (Cited in Reber and Renaud 2005: 252)

In August 2002 the Saskatchewan Justice Department announced that no criminal charges would be laid in the Neil Stonechild case. In the meantime, Aboriginal organizations had continued to press for a public inquiry. In November 2001 the Federation of Saskatchewan Indian Nations had reached an agreement with the provincial government to create the Commission on First Nations and Métis Peoples and Justice Reform. While the Commission's terms of reference authorized it to respond to justice-related issues of First Nations and Métis people, it was prevented from investigating specific cases (see Commission on First Nations and Métis Peoples and Justice Reform 2004). With pressure still building to address the issues that emerged in the RCMP investigation of the Stonechild case, the province finally relented in February 2003, when it announced the establishment of a provincial inquiry into Stonechild's death.

THE WRIGHT COMMISSION

Headed by the Honourable Mr. Justice David Wright, the Commission of Inquiry into Matters Relating to the Death of Neil Stonechild began sitting in September 2003. Its terms of reference specified its responsibility: "to inquire into any and all aspects of the circumstances that resulted in the death of Neil Stonechild and the conduct of the investigation into the death of Neil Stonechild for the purpose of making findings and recommendations with respect to the administration of criminal justice in the province of Saskatchewan" (Wright 2004: 4). The inquiry was prohibited from drawing any conclusions with respect to criminal or civil liability in Stonechild's death. In addition to Commission counsel Joel Hesje, legal counsel were present to represent ten parties granted standing at the Inquiry: Stella Bignell, Stonechild's mother; constables Hartwig and Senger; the Federation of Saskatchewan Indian Nations; the Saskatoon Police Service; the Saskatoon Police Association; Gary Pratt (who at one point was considered a suspect in Stonechild's death); Keith Jarvis; the RCMP; Jason Roy; and Deputy Chief Dan Wiks. The evidence examined by the inquiry included 137 exhibits and the testimony of sixty-three witnesses. The inquiry submitted its report in October 2004.

While constables Hartwig and Senger had continued to maintain that they had never encountered Neil Stonechild the night of November 24, 1990, Justice Wright disputed that claim. His report concluded that the officers had Stonechild in their custody that night. It also concluded that bloody marks found on the young man's face were most likely caused by handcuffs. The judge noted:

> I acknowledge that, in the final analysis, no one can ever know with precision, other than Neil Stonechild and Cst. Hartwig and Cst. Senger, what happened on the night of November 24/25. I say Cst. Hartwig and Cst. Senger because whatever other conclusion one may draw, there is no question that Stonechild was last observed in the custody of those two officers, and that he was later found in a vacant field near the Hitachi plant on 57th Street with injuries and marks that were likely caused by handcuffs. (Wright 2004: 191)

One of the key witnesses in the inquiry was Jason Roy. While police lawyers endeavoured to point out errors and inconsistencies in Roy's statements, Justice Wright deemed him to be a credible witness. The judge described him as "sincere and thoughtful" and "still deeply affected by the death of his friend and what followed." The judge also commended Roy for his "tenacity in pursuing this matter over many years" (Wright 2004: 49). Jason had told his story several times. On the night of November 24 and morning of the 25th, after returning to the place where he and Neil had been partying, Roy had told others about seeing his friend in the back of a police cruiser. He had also told Sergeant Jarvis several days after the body was found that he had seen Stonechild in police custody. In addition, Roy had met with Stonechild's mother in 1991 to tell her his story of what had happened. He had also disclosed his experience to a youth worker. While Roy's evidence was flawed, Justice Wright determined "the core of Mr. Roy's testimony — that he was stopped by police on November 24/25, 1990, and that he observed Neil Stonechild in the back seat of a police car — to be credible and corroborated by other evidence" (Wright 2004: 194).

Justice Wright also determined that on the night Neil Stonechild was last seen alive, constables Hartwig and Senger were dispatched to the Snowberry Downs apartment complex to remove him. "This fact was irrefutably established by police records and the officers' own notebooks" (Wright 2004: 72). While the officers might have easily forgotten a routine call, the discovery four days later of the frozen body of a young man they were looking for — and Constable Senger was the officer at the station who received the report when the body was found — should have led them to make a connection. Hartwig also knew Neil Stonechild because he had arrested him several times in the previous two years. As the judge noted, "The discovery of Stonechild's frozen body made the call on November 24th anything but routine. I would expect it to impress the search for Stonechild in the memory of both Hartwig and Senger." Constable Senger, however, littered his testimony before the inquiry with the response that he had "no recollection." In the judge's view, that neither officer made a connection between the young man they were looking for on the night of November 24–25 and the discovery of the frozen body was "incredible." That they kept quiet suggested to Wright that there was a "deliberate deception" designed to conceal their involvement (Wright 2004: 82).

The police lawyers argued that the officers could not have taken Stonechild to the northern edge of town because they did not have the time to make the drive before being dispatched to a call on the city's west side. The judge rejected this version of events: "I am satisfied that Constable Hartwig and Constable Senger had adequate time between the Snowberry Downs dispatch and the O'Regan Crescent dispatch to transport Stonechild to the northwest industrial area of Saskatoon" (Wright 2004: 194).

Justice Wright saved some of his harshest criticism for the Saskatoon Police Service, especially Sergeant Keith Jarvis. Citing a litany of errors and missteps committed by Jarvis during his three-day investigation, the judge asserted: "The deficiencies in the investigation go beyond incompetence or neglect. They were inexcusable" (Wright 2004: 199). Wright described Jarvis's theory that Stonechild was probably on his way to the adult correctional centre to turn himself in as "preposterous" (2004: 103). According to the evidence presented, Jarvis had learned that Neil Stonechild had been seen in the back of a police car and that constables Hartwig and Senger had been dispatched to Snowberry Downs in search of Stonechild, but the sergeant had failed to adequately follow up on that information. According to Wright, "The only reasonable inference that can be drawn is that Jarvis was not prepared to pursue the investigation because he was either aware of police involvement or suspected police involvement" (Wright 2004: 200).

Wright was also critical of the command structure of the Saskatoon police force. The deficiencies in the investigation, he said, "would have been identified and remedied before the file was closed if the file had been properly supervised" (Wright 2004: 200). In subsequent years, when confronted with both internal and external complaints about the Stonechild investigation, the chain of command chose to take a defensive and self-protective stand. For instance, evidence presented at the inquiry showed that senior officers held secret meetings to co-ordinate their response to the Stonechild affair, which included a strategy of lying to the media. In May 2003, Deputy Chief Wiks told a reporter that he was not aware that constables Hartwig and Senger were suspects in the RCMP investigation. As Justice Wright (2004: 207) noted, however, "Wiks was well aware by that time they were the only suspects." The Saskatoon Police Service had also conducted a "shadow investigation," called the Issues Team, to work alongside of the RCMP task force. According to Wright, "While the Issues Team undoubtedly performed legitimate tasks, it also evolved into a partisan forum for planning ways to rebut the evidence compiled by the RCMP against its members" (Wright 2004: 207).

In his concluding remarks, Justice Wright commented on the racial divide that exists in Saskatchewan: "As I reviewed the evidence of this inquiry, I was reminded, again and again, of the chasm that separates aboriginal and non-aboriginal people in this city and this province" (Wright 2004: 208). While he praised the Saskatoon Police Service for efforts made to reform itself, the judge acknowledged that much more work needed to be done: "The fundamental problem the service has to address is the public perception that it does not take seriously complaints about its members and that it defends its members against complaints" (Wright 2004: 208). Wright's report made eight recommendations, including more cultural sensitivity training, more Aboriginal officers, and an improved complaints process.

Stella Bignell greeted the inquiry report with a sense of relief. She told the media, "I prayed for something to come out of this. I never, ever want to see parents go through what I've had to go through all these years" (Smith 2004). Both the Saskatchewan Justice Minister and Saskatoon Police Chief accepted Justice Wright's findings. Justice Minister Frank Quennell described the findings of the report as "troubling" (Smith 2004), but indicated that there was not enough evidence to lay criminal charges against the two officers. Police Chief Russell Sabo responded by suspending constables Hartwig and Senger from the force and apologizing to the Stonechild family.

UNREST WITHIN THE SASKATOON POLICE SERVICE

The revelations of Starlight Tours and the events that followed had a profound impact on the Saskatoon Police Service. One of the police responses to these revelations was a "discourse of denial" (Tator and Henry 2006). For instance, responding to charges of racism in the force, Chief Dave Scott insisted that there was no trouble with his officers' attitudes towards Aboriginal people. "We've had lots of intense sensitivity training" he said (Hutchinson 2000). The police instead tended to put responsibility for the issue on Aboriginal people, placing the onus on them. Chief Scott held the view that if a problem did exist it lay within the Aboriginal community. His idea for a solution rested in the creation of more employment; but not just any jobs — jobs at the lowest level. "There's nothing worse than an unemployed person," he told a reporter. "We've got to make sure that there are menial jobs where these people with low skills can make some kind of living.... The root issue is alcoholism. Over eighty percent of the people coming to our detention facilities are sniffed up, drunk, or on drugs. I'm fed up with it" (Hutchinson 2000).

In June 2001 the mayor of Saskatoon, Jim Maddin (a former police officer), made the decision not to extend the contract of Police Chief Scott. Maddin had been receiving a litany of complaints about him. According to Reber and Renaud (2005: 251), Scott had been "accused of killing community policing initiatives" and "was shutting down a bicycle patrol and had made it clear there would be no new foot patrols either.... Scott also resisted police involvement in the city's race relations committee."

Scott's removal from the post created a wave of opposition within the force. He was replaced by Russell Sabo, who, drawing on his background in community policing, endeavoured to mend the rift that had been created between the Saskatoon Police Service and the Aboriginal community. He established ten new community liaison positions and opened the Little Chief Station in downtown Saskatoon (Hubbard 2004). Nevertheless, his initiatives to repair relations with the Aboriginal community, along with the dismissal of four officers in the space of three years, led members of the Saskatoon Police Service to close ranks. In June 2003 the Saskatoon Police Association held a vote in which 90 percent of the members said they had no confidence in Police Chief Sabo's management of the force (Parker 2003). Many of the officers maintained that the fired officers were innocent of any wrongdoing. Saskatoon Police Association president Stan Goertzen, for one, insisted that Hartwig and Senger never had Stonechild in their car and had nothing to do with his death (Burton 2004). More than two hundred officers voted unanimously to support their two comrades (CBC News 2004). Despite Sabo's efforts to manage the fallout from the Starlight Tour revelations, his contract as police chief was not renewed in March 2006.

COMPETING TRUTHS ABOUT STARLIGHT TOURS

The revelations of Starlight Tours prompted a wave of support from sectors outside the ranks of the Saskatoon Police Service. In March 2007 Calgary journalist Candis McLean released her documentary, *When Police Become Prey: What Lies behind Starlight Tours*. The main premise advanced by the documentary is that Starlight Tours are a myth perpetrated by "special interest groups" to advance their own political agenda (McLean 2006).

Featured prominently in the documentary are interviews with Ken Munson and Dan Hatchen, the two officers convicted of forcible confinement in the Darrel Night case. While Munson and Hatchen are presented as "exemplary officers" and family men, Night is decidedly "Othered" in this account. Described as a criminal offender with some twenty-two convictions and several aliases, Night is deemed to be "trouble" and therefore cast as unbelievable and untrustworthy. Although both officers admitted to having Night in their cruiser that night, they claimed that Night had asked them to be dropped off 3.2 kilometres from the Clancy Village apartment block where his relative lived so that he could "walk off his anger."

Hatchen admits on film to not recording the incident, saying, "In all fairness, police policy does state that we should have written something in our notebook." But he was adamant that he was not trying to hide something. Although Night was arrested, handcuffed, and then confined in the back of a police car, Munson's view was that "we did nothing that was against Darrell Night's wishes. Everything that happened that night *he was in full control of*" (McLean 2006; emphasis added). In the officers' view, they were being punished by the criminal justice system for "doing Night a favour." Evidence that might have helped to exonerate the officers was "either missed, ignored, or suppressed."

Critical of the court's decision to convict Hansen and Munson on charges of forcible confinement, the documentary puts forward the view that the officers, as well as Night, were "puppets" in a political game orchestrated by "activists and politically correct media." According to retired constable Larry Lockwood, "This is an agenda. It is an agenda by special interest groups to advance a sympathy cause." In particular, the film targets the Federation of Saskatchewan Indian Nations (FSIN). According to the documentary, while the FSIN claimed to have received 388 complaints to their hotline about police drop-offs, not a single allegation had been substantiated or led to charges laid — leading McLean to assert that allegations of drop-offs are "completely unfounded."

For its part, the FSIN offered a competing account. In its submission to the Wright inquiry, the Federation encouraged Justice Wright to consider the role that race and racism played in Neil Stonechild's death — and the Saskatoon Police Service's failure to investigate that role properly. The FSIN maintained that the Saskatoon Police Service

> intentionally or unintentionally discriminated against Neil Stonechild and his family when he died and that this discrimination continues to this day. It is a pervasive kind of discrimination that few people are comfortable recognizing and even fewer people want to acknowledge. Racism need not manifest itself in ugly name calling or overt stereotyping to be real but it is no less real just because it remains unspoken. (Halyk 2004: 5)

The submission also noted that the Federation had established a helpline in February 2000. The number of callers was so high and the mistrust of police so pervasive that in April the FSIN created a Special Investigations Unit (SIU) with the mandate to provide callers with a "complaint-friendly" alternative to traditional police agencies, which would in turn ensure that complaints were thoroughly investigated and provide complainants with protection from retaliation and discomfort in disclosing their experiences (Halyk 2004: 35). Some four years later Silas Halyk, legal counsel for the FSIN, noted that complaints were still being brought forward, and that over the period after its creation the SIU had received more than three thousand calls and "opened more than 695 files." By December 2000 the SIU had registered 310 complaints against the RCMP, along with 265 against local police forces and 120 aimed at other agencies (Halyk 2004: 35).

The FSIN hired Oliver Williams to lead its Special Investigations Unit. In Tasha Hubbard's documentary, *Two Worlds Colliding* — which offers a very different standpoint than the McLean video — Williams comments on the calls received on the helpline. Within the first few weeks the unit had received over eight hundred calls. Callers said that they did not report their experiences to police because they were "fearful of reprisal." With twenty-five years of experience as an RCMP officer in British Columbia, Williams was surprised by these revelations. He comments, "You think you've seen it all, heard it all" (Hubbard 2004).

In advancing its position that Starlight Tours are a myth, *When Police Become Prey* features statements from several Saskatoon police officers in which they claim no knowledge of such a practice. For instance, Sergeant Ernie Louttit, who is Aboriginal, comments: "Something of that enormity? There's no way. No way. Guys I work with wouldn't allow it. Would never do it. Would never allow it." While the documentary goes to great lengths to dismiss claims that Starlight Tours are a reality, other sources suggest otherwise.

In February 2000 the *StarPhoenix* reprinted a column published in 1997 by Brian Trainor, a Saskatoon police officer. Trainor had been writing a series of articles for the *StarPhoenix* on an insider's view of police work. This particular column featured a tale of two police officers who picked up an intoxicated Aboriginal man. They mocked the man's request to be taken to "the highest power in the land" by driving him to the Queen Elizabeth Power Station and dumping him there. The article ends with "Quickly gathering his wits, the drunk scrambled out of the car and into the thickets along the riverbank, disappearing from view. One less guest for breakfast" (cited in Reber and Renaud 2005: 199). The Saskatoon Police Service responded to the old column by stating that Trainor had written the piece on his own time and the force did not know if the story was fact or fiction.

In June 2003 Police Chief Sabo investigated the issue of Starlight Tours and discovered an incident that had occurred in May 1976. A police officer had driven three Aboriginal people — one of whom was a woman eight months pregnant — to the outskirts of Saskatoon and left them there. The officer was reprimanded by the chief of police and assessed a fine of $200 (see Reber and Renaud 2005: 113–15).

The issue of Starlight Tours also emerged during the Wright inquiry. Retired Staff Sergeant Bruce Bolton admitted during his testimony that in 1969 he and his partner had picked up an individual and dropped him off outside of town. The person lodged a complaint and Bolton was disciplined (Wright 2004: 123). Similarly, Constable Brett Maki testified before the inquiry that "from time to time he would arrest a person who was causing a disturbance and drop him off at a safe place several blocks away. He described this as 'unarresting' the person" (Wright 2004: 131).

When asked by a CBC journalist whether Starlight Tours occurred, Jim Maddin, a twenty-five-year-veteran of the Saskatoon police force, replied, "If somebody asked me does this happen — I couldn't look them in the eye and say absolutely no, it's never happened; never will happen. I couldn't say that" (Brass 2004). In the same report, Saskatoon law professor Sakej Henderson was quoted as saying: "It's been common knowledge in the profession, especially the defence bar, that this is what happens. These starlight tours are not new and they've been going on for a very long time. But there's very few times we have to bring it into court because of course when they drop them off, there's no charges laid usually" (Brass 2004).

Similarly, *Globe and Mail* reporter David Roberts (2000) cited sources inside the Saskatoon police force who claimed that "it was common knowledge among the force that some members would take unruly suspects out near the power plant and abandon them in the cold." One of Roberts' sources told him, "They've been doing that for years. ... I've never done it. ... But I know of people who have. If the guy pissed them off or if they didn't have enough to lock them up, they'd take him for a drive." Another police source confirmed the knowledge that some officers would take suspects to the outskirts of town and force them out in the cold: "It's been going on for years. Unfortunately, this time two guys ended up dead. If it's those guys who did it, let them fry," he said. "Who I feel sorry for is the rest of the guys; it gives the whole department a bad name."

Interestingly, retired constable Larry Lockwood admits in *When Police Become Prey* that he had engaged in the same practice as Munson and Hatchen "a hundred times." He says:

> I'll admit to it anytime — picked up guys in the wagon, they're drunk. "Guys, you know where I live. I live over in Sutherland,"

you know, we've got them in the back of the wagon on Broadway. "Look it, just let me walk home. I promise you I won't cause you any problems. If I cause you any problems lock me up for the next 24 hours." You used to get this song and dance continually.

Just as interesting, Hatchen remarked on camera: "Letting guys walk off their anger is a common practice in all police services in Canada, possibly even worldwide."

This "common practice" of police drop-offs — sometimes also referred to as "breaching" — does occur in other jurisdictions. At one point in the McLean documentary Munson laments that there are cases in other provinces where police officers have been accused in similar circumstances but received only internal discipline as a result — as opposed to the criminal charges that he and his partner were confronted with. In particular, Munson mentions a Vancouver case in which the officer received only a one-day suspension. That case involved the 1998 death of a forty-seven-year-old Mi'kmaq man named Frank Joseph Paul.

THE DEATH OF FRANK JOSEPH PAUL

Originally from New Brunswick, Frank Joseph Paul was sent to a residential school in Nova Scotia as a youth. He began drinking at the age of sixteen or seventeen and went on to adopt the itinerant life of a migrant worker, eventually settling in Vancouver in the 1980s. In poor mental and physical health, Paul suffered from both grand mal seizures and a medical condition that made him appear to be drunk. He was also a chronic alcoholic. As one of a small group of homeless men living in Vancouver's Downtown Eastside — many of them Aboriginal — Paul was well known to police and ambulance personnel working in the neighbourhood (Davies 2008: i–iv).

On the morning of December 5, 1998, two Vancouver police officers arrested Frank Paul for being in a state of intoxication in a public place. He was transported to jail by a police wagon, and held in a cell set aside for intoxicated people until 5:00 p.m. the same day. After he was released, Paul was seen leaving the loading bay area of the jail at about 6:30 p.m. At about eight o'clock that evening two other officers found Paul lying on the street in the rain. Believing him to be intoxicated, they arranged for him to be transported back to the jail in a police wagon. Once there he was unable to walk, and the police van driver dragged him the into the jail. The sergeant on duty, knowing about Paul's medical condition and that he had just been released a few hours earlier, disagreed that Paul was intoxicated and instructed the driver to take him to Broadway and Maple, where the sergeant understood Paul to have resided. The driver dragged Paul's soaking wet body back into the loading bay and pulled him into the wagon. After that the driver picked up three other men, putting them in handcuffs in the back of the van.

After another officer told him that Paul did not live in the Broadway and Maple area, the driver drove to the Detox Centre to deliver the three other men. Not believing Paul to be intoxicated, he did not ask to have Paul admitted to the centre but instead chose to release him out of the area — a practice known as "breaching" (Davies 2008: 9). The driver deposited Paul, who was barely conscious, at the end of a back alley, propping his body up against a wall. At 2:00 a.m. the next morning a passerby discovered Paul's dead body. The cause of death was determined to be "hypothermia due to, or as a consequence of, acute alcohol intoxication" (Davies 2008: 9).

As a police-related death, the case was assigned to a detective in the Homicide Squad of the Major Crimes Section of the Vancouver Police Department (VPD). While several civilian witnesses were interviewed, the detective did not meet with or interview police officers or jail staff. The report presented to Crown counsel on Paul's death did not offer any analysis of inconsistencies uncovered in the investigation and made no recommendations as to whether criminal charges should be laid. As the British Columbia Civil Liberties Association (BCCLA) noted, "The failure of the VPD to conduct a proper investigation polluted every subsequent investigation and review by the coroner's service, the police disciplinary body, and the office of the police complaint commissioner" (BCCLA n.d.).

The VPD's Internal Investigation Section conducted a professional standards investigation to determine whether any police officer had breached the Code of Professional Conduct Regulation. The sergeant conducting the internal investigation relied almost entirely on the report prepared by the homicide detective. According to the subsequent review, "He did not request further reports from, nor interview, the Jail sergeant or the police wagon driver" (Davies 2008: 11). The investigation recommended that the jail sergeant receive a two-day suspension without pay for failing to have Frank Paul medically assessed and failing to consider some other form of shelter (such as the Detox Centre). It recommended that the police wagon driver receive a one-day suspension without pay "for changing the location of Mr. Paul's 'breach' without consultation, and for failing to consider medical attention and proper shelter for him" (Davies 2008: 11). Both officers accepted the disciplinary action.

After reviewing the criminal investigation report, the autopsy report, and a video showing Paul being dragged in and out of the jail elevator, the coroner concluded that "Mr. Paul had not died while detained by, or in the actual custody of, police" and therefore a formal inquest was not ordered. Paul's death was deemed to be an "accident" and not a "homicide" (Davies 2008: 13). While it is the responsibility of the coroner's office to notify the next of kin, this was not done. Instead, an RCMP officer phoned Paul's sister and told her he had died in a hit and run accident.

As the civilian overseer of the police department, the B.C. police complaints commissioner received the report of the professional standards investigation. The Police Complaints Commission (PCC) office did further investigations, including obtaining the expert opinion of a forensic pathologist who was of the view that Paul might have been hypothermic while at the jail. While the PCC asked the Crown's office to reconsider criminal charges in the case, that request was denied. The PCC did not call for a public hearing. While the deputy police complaints commissioner considered the penalties imposed on the two officers involved to be inadequate, "He also felt that a public hearing would at most increase the suspensions to five days: the maximum suspension permitted under the regulation" (Davies 2008: 15). The deputy police complaints commissioner was also unsuccessful at having an inquest ordered and convincing the government to undertake a province-wide review, "including an examination of the police practice of 'breaching' a person" (Davies 2008: 15).

Almost nine years later, the provincial government finally acceded to demands for a public inquiry into the case. In 2007 retired B.C. Supreme Court justice William H. Davies was appointed to head a Commission of Inquiry into Frank Paul's death. In his 445-page report, the commissioner criticized the Vancouver Police Department for its treatment of Frank Paul and its failure to adequately investigate his death. The discipline meted out to the two officers, according to the commissioner, was hampered because it "depended upon the flawed criminal investigation" (Davies 2008: 4). He was also critical of the practice of police departments investigating cases of police-related deaths, calling it "fundamentally flawed, due to the conflict of interest inherent in police investigating their fellow officers" (Davies 2008: 18). Justice Davies recommended that an independent investigation office be established to conduct criminal investigations of all police-related deaths, and that a similar civilian-based model should be adopted for professional standards investigations.

The commissioner also highlighted the lack of resources and community supports available for homeless chronic alcoholics in Vancouver's Downtown Eastside. He suggested that although Aboriginal people constituted some 40 percent of that population, there were no Aboriginal organizations equipped to provide services for them. Drawing further attention to the role that race played in the case, Justice Davies stated:

> It also matters that Frank Paul was a Mi'kmaq man. The circumstances of his life and death are an account in miniature of the risks and struggles faced by many First Nations people of his generation. It is not surprising to learn that Frank Paul was burdened with having been sent to residential school, losing members of his family to alcohol abuse and struggling from his early childhood to make sense of a world in which his family was fragmented and fractured. It is not surprising that he came to Vancouver and isolated himself from his family and community for the last two decades of his life. We cannot know when the psychic injuries of childhood were compounded by the addiction and mental illness of his adult years. We must acknowledge, however, that the tragic arc of his life was that followed all too frequently by members of the First Nations in our community and that his death speaks out yet again of our need to revisit and refashion the important relationship between the First Nations peoples of Canada and the general community. (Davies 2008: 4–5)

In the end, the commissioner said, "our systems of justice and social service ultimately failed Frank Paul" (Davies 2008: 3).

While Ken Munson was correct in saying that there have been cases of officers receiving only minor discipline for their involvement in "drop-offs" or "breaches," cases such as the one he cited are certainly not without controversy.

MAKING SENSE OF STARLIGHT TOURS

As criminologists King and Dunn (2004) note, much of the literature on policing has concentrated on more visible police behaviours, such as the decision to arrest and the use of deadly force. This focus does not capture the majority of police-citizen encounters given the established norm of a police officer, on average, making only seven or eight criminal arrests a year, or one arrest every six or seven weeks (Sewell 2010: 10). King and Dunn argue that since police powers of arrest are subject to the legal requirement of establishing reasonable and probable grounds, police officers are encouraged to use more informal methods to handle what they perceive to be "troublesome persons." One of these strategies is "dumping":

> Dumping or PITT [police-initiated transjurisdictional transport] is a low-visibility police activity that stands outside the legal and moral norms of policing. PITT occurs when a police officer interacts with a mentally disturbed person, a person who is homeless, a prostitute, a juvenile, a drunk, or a person under the influence of drugs, the officer views this person as "troublesome," and the officer resolves the situation by transporting that troublesome person out of that officer's (or the department's) jurisdiction and releases that person into his or her own recognizance. (King and Dunn 2004: 341–42)

These criminologists suggest that a police officer's decision to transport a troublesome person can be influenced by a range of organizational, community, and situational factors. Organizationally, police departments that adopt a zero-tolerance or aggressive order-maintenance mode of policing may be inclined to engage in dumping practices in order to "quickly reduce disorder (as opposed to getting troublesome persons help or putting them under criminal justice control)" (2004: 347). Alternatively, those police departments that adopt community policing as a model will be more inclined to encourage the use of discretion by officers and informal solutions to problems, which may also encourage dumping practices. In this regard, the police culture may contribute to the practice, because dumping is a "low-fuss way of making bad people disappear, and police culture (or subtypes of police culture…) rewards creative, common-sense ways of handling problems" (2004: 348). Community characteristics, according to Dunn and King (2004: 348) include the availability of suitable dumping areas (for example, forcing a person to make a long walk over a bridge on a cold winter night) and the prospects of low visibility for the officers involved. The availability of alternative placements for troublesome persons (such as detoxification centres and homeless shelters) can also influence the practice. Finally, situational factors include the demeanour of the troublesome person (whether they are compliant versus belligerent) and the seriousness of the alleged offence.

While Dunn and King draw our attention to the police practice of transporting troublesome people as a routine and normalized activity, their analysis does not take in the role of broader systemic factors — such as race and racism — in the practice. Much of police work involves the difficult and challenging job of dealing with people who are both troubled and troublesome. In a Prairie city such as Saskatoon, dealing with the troubled and troublesome means frequent encounters with Aboriginal people. In 2006, 21,535 Aboriginal people were living in Saskatoon, which represented 9 percent of the total population (Anderson 2010). Much of the Aboriginal population — up to 30 percent in some neighbourhoods (Spence 2004) — is concentrated on the west side of the city, where poverty is also prevalent. In 2005, 45 percent of the Aboriginal population in Saskatoon was living below the poverty line, compared to 13 percent of non-Aboriginal people (Anderson 2010).

It is within this space of racialized poverty that police are delegated the job of reproducing order. In the process, they regularly encounter Aboriginal people whose lives have been ground down not only by poverty, but also by the other manifestations of the ongoing legacy of colonialism: violence, drug and alcohol abuse, and crime. There were two thousand arrests for drunkenness in Saskatoon in 2003. While Aboriginal people made up only 9 percent of the population, they were charged with half of the crimes in the city (Brass 2004). Indeed, Saskatoon is a city where young Aboriginal men are more likely to go to jail than to finish high school (Hubbard 2004).

In many respects, the stories of Neil Stonechild, Rodney Naistus, Lawrence Wegner, and Darrel Night epitomize the troubled lives endured by many Aboriginal people in this racialized space. All of them, for instance, had in common problems with drug and alcohol abuse. Given their regular contact with the Saskatoon Police Service, they were cast as "troublesome." Regardless of the name used to describe the practice — Starlight Tours, drop-offs, dumping, breaching, or unarresting — the act constitutes one of the racialized policing strategies that officers utilize in their efforts to contain and control this troubled and troublesome population. Whether emanating from frustration in dealing with repeat troublemakers, disillusionment with other sectors of the criminal justice system for being "too soft on crime," a sense of entitlement in imposing their own brand of "street justice," or simply being tasked with the insurmountable assignment of managing the effects of a systemic problem, police officers may well turn to this racialized practice as a way of fulfilling their role as reproducers of order. The consequences can be severe. Métis scholar Joyce Green (2006: 515) puts it most bluntly: "*Stonechild* shows us that racism kills."

Chapter Six

POLICING WINNIPEG'S INNER-CITY COMMUNITIES

Despite its moderate size relative to other Canadian cities, Winnipeg has garnered a reputation as a city ridden with crime and violence. In 2004 the city ranked first among the nine major metropolitan centres for its rate for homicides, robberies, and motor vehicle thefts. It ranked second for break-ins (Statistics Canada 2005). More recently, in 2009 Winnipeg ranked first among the census metropolitan areas on the violent crime severity index (Dauvergne and Turner 2010).

Much of this activity has been concentrated in Winnipeg's inner-city communities. A 2004 study by the Canadian Centre for Justice Statistics found that the closer one goes to the geographic core of Winnipeg, where the incidence of poverty and related problems is high, the higher is the incidence of crime. Robin Fitzgerald and his colleagues (2004: 8) concluded, "After taking into account all other factors, the level of socio-economic disadvantage of the residential population in a neighbourhood was most strongly associated with the highest neighbourhood rates of both violent and property crimes." Other studies (see, for example, Lezubski, Silver, and Black 2000; Kazemipur and Halli 2000) reveal that for Winnipeg, rates of poverty, unemployment, and limited labour force participation — in other words, "socio-economic disadvantage" — are considerably worse in the inner city than in Winnipeg as a whole. The poverty rate in Winnipeg's inner-city communities, for instance, was 39.6 percent in 2006 compared with 20.2 percent for the city as a whole (MacKinnon 2009). Crime and violence, therefore, correlate strongly with poverty and related conditions, and both are more prevalent in Winnipeg's inner-city neighbourhoods.

Much like other Prairie cities in Canada, Winnipeg is home to a large number of Aboriginal people. In 2006 about one-third of all Aboriginal persons in Manitoba lived in Winnipeg. Of major cities in Canada that year, Winnipeg had the highest density of Aboriginal people (68,385), representing 9.8 percent of the total Winnipeg Central Metropolitan Area population (United Way Winnipeg 2010: 40). Aboriginal people make up some 21 percent of the population of Winnipeg's inner-city communities (MacKinnon 2009: 32); 65 percent of Aboriginal households in those inner-city communities were living in poverty in 2006 (MacKinnon 2009: 30).

It is within this context of crime, violence, and racialized poverty in Winnipeg's inner-city communities that encounters between Aboriginal people and the police are most likely to occur.* Indeed, it is in this area and among these people that the Winnipeg Police Service has concentrated much of its resources.

RACIALIZED POVERTY, CRIME, AND VIOLENCE IN THE INNER CITY

Criminologists have long recognized the correlation between poverty and certain forms of criminal activity. One of the primary factors that can account for this poverty–crime correlation is the impact of changes in the global economy at the local level. Among the consequences of globalization — the integration of national economies into a global network — has been a shift in Canada from industrial to "non-standard" and service-sector jobs (Broad 2000; Broad, Cruikshank, and Mulvale 2006). Many industrial jobs that were unionized, paid a living wage, and offered reasonable benefits have relocated to other, lower-wage jurisdictions or, in some cases, have dramatically reduced wages in the face of external competitive pressures. At the same time the process of suburbanization that began in the post–World War II era has seen large numbers of people who can afford to do so moving away from inner-city locations to the suburbs. Many businesses followed suit. The result has been a hollowing out of many inner cities, Winnipeg's included. Those left behind in inner-city communities have been, for the most part, those least financially able to move.

The abandonment of Winnipeg's inner city by the more financially well-off placed downward pressure on housing prices in an area where housing was already the oldest and in need of repair (Deane 2006; Silver 2006b). As Ian Skelton and his colleagues (2007: 55) point out, 10 percent of Winnipeg dwellings are in need of major repair, which significantly exceeds the national average of 7 percent and is the highest percentage among Canada's twenty-five metropolitan areas. In many cases cheap inner-city housing was acquired by absentee landlords who used it as a "cash cow" while allowing it to deteriorate further. As Shauna Mackinnon (2009: 33) notes, 61 percent of Winnipeg's inner-city residents rent their living accommodation,

---

*   The discussion in the following two sections draws on Comack and Silver 2006 and 2008.

and are therefore reliant on landlords to ensure that buildings are properly maintained. The housing problem was accentuated by the continuation of a decades-long practice of severe underinvestment in public facilities in the inner city, and especially in Winnipeg's North End. Cheap housing attracted people with the lowest incomes, not surprisingly, thus concentrating poverty in large numbers in the inner-city neighbourhoods.

Aboriginal people began to move from rural and reserve communities to urban centres in the 1960s; their numbers increased significantly in the 1970s and 1980s (Loxley 2010). Many arrived in Winnipeg ill prepared for urban industrial life, a result in large part of colonial projects such as the residential school system, which had left many Aboriginal people without adequate formal educational qualifications (Knockwood 2001; Milloy 1999). They became concentrated in Winnipeg's inner city, at first because housing there was least expensive, and in subsequent decades because that is where other Aboriginal people already lived. But they were moving into neighbourhoods in which jobs — and particularly the kinds of industrial jobs that historically had been available to those with limited formal educational qualifications — had disappeared. With few well-paid jobs available, and facing a wall of systemic racism and discrimination because they were "different," many Aboriginal people became effectively locked out of the formal labour market (Cheung 2005; Silver 2006b).

In more recent years, growing numbers of immigrants and refugees from war-torn countries arrived in Winnipeg, many with low levels of formal education as a result of poverty and war. Most of them located in the inner city, and for the same reasons that low-income people had, for decades, located there (Silver 2010; Kazemipur and Halli 2000).

The result of these various processes — globalization, suburbanization, internal migration, and immigration — has been the concentration of racialized poverty in Winnipeg's inner city. Meaningful, well-paid jobs are scarce, housing is frequently inadequate, and opportunities (recreational and otherwise) are limited. This has been the case for decades. As a result, very large numbers of inner-city people have been "raised poor," and have never known anything but poverty and joblessness. For many Aboriginal people especially, the long historical process of colonialism has instilled a culture of despair (RCAP 1996; Silver 2006a) — a culture beyond the experience of most racially privileged Canadians.

It is not surprising that crime and violence flourish in this context. This is particularly so when street drugs are readily available as a means of escape and can be bought and sold at prices and in volumes sufficient for the traffickers to earn a living well beyond what they could earn from menial service-sector "McJobs" (Ritzer 2004). A self-reinforcing dynamic is set in motion. Many inner-city people reject such jobs on the grounds that the wages are insufficient to support themselves and their families and to create a financially secure future. Instead, some turn to the hidden economy — especially the drug and sex trades — to make a living. The illegal trade in drugs has become more and more insidious in Winnipeg over the last decade, with drugs such as crack cocaine and crystal methamphetamine being distributed on the street and via "crack houses" in inner-city neighbourhoods. For young — and disproportionately Aboriginal — women, working in the street sex trade is often their only recourse for getting by, which puts them at risk of violence and leads to drugging and drinking as a means for coping with the work (Brown et al. 2006; Seshia 2005).

Tied up with the drug and street sex trades, street gangs have become a more prominent feature of life in Winnipeg's inner-city communities. In the mid-1990s Winnipeg gained a reputation as the "gang capital of Canada," and Indian Posse, Native Syndicate, and Manitoba Warriors became part of the public discourse. While law enforcement officials were quick to locate these gangs within the parlance of criminal organizations (McLeod 2004), Aboriginal advocates and researchers were adamant in situating them as a contemporary manifestation of and response to colonialism (Fontaine 2006; Deane, Bracken, and Morrissette 2007). From this standpoint, the street gang is understood as a source of belonging and identity for many young Aboriginal men, providing a solution to the loss of family support and the grinding poverty they have encountered in their lives. With little education or training and few meaningful job prospects, the economic activity of the gang life seems like a rational solution to their dire circumstances. Nevertheless, it is also a life infused with masculine bravado, risk, and violence (Buddle 2011; Chettleburgh 2007; Comack 2008; Comack et al. 2009). While only some people may choose this pathway, all those who reside in the inner-city communities where the gangs operate are tasked with negotiating the violence that pervades their social spaces.

Increasingly, therefore, in Winnipeg, concerns about the prevalence of crime, violence, the drug and sex trades, and street gangs in inner-city communities have figured prominently. By and large these concerns are a product of broader processes tied to economic restructuring. In this regard, Winnipeg is not alone in experiencing the effects of globalization, suburbanization, internal migration, and immigration and the concomitant intensification of racialized poverty. As Loïc Wacquant (2008) documents, the widening gap between rich and poor has created a class of "urban out-casts" in Western cities worldwide, leading to alienation and disaffection and spawning heightened anxiety over crime, violence, and disorder.

The key state institution assigned the job of responding to these concerns is the criminal justice system. As the front line of the criminal justice system, the police are relegated to managing the fallout created by these broader processes.

MODELS OF POLICING IN WINNIPEG

As in other jurisdictions, police service delivery in Winnipeg has reflected a range of models adopted over time, in large part depending upon fiscal resources and the direction initiated by municipal leaders and/or police management. The dominant models have been traditional policing, community policing, and, most recently, zero-tolerance policing.

The traditional model of policing, with its roots in the early twentieth century, emphasizes a military style of organization with a focus on centralization and bureaucratization (hierarchies and chains of command), standardization (of recruitment, training, and patrol methods), reliance on technology (radio-equipped patrol cars and computerized dispatch systems), and specialization (youth units, morals units, homicide units, and the like). Envisioning police as "crime fighters," this model is reactive and incident-driven. Police work involves patrolling neighbourhoods in cars and responding to calls from the dispatcher. The focus is on serious forms of crime as opposed to maintenance of community social order or general service delivery, and success is measured by arrest statistics (especially for violent and property crimes) (Morash and Ford 2002; Herbert 2001; Greene 2000). This form of policing has predominated in most Canadian and U.S. cities; it still constitutes the core of Winnipeg's inner-city policing strategy.

By the 1970s, commentators coming from a variety of standpoints and locales began to argue that the traditional model was ineffective (Wilson 1975; Kelling 1974; Sherman 1974). An increasing scepticism about the traditional model's ability to "fight crime," coupled with a recognition that police on their own cannot solve crime and that communities also share in the responsibility for addressing crime problems, led to a community policing movement that found expression in Canada, the United States, and the United Kingdom. Described more as a philosophy than a specific program (Clairmont 1991: 471), community policing involves a more multiagency approach to service delivery, a generalist police role, and a greater community involvement at the local level (Linden et al. 2000; Brodeur, 1998; Murphy 1993; Hamilton and Sinclair 1991a). Rather than on "fighting crime," the emphasis is on crime prevention and community-building. Rather than focusing on arrest statistics, it measures success in terms of greater community satisfaction with the police, an increased sense of safety and security (reduction in fear of crime) in the neighbourhood, and a greater sense of ownership and partnership on the part of community groups and police in solving an area's problems (Clairmont 1991).

By the mid-1990s, researcher Barry Leighton (1994: 209) was able to assert that "community policing is firmly established as the dominant orientation or philosophy" in Canada and that "the overwhelming public rhetoric of Canadian police chiefs indicates they are committed to the paradigm shift, in principle and philosophy." Generally speaking, the success of these initiatives has depended upon the willingness of the police leadership to promote a community-policing philosophy and usher in changes in their departments. This was certainly the case in Winnipeg when David Cassels took on the position of chief of the Winnipeg Police Service (WPS) in May 1996. Cassels began implementing a community-policing model that included the assignment of twenty foot-patrol officers in inner-city neighbourhoods. As reflected on its official website <winnipeg.ca/police/AboutTheService/community_policing.stm>, the WPS continues to maintain a commitment to community policing. One form that this commitment has taken is a School Resource Officer Program, which places uniformed police officers in inner-city schools. Designed as a preventive strategy with a long-term focus, school resource officers become a regular presence in the schools with the aim of developing positive relationships and a sense of trust with students and staff.

Despite the professed commitment to a community-policing philosophy, concerns have emerged about the extent to which the initiatives have had an impact on the hierarchical structure and bureaucratic organization of police services. François Dumaine and Rick Linden (2005), for instance, have noted that initiatives such as community-police centres have been poorly integrated into the core functions of their departments. Jack Greene (2000: 332) has likened efforts to change internal police routines to "bending granite." Others have noted that individual police officers have tended to resist efforts to implement community policing because the model runs counter to a police culture premised on the exercise of force and a pronounced sense of morality ("getting the bad guys"). As Steve Herbert (2001) notes, both of those components are at odds with community policing.

Although community policing garnered considerable attention and support with its emergence in the mid-1980s, the 1990s saw the advent of yet another model. Zero-tolerance policing is similar to community policing in that it involves an increased police presence or visibility in the community and a more decentralized authority structure. Nevertheless, it differs significantly from community policing. For one, the main goal of zero-tolerance policing is to maintain order — and in a "hyper-aggressive" manner (Greene 1999: 175). The approach tends to target panhandlers, squeegee kids, street sex-trade workers, street-level drug users, the homeless, and the disorderly. To this extent, zero-tolerance policing shares in common the focus on law enforcement found in the traditional model. Like that model, it also relies upon a more aggressive, militaristic style of policing and typically involves giving police officers increased powers to stop and search citizens for minor law violations. As well, zero-tolerance policing tends to eclipse the active role of the citizenry by virtue of the more aggressive powers exercised by the police (for example, practices of intimidation and arrest), which is in contrast to the community-policing approach, which sees citizens and police as "co-equal partners in the construction and evaluation of tactics aimed at ameliorating community distress" (Herbert 2001: 446). With the zero-tolerance approach police measure "success" by counting field stops and the types of behaviour occurring in targeted locations (Greene 2000).

It was William Bratton who championed zero-tolerance policing while serving as the police commissioner of New York City in the mid-1990s. Bratton had been appointed by Mayor Rudolph Giuliani, who was elected to office in 1993 after a campaign strongly focused on issues of crime and disorder. Zero-tolerance policing meshed well with Giuliani's promise to reclaim the streets of New York for law-abiding citizens. As Judith Greene (1999: 173) notes, "Cracking down hard on the most visible symbols of urban disorder proved to be a powerful political tool for bolstering Giuliani's image as a highly effective mayor."

Under Bratton's lead, the New York City Police Department (NYPD) initiated a massive restructuring that saw the number of uniformed officers increase from 27,000 in 1993 to 41,000 in 2001. As Wacquant (2006: 104) indicates, this growth in personnel was only possible thanks to an increase in the police budget of 50 percent in five years, which allowed it to top $3 billion in 2000; during the same period social services in the city were cut by 30 percent. Bratton also decentralized authority in the NYPD in order to move power out to the individual precincts and boroughs. A computerized information system known as COMPSTAT — meaning "compare statistics" — was introduced to improve the police's knowledge of the occurrence of crime and disorder. And a Street Crime Unit was launched in 1994. This elite unit had a militaristic culture; members were known as "commandos" of the NYPD, and their motto was "We own the night" (Lynch 2000). By 1996 the unit had grown to 138 officers, and it was expanded further to 380 officers after Howard Safir replaced Bratton as police commissioner.

During his tenure as mayor of New York City, Giuliani credited the zero-tolerance policing strategy for realizing a significant reduction in crime and disorder in the city. Despite its detractors (see, for example, Herbert 2001; Grabosky 1999; Greene 1999; Innes 1999; Hopkins-Burke 1998), the zero-tolerance policing strategy found its way into a number of other locales (Newburn 2002; Jones and Newburn 2002; Wacquant 2006) — the City of Winnipeg among them.

In November 2005 the WPS launched "Operation Clean Sweep." Clean Sweep, as it came to be known, emerged on the heels of an inner-city, gang-related shooting death of a seventeen-year-old male bystander one month earlier. With an initial estimated cost of $1.6 million, the project involved the deployment of forty-five police officers, mainly in the West End, a part of Winnipeg's inner city. Described as a "take back the streets" and an "in your face" form of policing (Owen 2005), the goal of the project was to suppress street-level violence and disorder, "including, but not limited to, gang, drug and prostitution related offences" (Winnipeg Police Service 2006a). Like zero-tolerance policing generally, the success of Clean Sweep was measured by the number of warrants served, arrests, gun and drug seizures, and drug houses shut down. By the end of July 2006 this approach to policing had netted 873 arrests and 73 apprehensions. Some 5,555 spot checks were conducted, 42 search warrants executed, and 897 offence notices issued, while 6,689 police-person hours were logged walking the beat. The police reportedly seized $990,650 worth of illegal drugs and firearms. A "Clean Sweep Tip Line" set up to receive calls from citizens netted 322 calls (Winnipeg Police Service 2006a).

In May 2006 the City of Winnipeg sponsored a two-day, by-invitation-only summit comprising business and community leaders to examine the economic, social, and infrastructure development opportunities and barriers with the goal of creating new initiatives for the city. Giuliani of New York was the keynote speaker. He was reported to have told his audience at the $260-a-plate dinner that "Winnipeg can get rid of its image as a high-crime, rundown city by first cleansing the streets of aggressive panhandlers and squeegee kids" (Sanders 2006). He also expressed his enthusiastic support for the use of computerized crime-mapping techniques. Winnipeg mayor Sam Katz, a sports and entertainment entrepreneur turned civic politician, was quick to act on Giuliani's advice.

Initially designed as a pilot project, Operation Clean Sweep was subsequently bolstered by a $2-million contribution from the provincial government and an addition of $3.5 million to the Police Service's overtime budget to make it a more permanent feature of policing in the city (Katz 2006). Adopting the same name as the NYC unit, what is now referred to as the Street Crime Unit comprises some forty-seven officers who work on a city-wide basis. In addition to providing support to uniform patrol and investigative units, officers in the Street Crime Unit "provide a visible police presence in hot spots of criminal activity, carry out regular spot checks and execute warrants" (Winnipeg Police Service 2009). As well, in February 2007 the Winnipeg Police Service launched the first phase of "CrimeStat." The WPS website displays weekly statistical breakdowns of crimes committed across the city, and police utilize this information to identify and respond to crime patterns. According to Mayor Katz, "CrimeStat will measure police effectiveness, hold commanders accountable to delivering results, and use accurate and timely intelligence to assist in the deployment of officers to meet emerging challenges" (Katz 2007).

That Winnipeg's mayor is enamoured with this zero-tolerance approach to policing, delivered in person by a famous former NYC mayor to a congregation of the city's elites, is clear. There is also evidence to suggest that this "get-tough" approach to the problems of drugs, gangs, and violence in Winnipeg's inner city has popular appeal. Like Giuliani, Mayor Katz won re-election in both 2006 and 2011 on a platform that showcased his approach to crime control.

THE EXPERIENCES AND STANDPOINTS OF ABORIGINAL PEOPLE

While interviews with police officers can shed light on the challenges they encounter in policing inner-city communities (see, for example, Comack and Silver 2006; Huey 2007), it is just as — if not arguably more — important to explore the standpoints of the citizens whom the police are mandated to serve and protect. This is especially the case for Aboriginal people living in Winnipeg's inner-city communities. As Henry and Tator (2006: 119) note, qualitative research aimed at gaining access to these standpoints can help "to 'break the silence' and 'bear witness' to the lived experiences of people of colour and other minorities in the face of a hegemonic culture that distorts, stereotypes, and marginalizes that experience."

What can Aboriginal people tell us about their experiences with the policing of Winnipeg's inner-city communities? For one thing, during the interviews we carried out (see Appendix), some of the participants did report positive experiences with the police. One woman who suffered from mental health issues commented, "They're patient with the mentally ill, I think, for the most part.... 'Cause when I get sick it just, you know, I mean, I'm not really totally in control of everything (laughs)." Another woman who had worked in the street sex trade said, "I've seen a lot of cops who are very kind-hearted."

People also spoke about instances when they needed assistance and a police officer was there to help them. One twenty-one-year-old man told of a time when he had been badly beaten — to the point where he was having convulsions. He said the police "saved my life" — they had come to his aid and called an ambulance to get him to hospital. Another twenty-something man told of a time when he was drunk and having trouble making it home safely, but two police officers spotted him. They gave him a blanket to keep him warm and bought him a burger from McDonald's. "I think they totally saved me that day," he said. "They do good things too, you know. I don't really think they're trying to be bad people at all." A forty-something woman found police to be attentive when she encountered domestic violence from her partner. "I'd phone them and they'd be there right away."

These experiences showcase both the diversity of situations in which police are called upon for assistance when people are in trouble, and the invaluable role performed by police officers in Winnipeg's inner-city communities. They also suggest that some officers not only meet the demands placed upon them in the course of their work, but also do so with professionalism, kindness, and concern. Nevertheless, while some participants had very positive comments to make about the Winnipeg Police Service, others were more disparaging. We frequently heard comments such as "I hate the police," "I don't trust the police," and "I don't want nothing to do with them. I'm scared of them." More often than not, these judgments sprang from the negative experiences that people had with police officers.

Given the troubled lives of many of the participants, it is not surprising that they would report having regular encounters with the police. But that contact was not simply a function of their own actions or behaviours; it also emanated from their location in the racialized space of Winnipeg's inner-city communities. By and large, inner-city residents take considerable pride in their community and see its many strengths and benefits (CCPA–MB 2007; Comack and Silver 2006; Silver et al. 2006). Nevertheless, because of the inner city's reputation as a disorderly and dangerous place in which crime, violence, gangs, and the drug and street sex trades proliferate, police surveillance there is heightened. Just being present in that space, therefore, means that Aboriginal people are at risk of being targeted as the "usual suspects." In the process, encounters between Aboriginal people and the police become infused with questions of race and racialization. Indeed, while police officers all too readily define Aboriginal people as troublesome, some of the strategies that officers adopt in their endeavour to reproduce order are also troublesome, to say the least.

The "Usual Suspects"

A common theme to emerge from the interviews is that Aboriginal men who live in Winnipeg's inner city are regularly stopped by police and asked to account for themselves. Officers often carry out warrant checks. When the men ask, "What did I do wrong?" the typical response is "You fit the description" because the police are looking for an Aboriginal man as a suspect in a crime. In other words, the men are stopped precisely because they are Aboriginal. For many of the men we interviewed, this experience has become an all too normal occurrence.

Twenty-year-old Frank said that he is accustomed to being stopped by police "once a week, guaranteed. I can't even, like, count the number of times where I've been stopped just for walking down the street wearing, like, all black or something." When asked what the police say when they stop him, Frank replied, "Nothing. Just, like, put some cuffs on me and say, 'Oh, we have a guy fitting your description. He's breaking into garages or throwing stuff at houses.'" Frank says, "It makes me mad. But, like, there's nothing you can do."

Carl had similarly frustrating experiences with the police. While he had been charged and ticketed for squeegeeing, he did not have a criminal record. Only twenty-four-years old when we met, Carl said that since the age of sixteen he has been stopped "at least twice a month" by police because he fit the description of someone the police were looking for.

> And what am I supposed to say to that? I get stopped — "Hey, I'm not this guy. I'm not who you're looking for." They're still not going to believe me. They're still going to take my ID. They're still going to check my, if I'm wanted or not, you know. They're still going to do all that. So

what am I supposed to do? Like, am I supposed to say, "Hey, I'm not the guy who you're looking for so just keep on driving?" But it doesn't work like that. If they think that you're someone that they are looking for, they're going to stop you and going to check you.

Stan was in his early forties at the time of the interview. While he grew up in Winnipeg, much of his younger years were spent moving back and forth between the city and his reserve community. By the age of eleven, however, he was "hanging around with the wrong crowd" and got into trouble with the law. He went from the youth detention centre to group homes to foster homes. "In my teens," he said, "I didn't really grow up with my parents 'cause I was always in and out of youth facilities."

While he used to steal cars and go joyriding as a kid, as he grew older Stan's crimes "got more serious." At the age of twenty-one, facing some seventeen charges (including one for a home invasion), he began serving thirty months in Stony Mountain Penitentiary. When he was in Stony he "never associated with any gangs or anything like that, you know. I just kept to myself, did my time." When he was released in 1991 he "never looked back." However, Stan continued drinking. "It was with the drinking that really, that really it got me into trouble. When I used to drink I used to go and do stupid things." None of his crimes were violent, "just break into garages, break into houses or whatever, you know, whatever I could do to get my hands on, just to make money, just to get money." Stan said that during this period his contact with the police would involve them taking him "for rides down the back lane, try and get me to talk, trying to get me to admit to something I didn't do, to take the fall for something I didn't do.... Get a couple of shots, whatever. Get my hair pulled or whatever. Get called down, you know, 'You fucking Indian,' this and that, blah, blah, blah, you know."

In the last several years Stan had quit drinking and was trying his best to go straight. Nevertheless, he continued to attract the attention of the police simply because he "fits the description." Stan told us about a recent incident:

One day, this was last summer [at about two in the afternoon]. There was a cop car parked behind Mac's on Selkirk and Arlington, and they came across the back lane really fast. A cop got out and grabbed me without asking me, like, without even telling me what the hell is going on. Like, I asked him, "What's going on?" He says, "Quiet. You fit the description of somebody we're looking for." "Well, what's the description?" "White T-shirt, blue jeans, long hair, ponytail." I says, "Don't forget where you are, man. You're in the North End. How many Native people in the North End have long hair and a ponytail and are wearing a white T-shirt? Come on now, use your fucking head." Cop grabs me, throws me against the car, puts me in the car, doesn't, I'm not under arrest or anything but he's throwing me in the car and they want to take me for a ride. So they take me for a ride. And they're trying to get me, like, do I know this, do I know that. Like, I don't know anything.

Chris, age thirty, reported similar experiences. When he had long hair, he said, "I'd get picked up like every other weekend, you know, just for questioning because I looked like somebody else. And so I figured if I cut my hair it'd be a little bit easier." The strategy helped somewhat. Chris said he now got stopped by police "maybe once a month."

Owen, nineteen years old, talked about an experience that occurred on the night of his fifteenth birthday party. He was walking in West Broadway, an area in the most southerly part of the inner city, around midnight:

I was leaving my place and I was walking my friend to his bus stop and when I was on my way back home after I'd left him — I was with three of my friends. We had all gone on this walk and we were at the end of my block. And five cop cars pulled up and all the cops jumped out with guns drawn to our heads and told us to "Get the fuck on the ground!" And they all — and they didn't really give us a chance to say much. If one of my friend's parents hadn't been driving by at the time — 'cause my friend's dad was picking her up, so he saw us all laid down on the ground with the cops drawing guns to our heads and he asked, like, what was going on and he vouched for us. So they eventually let us go.

The police told Owen that someone had been assaulted nearby. As he surmised, "I'm guessing we just fit a description." Owen had been pulled over by police "countless times" since then. The police, assuming he was dealing drugs for a street gang, would ask him: "Who are you selling for?" "Who are you banging for?" "Where's the shit?"

One of the challenges confronting Winnipeg police officers is quelling the illegal trade in drugs that goes on in the inner city. Like Owen, several of the men talked about how police just assume they are involved in the drug trade. Thirty-year-old Bill, for instance, told of an incident when he had been standing in front of his house, "and my friend, my neighbour, he was giving me ten dollars so I can go get some beer for him. 'Cause I had a bike so I was going to the beer store for him." The police happened by and saw the exchange. "They grabbed me, searched me and everything, thinking I got drugs or something. I didn't have nothing." Even sixty-five-year-old Edward told of being stopped by police based on this assumption:

> Well, just recently, about two weeks ago, I was visiting my friend until about ten o'clock at night on Salter and Redwood. And I was coming home. And I come up to Salter and I hit Manitoba. Then I started walking down Manitoba, taking a shortcut. And I got pulled over and they got out of the car and slammed me against the car. "Where's your drugs? Where's your drugs?" "What drugs?" "You're selling drugs." I said, "I just came from my friend's place." I said, "Here's his address, here's his name." I said, "Do you want to go and check it out?" "Oh, you're lying, you bastard." I says, "Hold it. Hold it," I says. "There's no need to talk to me like that," I said. "I've got nothing," I said. "Look. You don't see no drug paraphernalia on me or anything like that," I said. So, you know, "What's with this?" "Well, we're pretty sure." I said, "You could be sure all you want, you know," but I said "that's not the way it is."

While police often assume that men found on the streets of the inner city are involved in the drug trade, several of our participants talked about how police also assume that they are gang-involved because of how they dress. Forty-one-year-old Mark commented: "Like sometimes I used to wear tracksuits and stuff. We'd get pulled over for no reason, thinking we're like Native gang members. And that's bullshit." Peter, in his thirties, said that police would assume he was gang-involved when he wore a white track suit (associated with the Deuce gang) or a red one (Indian Posse). "They would beat you up and they would try to make you rat out where drug houses are and that. It was scary, scary growing up being Native in this neighbourhood." When the same thing happened to Greg, he told the police officers: "That's pretty racial of you guys to think that I'm with the gang. Just 'cause I'm Native you think I'm with Indian Posse or something. 'Cause I grew up in the North End, you know. Just live this life. But not be in a gang. You don't have to be in a gang. Not everybody's in a gang."

While Aboriginal men are presumed to be involved in the drug trade or affiliated with a street gang, Aboriginal women encounter a different kind of stereotyping. Given the concerns with the street sex trade that operates in Winnipeg's inner-city neighbourhoods, police often assumed that Aboriginal women found in those spaces are sex workers. As one woman (and she does work in the street sex trade) noted: "They see a girl on a strip where prostitutes happen to roam, they automatically stereotype and think that they're, every girl is out there doing the same thing when, in reality, you know, half the girls that are out there aren't even working. They're just walking by or whatever."

Dianne, twenty-four years old, told us about an incident that happened in the winter of 2008. She had been visiting her uncle in the downtown area. On her way home to the North End, she walked across the Slaw Rebchuck Bridge and stopped to use a pay phone to call her dad and ask for a ride the rest of the way. A police car pulled up, and the officers proceeded to charge her with a prostitution offence.

> *They said I was standing around trying to work the streets.... They grabbed me and they handcuffed me and they took me.... I did get a lawyer and did get it dropped because there was no evidence or nobody saying that, like, no undercover cop saying that I was talking to them or anything. So they just said that they, the cops said that they saw me going to a car, which I wasn't. I was going to the pay phone. So if they don't know the difference between a pay phone and a car, then, I don't know, something's wrong with them.*

Similarly, Christine, a thirty-three-year-old, told of being stopped by police on her way to the corner store. The police assumed that she was a sex-trade worker.

> *I live in an area where there is prostitution happening there and, like, sometimes I go to the store and, like, right away they're driving by and then they slow down. Like, "I'm going to the store," and, like, "Oh, you're lying." Like what — a woman can't even walk the street today? Every woman that walks the street today is what, supposed to be a hooker?*

Simply, then, because of their location in the racialized space of the inner city, Aboriginal people are subject to the racialized and gendered stereotypes associated with the "usual suspects." Those of us who have never been the target of such stereotyping (especially by police officers) can only imagine how scary and unsettling that experience can be. Racialized policing, however, runs deeper than the use of stereotypes; it is also implicated in the particular cultural frames of reference or stocks of knowledge that officers adopt in the course of their work.

Racialized and Sexualized Frames

As one Aboriginal man, Stan, told us, "We're the dirty ones. We're bad. We're drunks, sniffers, crackheads, the whole, like, we're everything, you know what I mean? That's the way they look at us."

Winnipeg police officers are tasked with the difficult job of responding to situations when — as Egon Bittner (2005) describes it — "someone-had-better-do-something-now!" These situations include break-ins, assaults, robberies, and other forms of crime. That is their mandate. In the course of fulfilling that role, and particularly in their encounters with Aboriginal people, the police officers see matters through racialized frames. As officers go about their daily work, these frames inform what Clifford Shearing and Richard Ericson (1991) refer to as the "storybook" or particular way of seeing that develops over time.

Sometimes these racialized frames are invoked to question the credibility of complainants. Thirty-eight-year-old Janice, for instance, talked about an experience she had with police officers when she was just twelve years old. Janice had been sexually molested while staying in a foster home. She told her dad's girlfriend, who took her to the police station. Janice explained:

> *The cops took me in the room and they asked me what happened and I told them. And they straight up didn't believe me, like I was lying. I was making this whole story up. And they treated me like I was the worst thing ever to walk into the police station. And I just felt really cheap. Like, it really, really hurts when somebody doesn't believe you. You know, there's nothing you can do to make them change their mind. If they believe you, that's it. And I felt like, why wouldn't they believe me? Because I'm an Indian? That was the only reason I could see why they didn't believe me. So the guy got away with what he did to me because the police didn't believe me. So when the police told my dad's girlfriend that they didn't believe me then she didn't believe me. So then it seemed like everybody thought I was a liar and that I was making this up.*

When the two male officers asked her what had happened, Janice told them she was sleeping when the man came into her room. They responded with, "Couldn't you dream that that was happening to you? Are you sure you were awake?" Janice told them, "I'm sure I was awake. I know what he did to me, you know." Janice was placed in two more foster homes after that — and sexually molested in both of them. "I never told anybody 'cause they're not going to believe me, right?" Janice remained convinced that, as she said, "I wasn't credible for anything because of who I was, 'cause I was an Indian. Had I been white I think they would have believed me. I honestly do."

One month prior to our meeting, Owen was at a birthday party for a friend who had just turned eighteen. It was a hot summer's night and they were sitting in the backyard of a North End house. Earlier that evening, Owen and his friends had heard a house alarm going off, but thought little of it. Owen explained what happened next:

> *After a while a cop came, just one cop in a car, like, not two of them, just one guy. And he came out and he approached us. We were sitting in the backyard. And he said, "Where's your guys' ID's?" And he pointed at me and my girlfriend… and he only wanted our ID's, like, he didn't care for anyone else's around, like, my friend or his sister. So I gave him my ID and I told him my name or whatever and he wrote it down in his little log book. And my girlfriend told him her name too, but she didn't have her ID on her, so he started giving her attitude. Like, he said, "How am I supposed to believe you if you don't have ID on you?" And he came on to our property there, you know, and giving her heck for not having ID when she's on private property anyway. So she gets pretty steamed and she walks inside. And he continues talking to me, "Where have you guys been all morning?" and "Where are you guys going?" or whatever. And I said, "We've been here the whole time, like, I slept here last night. I've been here since yesterday." Then my friend's sister was outside, like, they were kind of standing around and she starts going inside, and he goes, "Hey," and he goes, "Where did that other girl go?" And he was talking about my girlfriend. And she's like, "I don't know." And then she walked inside and he said, "Jesus. How come I can never get a straight answer from you people?"*
>
> *So then my friend walks inside and I'm starting to walk inside too at that point, 'cause I'm just kind of, like, it feels like it's just a waste of all of our time, right. Like, we didn't do anything. There was no reason for him to come onto the property. So I was about to walk inside and then he starts stepping into the door. And then I stood in the doorway and I said, "You have no warrants. You can't come in here." And then he goes, he steps back and he goes, "What. You want to fuckin' fight me?" And I'm like, "No." And he's like, "Well" — and then he leans in the doorway 'cause he sees my friend's sister, the one that had gone in earlier and he says, "Where's that girl? Go get that girl and bring*

her out here." And then, so then my girlfriend comes back outside and we're both standing there and he goes, "So this is your real name?" And she's like, "Yeah." And he's like, "Well, if I look up both your names in my computer right now, you guys aren't going to have any warrants?" And we both said, "No." I said, "Why would we have warrants?" And he said, "'Cause most of you people do." And I said, "What's that supposed to mean?" And he said, "Figure it out."... He sat around in his car there and probably ran the names through first and then he took off.

Comments such as "Jesus, how come I can't get a straight answer from you people?" and "'Cause most of you people do" signal the racialized frame that the police officer adopted in carrying out a routine investigation. One has to wonder if the response would have been the same if the citizens the officer encountered resided in a wealthier neighbourhood instead of being Aboriginal residents of Winnipeg's North End.

The use of racialized frames by police officers is reflected in another encounter. This time the frame adopted drew upon the racialized discourse of the "North End drinking party" (Comack and Balfour 2004: 93). Harold is a sixty-four-year-old who lives with his common-law partner. His partner's sons had come to the city one weekend on a break from working at a northern fishing camp, so the family decided to have "a little get-together, having a few drinks." At around three in the morning they ran out of cigarettes, so decided to head to the nearby gas station. Harold and his older stepson went into the station to buy cigarettes while the younger stepson waited outside for them, where he began talking with another Aboriginal man on a bike. "The one fellow that's outside," Harold said, "he's not very, what you call it, he doesn't get to the city very often, he's telling that guy, 'Oh, my brother's got lots of money. We just come from fishing, blah, blah, blah.'" As they left the gas station to begin the short walk home, the man on the bike began following them. Harold became concerned, telling his stepsons, "Keep going, keep going." Then the man on the bike went ahead of them, dropped his bike, and came over to them. Harold said, "I heard him say, 'I've got a knife.'" Next thing Harold knew, his older stepson was "bleeding like crazy." They managed to get him back to the house and Harold's wife ministered to her son while Harold called for an ambulance.

The police arrived along with the ambulance. "And I guess their first assumption they take is because we're all Native people, that there was a big fight in the house, blah, blah, blah." Harold tried to tell the officers about the man on the bike, but they wouldn't listen to him. Instead, Harold and the younger stepson were put in the back of a police car and taken to the police station. "They wanted us as witnesses but we were being treated more or less like the criminal, eh.... We were locked up the same as if we had committed a crime, eh."

Harold was frustrated by the experience. He believed that if the police had taken the time to listen to him they would have been able to apprehend the culprit.

> I can understand if there was a weapon there that had created the conflict and, right on the premises, like, say, a gun or a knife or a piece of wood that created the — "Okay, this happened here." Like I say, jump to the assumption. But when you're trying to tell them, "No, no, this didn't even happen on the premises. We got home from going to buy cigarettes." That's what I was trying to explain. By the time I got through to one of those, one police woman and two or three other police, and there was a couple police cars there. It only took one to get the information. The other ones could [say] "Okay, I'm going to go look for this person you described."

Racialized frames also come into play when police see a group of Aboriginal people congregating. Fifty-three-year-old Florence said she likes to meet up with her friends at Thunderbird House, located in the heart of the Main Street strip. Florence said they were regularly approached by police, who "assume that everybody drinks, you know, but a lot of us don't. We just go there to say 'Hi.' And they come there and they start swearing." The police, Florence said, "sometimes just come and hassle you for no reason. Or they say, 'You got any warrants?' We'll say 'No.' They're coming to check you out anyways." According to Florence, "They figure because you've got a criminal record, you know, that's why they hassle you. They figure that you're going to be in trouble all the time, you know, 'cause you got a criminal record."

Several other people talked about the stigma they encountered because of past conflicts with the law. As Valerie commented, if you have priors, the police assume you haven't changed. "You're still just a criminal in their eyes." Dianne maintained, "Whether I have a criminal record or not, that don't entitle them to talk to me like that. That really bothers me, it really does. Yeah. I'm really upset about that, the way they talk to me."

The frames used by police officers are not only racialized but also sexualized. Women and transgenders working in Winnipeg's street sex trade are at great risk of encountering violence from their customers (Comack and Seshia 2010). Thirty-year-old Jessica had worked in the street sex trade up until three years before we spoke to her. She talked about being raped by a john, an experience that had happened seven years previously. She ended up at the hospital, and the medical staff summoned the police. Two officers attended who knew Jessica from seeing her working on the street. They chided her, "What's wrong, Jessica? Did he not pay you enough? What, he didn't give you enough money?" Jessica was so disturbed by these comments that she left the hospital — even though she had bruises all over her body and required medical attention. "And, like, I got raped so many times after that. And I didn't even bother calling the cops because I thought, you know, they'll be the same way." Fortunately, the last time Jessica was raped officers from the Sex Crimes Unit of the Winnipeg Police Service came to the hospital. Jessica said, "They were really good. They didn't make me feel shitty or anything."

Margaret, a thirty-one-year-old, had a similarly troubling encounter with police officers. She phoned the police after being assaulted by a man she knew. When two young officers arrived at her doorstep the next day, she said, "They asked me if I saw his penis. And I was like, 'What?' Like, that totally shocked me. And they were like, 'Well, did you see his penis or not?' And I'm like, 'I don't see what that has to do with anything.' And they're like, 'Well if you seen his penis then it's a domestic.'" When Margaret finally relented and replied in the affirmative, the officers were "smirking and smiling," she said. "They were getting a good kick out of this."

The Use of Racist and Sexist Language

For many of the participants, how the police chose to interact with them is a matter of importance. In particular, many people spoke of the way police officers put them down. As one woman queried, "Why do they have to treat us with such disrespect?" More often than not, this attitude shows up in the words they use, the unprofessional language. Edward had this to say about his experience of being stopped by police when they assumed he was a drug dealer:

> It bothers me more not so much that they stopped me, but it's the way they talked to me. Like, there's no respect whatsoever, you know. Like it's a "F-you" and "F-this and that," you know. Like, sure they're going to deny it and say, "Oh, no. We never said that and this and that." But that's exactly what they do to people when they got you alone where

there's nobody around to witness it.... They sure don't use very good vocabulary when they get you alone, I'll tell you that.

Twenty-year-old Susan told of an experience that had occurred three years previously. The police were called to the house because of a disturbance between a female cousin and her boyfriend. When they arrived, one of the officers was rude to her auntie, who was upset and talking in a loud voice. The officer turned to her auntie and said, "Can you just shut the fuck up!" Susan intervened and told the officer, "Don't talk like that to my auntie! That's really disrespectful." While the officer apologized, Susan had to wonder, "I bet he wouldn't talk like that to his mother."

Other officers were not as forthcoming with apologies. At one point when I was doing interviews at the Indian and Métis Family Centre, located in the heart of the North End on Selkirk Avenue, I met up with a woman who had come to the centre to use the phone. She heard about the study and wanted to be interviewed. Just that afternoon she had gone to the nearby school to drop off her kids. A police cruiser was parked out in front of the school. One of the officers rolled down the window and called for her to come over to the car. "So I told them [the teachers] to come with me. I said, 'Watch them be rude to me.'" As the three women started to walk towards the car, one of the officers came out of the vehicle and said to the teachers, "No. I'm not talking to you squaws." The woman pointed out that "those are my kids' teachers," and the teachers responded with "Yeah. We work for [school name]. We're the teachers here. There's no use for language like that. We're not called squaws. We're called Native people." The police officers did not apologize. They just said "Keep your nose clean, Mrs. G." and they "just laughed and drove away."

According to many of the participants, police officers regularly use words like "squaw," "dirty Indian," or "fuckin' Indian" in their encounters with Aboriginal people. Florence said she had been called a "cunt," "slut," "whore," and "crackhead." In her experience, police used "lots of bad language, especially against Natives, 'You're nothing but a squaw. Your mom and dad are alcoholics.' I've heard it so many times from their mouths I just don't say anything anymore." The use of racist and sexist language by police obviously runs counter to the professional image of the police officer and the "core values" of honesty, integrity, trust, respect, accountability, and commitment to excellence that the Winnipeg Police Service professes to uphold (Winnipeg Police Service 2009). While the use of such language may emanate from the effort to reproduce order, at its core it constitutes a power move that has the effect of silencing and marginalizing Aboriginal people. When such language is heard "so many times from their mouths" it becomes a routine part of the everyday life of Aboriginal people living in Winnipeg's inner city, thereby contributing to a wider system of racism and racial inequality.

Aboriginal people are not always passive recipients in these encounters. In this regard, the disrespect and use of troublesome language work both ways. Stan, for instance, says that when police officers say things to him like, "You're just a fucking Indian," he gives it back to them:

> I could respect people up to a point. Once they start coming down on me for nothing then I just kind of bite back a little bit, you know what I mean? Just to let them know that, "Hey. I'm not going to sit here and let you talk to me like that. I don't care who you are," you know? Cop or no cop, whatever, you know. I mean, I can be a nice person but then I can be an asshole too.

Because of his negative experiences with police, Carl said that he too "gives it back" when he does meet up with a police officer. "I'll treat them how they treat me. I swear at them. I call them 'fucking pigs.' I'm straight, a dickhead to them. I know I am." Carl believed that the negative experiences he had with police stemmed from the stereotypes that police officers hold about Aboriginal people.

> They don't even take the time to, you know, realize who we are, like, an individual person. They think that all Aboriginals are the same because they see the people on Main Street. Like, I know all that. But that's not me. So I don't know, they treat me all fucked up every time. I rarely get a cop who's nice to me, so fuck 'em. I hate them all.

Given the authority invested in police officers, efforts to resist or "give it back" have consequences, including the possibility of being charged with a criminal offence. Ellen, thirty-seven years old, told of an incident when she was intoxicated. When the police came to the house they were calling her a "drunken Indian" and saying, "All you Indians are drunks and drink and whatever." As Ellen remarked, "It's just, like, not all of us are the same, you know? And they were just, they were just being rude." So Ellen became "belligerent and rude" too. In response, she said that the police

> slapped me up against, on the street, on their cruiser, like my face was

all bruised. And, like, I had scrapes on my face from slamming me into
a concrete wall. And they were just going to take me to 75 Martha [the
Main Street Project]. But then I just couldn't take no more, of them
like just knocking down Indians and, you know, stuff like that. So I spit
in their face and they charged me with assault.

Ellen took issue with this result: "I think it's wrong, like, it's okay for them to beat me up but when I fight back I get charged with assault? I told my lawyer, 'Look at my mug shot,' I said. 'My face wasn't like that when they come to my house.'"

Troublesome Police Practices

While race and racialization are evident in the assumptions, frames, and language that police officers adopt in their encounters with Aboriginal people, there are also several troublesome police practices that emerged from the interviews with participants.

The Drunk Tank. As Richard Ericson (1982) suggests, the police use the law according to what other forms of social control are available and can be used effectively to achieve their role as reproducers of order. In that regard, one of the options that Winnipeg police officers have in dealing with troublesome people is to invoke the province's Intoxicated Persons Detention Act and deliver them to the Main Street Project. Housing a drop-in centre, an emergency shelter, and a twenty-five-bed non-medical detoxification centre, the Project is designed to provide a safe place for supervised withdrawal from the effects of drug and alcohol abuse. Several of the people interviewed, however, told us about being taken to the Project — otherwise known as the "drunk tank" — when they weren't drunk or under the influence of drugs.

Christine told of an experience when she was pregnant with her now six-year-old son. The police came to her home at around nine o'clock in the evening and arrested her. Christine explained, "There was drinking and that going on in the building and I guess they must have thought that was me and didn't give me time to explain myself or anything. And they just took me in." Believing her to be intoxicated, the officers delivered Christine to the drunk tank. Christine recalled what happened next:

They were demanding that the people running the place there strip-
search me and my purse and everything. And, uh, [the workers] told
the officers that that wasn't one thing they do at the Project, and that

they had no reason to keep me because I was sober. And they were even telling the officers that I shouldn't be treated this way and that they were going to take their badge and their number down and everything. And they said, "Well if you aren't going to take her," so they took me out and they drove around with me for about an hour. Kept me down in the [Public] Safety Building, down in a parking lot while, I don't know, they went and did their whatever, work or a coffee break.... And then they took me back to the Project and the people told them there, "Well, we got no reason to keep her. Once you guys are gone then we're going to let her go." So and then "Well we're not going to leave her here then." Then again we went to drive around, drive around. And then I said, "Well, where are you guys going to take me?" They said, "Do you have friends or somebody?" And so I gave them a friend's address and they drove around with me a bit longer and then finally took me to my friend's, I don't know, about two or three in the morning.

Forty-eight-year-old Linda had a similar experience. Several years ago she was coming out of the Savoy Hotel on Main Street.

I was coming out of the side door and I almost, like, tripped but I was sober. I was just going to catch the bus and come back to the North End here, eh. And just for that they just grabbed me and handcuffed me and said, "You're drunk." I said, "No. I haven't even been drinking, maybe one beer." But they still dragged me to the Main Street Project and I had to get in that cold little cell with just a blanket.

Valerie, forty-six years old, also talked about her experience of being taken to the drunk tank saying, "and sometimes you don't even need to go." One time she had phoned the police because a former partner was at her door, threatening violence. When the police arrived they put both of them in the back of the cruiser, telling Valerie it was for her own safety. But instead of letting her go back into her house, the police took her to the Main Street Project. As Valerie explained, "I'd had a few [drinks] but nothing to the point where I needed to be in the drunk tank. And they take me away with no shoes, no jacket, nothing. I just had on a pair of shorts and they throw me in there, eh." Valerie was frustrated by the experience, feeling that the police "weren't listening to me at all." In her view, the police operate on assumption that the drunk tank is Aboriginal people's "home away from home" — and so rely on it as a strategy for dealing with troublesome people.

The Use of Force. While the use of force by police officers is officially sanctioned, the conditions under which officers use force and whether the amount of force used is reasonable under the circumstances are contentious issues (Hoffman 2011). In this regard, one of the ironies to emerge from the interviews with Aboriginal people is that police are tasked with the job of responding to the violence that occurs in the inner city, but, in the process, violence appears to have become one of the strategies that police themselves use in the reproduction of order.

People who are involved with gangs appear to be especially prone to encountering violence from the police. Twenty-eight-year-old Jason, for instance, reported that he was part of a gang when he was a teenager, and that brought him into conflict with law. He acknowledged that his crimes were "pretty violent." So too was the response of the police. "And so, when they were violent, the cops treated me as violent, as violent as my crimes were. So when they caught me, it was bad, you know. I was so scared of them, you know. And they instilled that fear in me. So I still have that fear, you know, every time I see a police officer. It just reminds me of being hopeless, you know, being young again, where I can't do nothing."

Jason remembered one night when the police apprehended him while he was sleeping:

> *I woke up and there were cops standing all around me. And then they told me to get up but they grabbed me by the hair. And so they grabbed me by the hair, they put me in a choke hold. And then the next thing I know I blacked out and then when I came to I was in the back of the police car in handcuffs. I had no shoes, no shirt on, just the pants on, and then that was it.*

The police took Jason and his two friends to the Public Safety Building.

> *They put us each in a cell and they confined us to three cells, side by side. And they started doing interviews? And the interviews, they were not interviews, there were five guys walking, five un-uniformed officers walking into the cell and beating the living daylights out of you to try to make you confess for what you did. And so I listened to the guy in the next cell. And he was just screaming and hollering. And then my turn came around and then I just gave up.*

Jason said he told the police "everything because I couldn't stand the assaults. I couldn't take it. So I just, whatever they said, I just agreed, and that was it." Jason was charged with several offences, and also labelled a "rat" by his gang associates.

In Jason's estimation, police treat gang members more harshly: "If you're in a gang they'll be really violent to you. But if you're not in a gang they'll just, you know, they'll just give you maybe a slap in the back of the head or something, kick you once and then that's it. But they won't severely, like, try to beat it out of you? Because that's what they did to us three, they beat it out of us."

Other participants told of being subject to the use of excessive force but then ending up with charges of assaulting a peace officer or resisting arrest. As Scot Wortley (2007: 11) notes, because of the emphasis placed on receiving respect from the citizenry, the police subculture reinforces the belief that "it is sometimes okay for officers to respond to citizen hostility, disrespect or disobedience with violence." The police deem the offence of what is colloquially referred to as "contempt of cop" to be deserving of punishment. That would appear to be the case in an incident described by one of our participants, Margaret.

Margaret called 911 because a male friend who had come to her house to collect on a debt was assaulting her. The police and ambulance arrived shortly afterward. Margaret had a bite mark on her arm from the assault, and the paramedics wanted to take her to the hospital for antibiotics. Margaret told them, "I can't afford an ambulance. I don't need a bill coming, like, weeks later for three hundred bucks for an ambulance ride just because I have a bite mark on my arm. Like, I'll go to a doctor later. I'm really tired and I just want to be at home." The police responded by grabbing her, "one on each arm, and twisted my arm, like, you know that hold where they restrain you? They proceeded to take me out of my house. They didn't let me grab my keys." The police were trying to say that Margaret was intoxicated and verbally confused. Margaret told us, "I wasn't like that at all 'cause I hadn't been drinking. I had been up for most of the night but I wasn't drinking or anything. I had just been assaulted and here's two men grabbing me." Margaret said she "panicked" and bit one of the officers. She knew she shouldn't have done that, she said, but "I was in a panic mode." The result was that they threw her on the ground and "beat the crap" out of her. So that was the second time that night she had been assaulted. "And this time my face was like this [all swollen up], 'cause they were kicking me repeatedly in the face." Margaret took issue with the police officers' version of what happened:

They in their report said that they had used minimal force, like, all they did was punch me in the face a couple of times to make me let go. That was a lie. They beat the crap out of me. They both laid their boots on me and they had me on the ground and then the door slightly opened and that's when they stopped and they had me handcuffed behind my back and they proceeded to call me all sorts of names, like "You stupid squaw," "You're just a dumb dog" and "You want to bite, you dumb dog? We should stick you in the back with the dogs, like, have the dogs go at you." And calling me every derogatory name, "bitch," "slut," "whore." They called me right down.... And then by that time two more had come and they proceeded to kick me down my stairs and slam me against the car, slam my head against the car, throw me into the back of the squad car. And by that time I was mad. I was freaking. I mean, I was so mad and I was crying and they just kept on with the insults. Like, they wouldn't stop and they were talking on their, their things to each other, like "Oh, we're bringing a live one in. We're bringing this dog. She bit the cop."... And then they charged me with assaulting a peace officer.

Margaret was given the option of making a complaint to the Law Enforcement Review Agency. "I wanted to pursue it 'cause I thought who gives them the right to come into my home and grab me after I was just assaulted? They have no right to grab me out of my own house when I'm fine, I'm not verbally abusive, I'm not yelling at them. I'm, you know, I just wanted to feel safe and I was safe at that moment and they abused their power by grabbing me out of my own home, treating me like I was a criminal." But she decided not to lodge a complaint. "I'm not complaining to the cops about the cops 'cause I know how cops are and they just defend each other and they'll say whatever. And I didn't have that will or that support to go through with making a complaint like that."

Her case went to trial two years later. Margaret's lawyer advised her to plead guilty. "My lawyer advised me that if we did go to trial that they have all these, like, the other cops to collaborate and testify against me to say that I did actually bite him. And that was what the charge was, if I bit him or not. And I knew, I did bite him, I knew I was in the wrong for that but I told my lawyer, 'I just want my story told, you know, I don't want them to get away with what they do to us.'" She took her lawyer's advice and ended up with a conditional sentence of eighteen months, with the proviso that if she stayed clean all her charges would be dropped and she wouldn't have a criminal record. "And to me that sounded like a good idea … that was my main concern, that I would have a criminal record as an adult and I don't have any charges prior to this."

The "Phone Book Treatment." One of the troubling practices related to the police use of force is referred to as "the phone book treatment." Several of the participants had experience with this practice. As Peter explained:

> They put a phone book on you and they hit the phone book with a belly clip, so they don't bruise you. They put it on, they'd say, "Look in the phone book. See if your name is in there or your family name." And if you, if you wouldn't they would put the phone book on the side of your head and they would hit the phone book with the belly clips, so they wouldn't bruise your face and that.

Carol told of being taken to a police station and held in a room for sixteen hours. Her sons had a history of getting into trouble with the law and the officers — four of them — wanted information about their whereabouts. The officers told Carol they were going to charge her if she didn't tell them where her boys were. "They kept hitting my head with a phone book, you know, put the phone book against your head and punch it. … Even my boys too when they get arrested, that's what they do to them."

Stan had also experienced the phone book treatment some ten or eleven years earlier in the elevator of the Public Safety Building: "What they do is they'll take you for an elevator ride and they'll have a phone book with them, and they'll hold the phone book to your pelvis.… It hurts, it really does." Stan said he "caught on right away" to what was happening "when they put me in the elevator and they came in and the cop had a phone book. I knew it, I'm not stupid." Why indeed would police officers be carrying a phone book into an elevator? Were they planning to make a call?

> I'm pretty sure there's phone books on every floor wherever, wherever there's a phone. And I knew right away. So I'm standing there and cop holds the book and then he puts it to my side and he just hit me. He hit me hard. I fell down, but I'm handcuffed. Cops grab me by the arm, tells me, you know, "Stand up." "Fuck you, I don't have to," you know. "Fucking goof, fucking asshole" whatever and, you know, "Tough guy, eh." "I'm not a tough guy. I'm not tough at all," I said. "I'm not stupid, that's all. I'm not stupid at all." So whatever information they were trying to get out of me, they didn't get it. They didn't get it out of me.

Getting "Red-Zoned." While inner-city communities are cast as spaces of disorder and danger, other spaces are cast as respectable, as spaces of civility. In reproducing order, police officers maintain this divide by cleansing certain spaces and containing "disorderly" people in other spaces. Being found "out of place," therefore, prompts police attention and action. Twenty-seven-year-old Don, for one, told us about being stopped by the police when he was visiting a cousin in Tuxedo, which, as the name suggests, is one of the wealthiest neighbourhoods in Winnipeg:

> *And they asked — I was coming back down where the number 18 bus stops, and I was walking through Tuxedo — and they were "Oh, what are you doing out here?" I was like, "I'm visiting a cousin." "You don't have a cousin out here." I was like, "Why can't I have cousins out here?" "Oh, because you're a dirty bum, blah, blah, blah. We see you in the Village all the time." I was like, "Whatever. You don't know nothing." And then they were, "Okay, we're going to write you up for jaywalking. We just saw you jaywalk." I was like, "I didn't jaywalk. I used the crosswalk thing." Then they told me to sit on a bus bench, and I sat down. And they said, "If you move, we're going to pepper-spray you." And I was like, "Whatever." I didn't say anything. I just sat there. And I told them, "I'm going to sneeze." He's like, "You move, we're going to pepper-spray you." And I said, "I'm gonna sneeze." And then I sneezed. Just — sprayed me down. And then they left. So I was just sitting at the bus stop, rubbing my eyes.*

Don also commented that the police "also try and ban you from certain areas of the city, which I know they can't do." One of the areas where police will "red-zone" young men is Osborne Village, a trendy neighbourhood filled with restaurants and shops. Don said the police "have been doing it for as long as I can remember, ever since I was hanging out in the Village." The police will tell him, "You're red-zoned from that area, so if we see you in this area we're going to arrest you.... And if they do see you, like, they can't arrest you for anything so they'll pick you up and drive you out of the area."

Twenty-one-year-old William also spoke of being "red-zoned" or banned from the Osborne area. Like many of the other young Aboriginal men interviewed, William had experienced frequent contact with the police — "about six or seven times a month." On one occasion he was walking down Osborne Street when a police officer told him to "take a different route or get the hell out of here. I'm banning you from Osborne." William said he had been "banned more than once in Winnipeg." On one occasion he was living in the Elmwood area, "right behind" the high school, and got picked up there. "They said I lived in the North End. They said 'Get back on Mountain.' I said, 'My address is down the street.' Said 'We're banning you from Elmwood.'" William ended up moving to one of the city's suburbs to avoid being stopped and harassed by police all the time.

Starlight Tours. The police practice of detaining a person, driving them to another location, and then leaving them there to find their own way home, Starlight Tours — already a contentious public issue given the events in Saskatoon in 2000 — also emerged in thirteen of our seventy-eight interviews.

Carl was one of the people to raise the matter, and both the location and timing of his experience was unsettling. "When I was sixteen," Carl said, "when I lived in Saskatoon, I don't know if you heard but a couple of times the police would pick somebody up when they're really intoxicated and they would take them to the outskirts of town. And they just left them out there. I had that happen to me one time." His experience occurred "right before they took those two Native guys out there and two times both of them died." Carl explained that he was drunk and on his way home at about two-thirty in the morning.

> I was about ten blocks away from my house. But I was, you know, visibly staggering. And they pulled up to me and they're like, "Hey. Where are you going? Blah, blah, blah, you know." At first I thought they were trying to find out if I was alright and if I could make it home, the way they were asking? Anyway, the first, the passenger of the police car got out first and then he said, "Hey, come, you know, stand in front of the car. Put your hands behind your back." So I complied at first and then they took my ID out and they threw it away. They threw my ID's away. And I was already in handcuffs while they were doing this.

When we asked him why he thought the police officers had thrown his ID away, Carl replied: "So I don't have no identification on me so I would be able to get ID'ed. First of all, that's what I think, why they would throw my ID away. And yeah, I got handcuffed. I got put in the back seat. I thought that I was getting taken to the drunk tank. But after about ten, fifteen minutes driving in the car I realized that we were heading out of town." The police officers drove Carl to an area about fifteen minutes outside of Saskatoon.

"We got out there and obviously I was worried and, you know, realizing where we were at." The officers let Carl out of the car. Carl reported that they told him, "Okay, we're not taking you to the drunk tank and hopefully this experience will tell you that, you know, not to drink." They removed the handcuffs and then "just took off." It took Carl two and one-half hours to get back to town.

Carl told his mother what had happened, but didn't report his experience to the authorities. "If I'm going to report it, I didn't get their badge number or their car number or nothing like that. Like, who's going to believe me, right, if I go to the cop station and say, 'Hey, two of your guys took me out of town and they just left me out there'?" Nevertheless, this experience left him hating the police. "I don't even care if there's a nice cop anywhere. I hate you. If you're a fucking cop, I hate you. That's just how I think."

Peter was in his forties at the time we interviewed him. When asked about his experiences with police he replied: "I've been harassed from these two officers. They were officers and then became detectives, and they kept harassing me through my life." When asked what the officers would do to him, Peter replied: "They would see me on the street, me and my friend, 'cause they knew my friend was bad, and they'd pick us up and take our brand new runners, and they knew I'd get a licking from my dad when I'd get home." We wondered what he meant by "take our brand new runners." He explained:

> Yeah, they would take us out of town, like, in the evening, just, like, they would be waiting around the area for us to get out of school and they would pick us up. And, like, after so many times, they'd say, "You know the routine." So they would take us just on the outskirts of the city and take my brand new shoes. And they knew my dad would give me a licking for that, 'cause my dad thought I would sell them for dope or whatever. And I kept telling him the cops were taking my shoes and he wouldn't believe me. And I'd get a licking with a belt.

Sometimes the drop-off would happen in the summer, sometimes in the fall — "It'd be raining, rainy season. And then nighttime, like, in summer, a lot of mosquitoes, yeah." Peter estimated that the experience happened to him "maybe ten times" between the ages of thirteen and sixteen. On one of those occasions, Peter said that he finally "got sick of it":

> As I was taking my shoes off I told my friend, "I'm going to throw a handful of rocks at his face, and I'm running into the cornfield, whatever." And it was, it was practically nighttime. As I was bending over to

untie my shoelaces, I grabbed a handful of rocks and I threw it at the officer's face, and I ran into the field. My friend ran into the field too. I only had one runner, and we made our way back to the city from Birds Hill Park that night. When I got home I showed my dad that I had one shoe left. I told him that the cops took us out of town. And that's when he finally believed me.

Although Peter's father phoned the police station to report this experience, "they just kept hanging up on him. They wouldn't believe him."

Like Peter, Robert was in his forties at the time of the interview. Nevertheless, he could recall very clearly a Starlight Tour he had as a thirteen-year-old. It was in the late fall, shortly after Halloween — Robert remembered that he still had candies left over from trick or treating. Robert was living with his dad in a house in Gilbert Park, an area that people in the Aboriginal community refer to as "Jig Town." That evening stood out in Robert's mind because his father, in a rare move, gave him five dollars to go to the store. The two of them had been watching television. It was around eight or nine o'clock in the evening.

With the five dollars in his pocket Robert headed across the baseball field in front of their house to the Speedy Mart store. He remembered buying himself a Big Gulp, a bag of salt and vinegar potato chips, and a chocolate bar. When he was heading back home across the field, Robert saw a car coming up the street nearby, so he started running to cross the street before the car passed. All of a sudden he heard someone yell, "Hey. Stop!" He turned to see a police cruiser pull up beside him. One of the two police officers asked him, "Where did you come from?" and Robert told them he had just been at the Speedy Mart. They replied, "So, who do you think you are?" He answered, "Well, I'm nobody. I'm just going home. I can see my house. It's right there. My dad is in the window. He's watching television. I can see him from here." One of the officers said, "Well, I want to talk to you for a second. Jump in." Figuring that he had nothing to worry about because he had done nothing wrong, Robert climbed into the back seat of the police car.

The car backed up and began driving up the street. Robert asked them, "What are you guys doing?" I thought you said you just wanted to talk to me?" One of the officers responded, "We're going to take you for a little ride, and ask you a few questions." Although Robert asked to be taken back home, they kept on driving, saying "Stay quiet for a little while. We're trying to listen to something here."

As they passed the Speedy Mart Robert told them, "That's where I was. I was at Speedy Mart." The officers said, "You were gonna run away from us, weren't you?" Robert denied it, saying he was just running home. "I'd like to get home, out of the cold. It's cold outside." But the officers kept driving — farther and farther away from where Robert lived. When the car started to head down Keewatin Street towards Inkster Boulevard, Robert asked, "Where are you guys taking me?" They responded, "We're not talking to you, are we?" He said "No" and kept quiet.

The officers drove Robert about two miles from the perimeter road that circles the city. They stopped the car and told him to take off his clothes. At that point Robert tried to run away, but one of the officers grabbed him. He was scared and did what he was told. He took off his jacket, shirt, pants, runners, and socks. The officers then said, "Good luck, kid," got back in the car, and drove off, leaving him at the side of the road dressed in only his underwear. Robert watched as the cruiser drove away. When the brake lights came on, he thought the officers were coming back for him, but the car just turned left and disappeared from his view.

Asked how he made sense of the experience, Robert said: "I thought maybe they thought I stole something or that's why they're taking me back in the direction of the Speedy Mart. Maybe they thought I stole something. I didn't know what I did wrong.... I just simply didn't know what I did wrong. And to get taken out that far, out there, and I got left out there. It was starting to, I don't know, if it was slushy rain, it was, you know, snowflakes started to fall on the ground. It was pretty cold that evening."

About three vehicles passed Robert as he walked down the road. Finally, after about twenty minutes, a Duffy's cab drove towards him. Robert managed to stop the vehicle. The cab driver asked him, "What the hell are you doing up here?" Robert told him that the police had brought him out there and made him take off all his clothes. The cab driver offered to give him a ride home, saying, "You should tell your father to phone the police." Robert replied, "How can I phone the police on the police?" So he didn't say anything about his experience once he returned home. Robert made it back home around 11:00 p.m. Entering through the back door, he went downstairs and put on some clothes. "And my father didn't say nothing and I didn't say nothing to him either on the subject. Because in those days, we couldn't never do anything wrong, like, if it involved police officers. I already knew, in that era, that the police officers could never do nothing wrong. So no use in even telling anybody that they did something to you or whatever because they were always right and you were always wrong."

Over the years Robert managed to disclose his experience of a Starlight Tour to a few friends. But the actions of those two police officers had a lasting impact.

> *I had to let things go to heal and recover. And I tell you, in these last fifteen years I've been, a lot of things have been racing through my head about a lot of things. But that's the main one, right there. And I remember it fully. It was pretty cold and they did pretty bad things. I don't know how many other people that they did it to. And I heard over the years that it could happen. It happened to people in Saskatoon and stuff like that. So I was thinking, well, those people in Saskatoon, so that's the same time, that around the same time that happened to me, so, it's just what they were doing back then in those days.*

While Robert commented that Starlight Tours were "just what they were doing back then in those days," reports from other Aboriginal people suggest that such practices are still going on.

Sheila, a woman in her thirties, told of an experience that happened to her just a few months before our meeting. It was a bitterly cold, minus-40-degree Celsius evening. Sheila said she was sitting on Main Street near a park when two police officers came by. She knew one them by name. "I was sniffing and I was just sitting around there. I wasn't bothering anybody. I was just minding my own business, just sitting there. Next thing you know he comes flying at me and grabs me. And then his partner, I don't even know who that other guy was, they grabbed me and put me in the car." Sheila thought the police officers were taking her to the Main Street Project, but instead they told her, "We're going to take you for a joy ride." They drove her down Main Street to the outskirts of the city, where they took her shoes and her jacket. Sheila downplayed the loss of her shoes, saying, "I didn't care — they were ugly looking shoes anyway." But the officers then abandoned her there to find her own way back, telling her, "Well, it gives you time to think." As Sheila remarked, "I was thinking about freezing and all that." Sheila explained what happened next:

> *I walked back. I stopped there once at that Robin's Donuts store. I stopped there, warmed up a while, and then I got kicked out of there 'cause I wasn't dressed properly. So at least I warmed up enough and I made it back downtown. I made it back to the [Main Street] Project. And they asked me what happened. I didn't want to say what happened because I was scared they were going to call the cops. I was*

> *scared they're going to call the cops and I'd get more harassed again.*
> *So I just left it at that and I didn't want to tell nothing to nobody.*

Carol told of an experience that had happened two years prior to our meeting. She was coming home from a social one winter evening when she was picked up by two male police officers outside of the Northern Hotel on Main Street. The police had another woman in the back of the car. At first Carol thought they were both being taken to the district police station. Instead, "they dropped off that other woman first" and then dropped her off "way on the outskirts of the city." Carol recalled that the police officers "took my jacket. But I kept my shirt, like, my arms in my shirt like that tucked in, and I was freezing."

When asked what the police officers said to her when they dropped her off, Carol replied, "They just called me a 'stupid Indian.' 'You guys won't be missed,' that's what he said. And I said 'What about my jacket?' and then he threw my, just tossed my jacket in the trunk. And they just drove off and just left me there. And I started crying 'cause I was cold." Luckily, a car drove by. Carol said she "was screaming and that car stopped and pulled over and gave me a ride back to the city and dropped me off at home. And I just took a hot bath and I just cried to myself."

"A PROBLEM OF CONSIDERABLE MAGNITUDE"

Over two decades ago AJI commissioners Hamilton and Sinclair (1991a: 593–94) came to a harsh conclusion about relations between Aboriginal people and the police in Winnipeg.

> We heard testimony that police-Aboriginal relations in the city of Winnipeg are not good. We heard complaints about the police refusing to follow up on allegations of assault. We heard of Aboriginal people being stopped on the street or in cars for no reason. Those arrested were afraid of the police and many reported being beaten by police officers. The large number of complaints which we received points to a problem of considerable magnitude concerning how Aboriginal people are treated by Winnipeg police. (Hamilton and Sinclair 1991a: 593–94)

Judging from the reports from Aboriginal people about their encounters with Winnipeg police, that problem persists into the present day. How are we to account for it?

Certainly, a few "bad apples" or rogue officers do appear to exist in the Winnipeg Police Service. The interviews with inner-city residents reveal that in the same way that the police come to view certain people in the inner city as troublesome, inner-city residents have come to learn that certain police officers are equally troublesome. For instance, the name of one particular officer came up more than once in the interviews. As Mary described him, "He was violent and so mean." Sheila referred to this same officer as "that's the mean cop, that one." According to Mary, the officer would "drive his car right up at Higgins Park, right on the grass, and park and "start kicking" people around. "He'd say, 'Oh you shouldn't even be walking Main Street.' And I said, 'I've got to walk Main Street. This is where my family is.' And then he'd threaten me. He said, 'Oh all your family are fucking sniffers. You guys are no good.' And I'd say, 'Why do you say that when you don't even know them?'… He'd beat me up in the park, then he'd leave."

Nevertheless, while certain police officers are deemed to be more troublesome than others, the range and extent of the negative experiences reported by Aboriginal people in their encounters with Winnipeg police suggest that the source of the problem involves more than just "a few bad apples." Pinning an explanation on the actions of individual officers only evades scrutiny of the broader systemic factors — including the political context — that give shape to the policing of Winnipeg's inner-city communities.

The intensification of racialized poverty in Winnipeg's inner-city communities has been largely produced by processes occurring *outside* of those communities. Over the past three decades, the increasingly global or international nature of the economy has led to significant transformations within particular nations, including Canada. Corporate restructuring and downsizing — designed to keep up with these new production relations and financial systems — have led to heightened levels of inequality. A Statistics Canada survey of assets, debts, and wealth, for instance, documented how millions of Canadian families and individuals were living on the brink of financial disaster at the same time as a small proportion of people were managing to obtain huge slices of the wealth pie (Kerstetter 2002). For instance, during the strongest period of economic growth in the past thirty years, between 1997 and 2007, a third of all income gains went to the richest 1 percent of Canadians (Yalnizan 2011). In tandem with this widening gap between rich and poor has come a decided shift away from a professed commitment to social welfare on the part of government towards an emphasis on enhancing economic efficiency and international competitiveness. Commentators have termed this new governmental rationality "neo-liberalism," as it is premised on the values of individualism, freedom of choice, market security, and minimal state involvement in the economy (Rose 1996; Pratt 1999; Larner 2000).

The impact of this shift from social welfare to neo-liberalism has been profound. The social safety net — historically designed to assist those who were out of work or in need of social assistance — has been unravelled, and more and more people are being left to fend for themselves. Joblessness has been deemed to be an individual rather than a social problem, while the increasing numbers of people living in poverty are stigmatized and personally blamed for their dire circumstances. But it is not just the poor who feel the impact of these transformations. With the disappearance of secure, well-paying jobs and the stable communities that went with them comes increased social anxiety and unease. This social anxiety and unease have been translated into a widespread fear of crime and violence.

Public anxiety over crime and violence has actually occurred at a time when crime rates in Canada have been on the decline. Both the severity and the volume of police-reported crime dropped in 2009, continuing a general decrease seen over the past decade (Dauvergne and Turner 2010). Nevertheless, politicians have been quick to tap into this anxiety, promoting "law and order" and "get tough on crime" strategies as the solution to the troubles confronting contemporary society (Wacquant 2006; Garland 2000). Mandatory minimum sentences, prison expansion, parole-release restrictions, community notification laws, boot camps for young offenders, and zero-tolerance policing have become the order of the day. As Laureen Snider (1998) observes, these types of criminal justice policies constitute a form of "compulsory criminalization" in that they target groups — such as inner-city Aboriginal people — who lack the power to resist these political strategies.

Indeed, inner-city communities — arguably places where economic restructuring has been most acutely felt — are targeted as a primary location of these "law and order" and "get-tough" strategies. A site of racialized poverty, Winnipeg's inner city has come to be defined as a disorderly space. To this extent, the police have been called upon to control and contain the disorder that crime, violence, the drug and sex trades, and street gangs signify. But given that these are problems whose genesis is systemic, the product of larger global forces that are bearing down on those inner-city communities, the police have been confronted with an insurmountable task. To this extent, Candis McLean (2006) perhaps has it partially right in her documentary *When Police Become Prey* when she asserts that the police are controlled by political forces and agendas of "special interest groups." The "special interest groups," however, are not Aboriginal people and their organizations, but the wealthy and the corporations benefiting from global neo-liberalism.

Compounding the situation is the manner in which police in Winnipeg have responded — and that is where racialized policing enters into the picture: as one of the projects through which race is interpreted and given meaning and the means by which the racialized order of society is reproduced. The experiences of Aboriginal people with the policing of Winnipeg's inner city suggest that race and racialization have become deeply implicated in the routine practices of police officers. In their endeavour to reproduce order within this space, the storybook (the vocabulary of precedents) that police officers have adopted in the course of their daily work casts Aboriginal people as the "usual suspects." But the issue is more complicated than simply racial profiling or the stereotyping of Aboriginal people. Race and racialization also define the spaces in which Aboriginal people are found and the cultural frames of reference that police officers adopt in their encounters with Aboriginal people. Having defined (and experienced some) Aboriginal people as troublesome, the police respond with troublesome practices of their own — a response that has the effect of exacerbating the already fractured relations between Aboriginal people and the police and generating animosity and mistrust on both sides.

The policing models adopted by the Winnipeg Police Service may account for some of this animosity and mistrust. For instance, to the extent that police officers define their role as "crime fighters" and "law enforcers" intent on "getting the bad guys" — as the traditional model of policing encourages — they will be emboldened to use their authority in reproducing order. Sometimes this approach involves engaging in practices that exceed their authority, such as the phone book treatment and Starlight Tours. The zero-tolerance policing model — heralded by politicians as the solution to crime and disorder — encourages that same aggressive style of policing. For instance, several of the young men interviewed worked as squeegee kids to earn money. Their visibility on busy street corners often resulted in negative interactions with the police. Don, who had worked as a squeegee kid, told of an experience of being arrested by police. The officers put him in the back of their car, slamming his head on the top of the doorway in the process. Don responded by swearing at the officers. As they were driving to the district police station, the officers pulled the car off onto a side street. Don reported on what happened next: "The driver got out, opened the back door. And I was handcuffed, with my hands behind my back. He walked out and he punched me in the face, like, six times." Zero-tolerance policing also encourages the practice of red-zoning. In Winnipeg's Clean Sweep operation, the aim was to "sweep the streets" of those cast as troublesome. According to one of the young men interviewed, one officer was even known in the squeegee community by the nickname of "Super Cop" because he worked so hard to get them out of his district. To the extent that policing models encourage such practices, they only serve to exacerbate the problematic relations between Aboriginal people and the police.

While police have come to associate Aboriginal people with the "usual suspects" — or, in Jerome Skolnick's (1975) words, the "symbolic assailant" — aggressive policing practices that target Aboriginal people have the cumulative effect of engendering animosity and suspicion towards the police. Over time, therefore, a vicious cycle is produced that works to perpetuate conflicts between Aboriginal people and the police. As forty-three-year-old Helen explained:

> With Aboriginals, I see that a lot of young people when they see the cops, they don't like the cops 'cause they assume right away that the cops are going to beat on them or they're going to do something to them wrong. So they'll just automatically give them attitude. Just because automatically they assume right away they're going to get shit from them so they might as well give shit back, you know.

Indeed, by engaging in racialized policing Winnipeg police take on attributes not unlike those they are endeavouring to contain and control. Several residents, for instance, referred to the police as a "gang." Chris commented, "From what I know about gangs, they operate kind of the same way.... I just see them as bullies and people just forcing their little bit of power that they've acquired on other people." Fiona also thinks that the police are a gang, as "they stick together, they back each other up." Gregg described the police as "another gang with a badge that run the city.... They can do what they want. They run the show." The Winnipeg Police Service has actually encouraged this reading. In the 1990s, one of their recruitment posters read: "Join our gang."

One outcome of racialized policing, then, is that the police become part of the problem, as opposed to the solution, amid the violence and disorder they are endeavouring to contain. Edward, for one, was of the opinion that the street gangs actually posed less of a problem for him than the police did:

> *To tell you the truth I'm more afraid of the police than I am of the gangs. 'Cause the gangs, you know, you can walk by them, you don't bother them or say anything, you know, they don't bother you. But it seems like if you're walking home or walking home from the beer parlour or walking home with a case of beer or anything, it's harassment, harassment, harassment, you know, and it gets out of hand.*

Racialized policing and the strategies that accompany it therefore set up the potential for things to "get out of hand" — and, once again, with tragic outcomes.

Chapter Seven

THE SHOOTING OF MATTHEW DUMAS

On the early afternoon of January 31, 2005, Winnipegger Ken Warren was at the East Kildonan home of his girlfriend when he heard a knock on the door. A small boy was there. He asked for a name Warren didn't recognize. "You've got the wrong house," Warren told him. All of a sudden a man jumped into view and snatched the silver chain that Warren was wearing around his neck. The man turned to yet another guy who appeared out front and said, "Shoot 'em." This third male appeared to have something up his sleeve. The three intruders then left in a cab that was waiting for them in front of the house.

Warren slammed the door and called 911, saying "I got three Indians outside, threatening me with a gun." He gave the operator a description of each of the perpetrators and the number of the Spring Taxi cab that had taken them off. Police arrived at his door within minutes.

When the police learned that the cab driver had dropped his passengers off in Winnipeg's North End, they put out a high priority alert over their radio system, providing descriptions of the three males: "Native, fifteen to sixteen years, blue toque with hood up, a white Nike parka. He put a handgun into his parka jacket. Second male he was with was Native, twenty-five, with a black parka, no shots were fired. … The third male was a Native male also, nine to ten years old wearing a parka." Police cars quickly flooded the inner-city community and began doing spot checks. There were reports of five young males being observed in the neighbourhood.

A community policing officer was on his way back to East Kildonan after a meeting downtown when he heard the broadcast on the police radio about the robbery and how three Native suspects, one possibly armed with a gun, had been dropped off by a taxicab in the North End. After radioing in that he would join the police search, he too began doing spot checks. The officer stopped a young male near Dufferin Avenue and King Street, and then stopped another man in his fifties on Selkirk Avenue to ask him if he had seen a group of five males who had been reported in the area. Continuing down Selkirk Avenue he pulled his vehicle over to the curb to check his computer for updates. That was when he saw a young man who, he later said, kept looking at the police car and appeared to be nervous. As the young man began to walk away, the officer turned his car around and went along after him. Seeing the young man push something up his sleeve, the officer opened his car door and called to him. In response, the young man started to run.

The officer followed the suspect — and the pursuit, by foot and through back lanes and backyards, was quickly joined by other police officers. Moments later, on a sidewalk, shots were fired, and the young man being pursued fell to the ground. He was taken by ambulance to hospital, where he was pronounced dead.

The media quickly circulated news of the police shooting. The deceased young man was identified as eighteen-year-old Matthew Dumas, but initial police media releases contained several factual errors. Dumas was identified as a robbery suspect (he had played no part in the East Kildonan incident); he was reported to have been with a group of young men when stopped by police (Dumas was on his own); he was said to have been brandishing a knife (and not a screwdriver); and he had reportedly been shot once by the police officer (it was twice) (Winnipeg Police Service 2005a, 2005b).

As the news spread, charges that the incident was racialized soon followed. Aboriginal spokespeople decried Dumas's death as another instance of racism, a manifestation of the tense and troubled relations between police and the Aboriginal community in Winnipeg. Roseau River Anishinabe First Nation chief Terry Nelson, for one, stated, "There is a racial issue in terms of the way Winnipeg police have been dealing with Aboriginal people" (Castagna 2005). Several commentators made comparisons to the 1988 police shooting death of J.J. Harper, suggesting that police and government officials had not learned from the past.

Hymie Weinstein, legal counsel for the Winnipeg Police Association, responded to the allegations of police bias and racism from the Aboriginal community. "Race does not enter the picture," he said. "That's not relevant to the situation. There comes a point in time when an officer is faced with a split-second decision and has to use deadly force. The fixation is not on the person's colour or creed. It's on the real threat being advanced" (Castagna 2005). Weinstein also noted that the officer who discharged his firearm was Métis.

Police Chief Jack Ewatski held a press conference one week after the shooting (Winnipeg Police Service 2005c). He began his remarks by noting how "numerous lives were changed in a matter of seconds" when Matthew Dumas's life ended. While family, friends, and members of the community were faced with a wide range of emotions — from loss and sorrow to anger — the officer who shot Dumas "will be forever burdened by the memory of an incident that is indeed tragic. His life, the lives of his coworkers and all of their families have been and will continue to be affected." The police chief also noted that the event had exposed feelings of mistrust against the police force. While he was confident that the investigative process would produce a careful and fair examination, he was aware that some members of the community were not as confident. As he acknowledged, "The relationship between the Police Service and some members of the Aboriginal community is not at the same level as with the majority of members of the community." Chief Ewatski also commented that a series of reviews of the incident would take place to "increase the level of trust in the police service." In addition, he reported that he had met with Chief Denis White Bird of the Assembly of Manitoba Chiefs (AMC) and had extended an offer to appoint an Aboriginal representative to observe the process of the police investigation.

Ewatski made two further comments with regard to the investigation itself. The first was that the use of force policy of the Winnipeg Police Service was consistent with other police forces, and that police officers employed a level of force that was necessary in response to a person's actions "regardless of that person's race or colour." His second point was that while members of his department had been subject to "criticism, taunts, and at times extreme verbal attacks" and had been "unfairly labeled in most disturbing terms" as a result of the incident, he was proud of his officers for the emotional restraint and professionalism they had demonstrated. Ewatski concluded his remarks by extending his sympathies to the family and friends of Matthew Dumas for their loss, and affirming his support for the officers involved.

Following police protocol, the WPS Homicide Unit began an investigation, which was later forwarded to the Calgary Police Service and the RCMP for external review. Chief Denis White Bird of the AMC had declined Ewatski's offer to participate, saying that the investigation was already near completion and that he "didn't want to get involved in a process that is flawed" (Lambert 2005). While the government announced that an inquest would be held to determine the circumstances surrounding Dumas's death, the Southern Chiefs' Organization called for an Aboriginal-led inquiry into the shooting.

The internal police report, completed by October 2005, concluded that the death of Matthew Dumas was justified on the basis that police had reasonable grounds to stop him (he was wearing a blue bandana similar to the blue toque described in the police radio broadcasts of the robbery suspects); that Dumas had tried to run away from the officers who stopped him but later turned towards them armed with a screwdriver; that he was warned four times to drop the screwdriver, and pepper-sprayed once, yet continued to advance; and that he was only one metre away from the officer when two shots were fired.

Members of the Aboriginal community were not content with the findings of the police investigation. Sandy Bay Ojibway First Nation chief Irvin McIvor, who held the justice portfolio for the Southern Chiefs' Organization, stated:

> The shooting death of Matthew Dumas by the Winnipeg Police Service and the subsequent conclusions of their internal investigation, in which no criminal negligence or liability has been found, illustrates that in Canada there are two justice systems in effect. One that operates by oppressing and the other by maintaining its power and control over our people. Police consistently target and classify our people, to the point it's not even safe to walk down the street. (*South Wind* 2005)

In August 2006 Police Chief Ewatski announced that the Calgary Police Service had completed its external review of the investigation by the wps Homicide Unit. The review concluded, "The Winnipeg Police Service Homicide Unit carried out an open, transparent and thorough investigation of this incident" (Winnipeg Police Service 2006b). On January 29, 2007, the Dumas family filed a statement of claim against Police Chief Ewatski, the two (yet to be named) officers involved, and the City of Winnipeg under the Manitoba Fatal Accidents Act, on the ground that Dumas's death was "caused by wrongful act, neglect or default" (*South Wind* 2007). The calls for an inquiry — and not just an inquest — into the shooting were repeated. While the lawsuit sought a sum of $120,000 in damages, Dumas's sister Jessica indicated at a news conference that the claim was not about money but about securing a more thorough investigation into her brother's death. (Although money did become an issue because the family did not proceed with the lawsuit because of a lack of financial resources to pay for the legal fees involved.) Manitoba's justice minister, Dave Chomiak, held to the view that an inquiry was not necessary. Unlike the J.J. Harper case, the public investigation into the Dumas shooting was confined to an inquest.

The inquest proceedings examined several questions. What were the descriptions of the robbery suspects broadcast over the police radio? Before being shot by the police officer, did Dumas raise his hand to wipe pepper spray from his face, or was he attempting to "lunge" at the officer while brandishing a dangerous weapon? Did the officers have choices other than the use of lethal force to subdue him? In addressing these questions, the inquest focused squarely on individual actions and standard police operating procedures.

As the inquest proceedings unfolded, the main character in the event — Matthew Dumas — remained obscured. Observers to the proceedings learned very little about him. Observers gained little information that might explain why Dumas made the decision to run when the officer called to him on the street, and why he was in possession of a screwdriver. Even the "involved officers" — any officers at the scene when a firearm is discharged — were without accurate information about the case. It was only during his testimony at the inquest that the officer who fired the shots learned that Matthew Dumas was not a suspect in the robbery. Other officers testified that they learned this information only just prior to the inquest, held more than three years after the shooting.

Despite the lack of information about the main character in the event, two competing constructions of Matthew Dumas did emerge during the inquest. One depicted him as a "scared kid." The other cast him as an "angry and armed menace," the author of his own misfortune — and that was the construction that came to dominate. What also became apparent during the testimonies was not only the "feelings of mistrust against the police force" that Police Chief Ewatski had called attention to during his press conference in February 2005, but the mistrust that Winnipeg police officers held towards residents of Winnipeg's inner-city communities.

Nevertheless, while the inquest focused on clarifying police protocols and specific details surrounding the shooting, one question was never fully addressed. What role did race and racism play in the death of Matthew Dumas?

THE DUMAS INQUEST

In May 2007, under the authority of the Fatality Inquiries Act — whereby an inquest is mandatory when a person dies "as a result of an act or omission of a peace officer in the course of duty" — the province's chief medical examiner called for an inquest to determine the circumstances relating to Matthew Dumas's death and what, if anything, could be done to prevent similar deaths from occurring in the future. The inquest began on June 9,

2008 — what would have been Dumas's twenty-second birthday — and ended on June 20, 2008. It was presided over by Provincial Court Judge Mary Curtis. Three lawyers were also present: Robert Tapper, an attorney appointed to represent the Crown; Kim Carswell, counsel for the Winnipeg Police Service; and Donald Worme, counsel for the Dumas family (Worme had been counsel for the Stonechild family and for Darrel Night). The inquest heard testimony from fourteen civilian witnesses, eight police officers, a pathologist, and an RCMP use of force expert.

The Inquest Testimonies

The first witness to testify at the inquest was Ken Warren, the man who had phoned 911 to report a robbery at his girlfriend's East Kildonan home.* Warren testified that while he heard one of the men who appeared at his door tell an accomplice to "shoot 'em," he had never actually seen a weapon. In describing the three perpetrators, he told the 911 operator that one of them was about twenty-five years old; another was fifteen or sixteen years old, tall and skinny with baggy clothes. When the 911 operator asked, "Where is the gun?" Warren replied, "It's in a kid's hand who can't be a day over sixteen. He's in a white Nike parka with his hood pulled up." When asked "What kind of gun? Handgun or rifle?" Warren replied, "I don't know."

The next witness to testify was Julius Wirffel, the cab driver who had driven four people (three males and a female) from the North End to Warren's house in East Kildonan. Because his passengers were speaking in an Aboriginal language, Wirffel could not report on the nature of their conversation. Nevertheless, he testified that when they arrived at their destination the three males got out of the cab and were gone for four or five minutes. The young woman remained in the cab waiting for them. Wirffel was under the impression that when the passengers returned to the cab they seemed happy, as if they had gotten what they wanted. They asked to be taken back to the North End and paid the driver $20 for a $16 fare when they were dropped off.

Roderick Pelletier was a fifty-year-old Aboriginal resident of a house on Dufferin Avenue. Matthew Dumas had knocked on his back door in the course of his flight from the police officer. Pelletier described Dumas as a "young boy, shaking and scared." Dumas asked Pelletier if a boy named Jason or Justin lived at the house. "He was out of breath. He asked me for a

---

*   Unless otherwise indicated, quotations in this section are drawn from notes I took while observing at the Dumas inquest.

light for his cigarette. He couldn't light his cigarette … he was played out." Pelletier said he then saw a police officer "sort of running" towards them. He turned to Dumas and said, "Look man, you're caught." According to Pelletier, the police officer took Dumas roughly by the arm and told Pelletier to "get the fuck back in your house" — which he did. Pelletier's daughter looked out the window and said to him, "Look Dad, they're fighting." The police officer then fell, "saying bad words." When the officer got up and chased after Dumas, Pelletier went back into the living room. A minute or so later, he heard two gun shots. Pelletier's reaction was, "Oh man. They shot him." During his testimony Pelletier was candid in stating that he did not trust the police. He told the court, "I'm kinda scared of them too," and said it was because he was shot by police several years earlier. Pelletier also wondered why the officer hadn't handcuffed Dumas when he took hold of him in Pelletier's backyard.

Willie Sinclair, an Aboriginal witness, had a very different encounter with Dumas. "I feared for my life," said Sinclair, who tried to block Dumas as he was running away from the police officer. Sinclair had been in his house on Dufferin Avenue when he saw someone run by his front window. A minute later he saw a police officer running by. Sinclair described the officer as "distressed." The policeman had no hat on, and his jacket was hanging open. Sinclair left his house and followed the officer up Dufferin Avenue. The officer saw him and told him to "go back in your fucking house." As he was stepping back to comply with the officer's command, a neighbour pointed in the direction of where the young man was hiding behind a house on Dufferin. Sinclair watched as the police officer escorted the young man towards the back lane, with his left arm twisted up and walking on "tippy toes." As the officer was speaking on his portable radio, Dumas "sucker punched" him on the right side of the face, knocking the radio from his hand. Like Pelletier, Sinclair told the inquest that he could not understand why the police officer did not handcuff Dumas right away.

With Dumas in flight, Sinclair thought he could assist the police by trying to stop him. Dumas, according to Sinclair, made two attempts to "poke" him with what Sinclair thought was a "shanker." Sinclair ran from Dumas and scrambled over a snow bank to safety, just in time to witness the officer pepper-spraying Dumas, which he said "had no effect." Sinclair testified that officers were calling on the young man to put the weapon down. He also said that he saw Dumas "lunge" at the officers twice. He then heard two shots and Dumas dropped to the ground. Sinclair also told the court he had been unable to sleep or eat and had lost a hundred pounds since witnessing the shooting. He had been given a card with the phone number of Victim Services on it, but seemed unsure of what he was to do with it.

Another civilian witness was Stuart Hourie, who was on his way to a walk-in clinic on Dufferin Avenue when he heard footsteps behind him. At first he thought the officer was after him, but then saw an "Aboriginal fellow" in front of them. He testified to seeing the screwdriver in Dumas's hand, and hearing the officers telling him to "drop the weapon." He also saw the officer pepper-spray Dumas, hitting him on the face. After Dumas lunged at the second officer, two shots were fired. Like Sinclair, Hourie told the court that his presence at the event had a tremendous, lasting emotional impact. He had difficulties sleeping and was experiencing nightmares. He also could not understand why two officers shot to kill the teen, whose face was "scrunched up" from the pepper spray. In Hourie's view, "They could have disarmed him in a different fashion." Like the other civilians, Hourie was never offered counselling or support to deal with what he had witnessed.

Israel Kleiman, who watched the confrontation from the window of his Dufferin Avenue business, testified that he saw no "lunging" on the part of Dumas. He suggested that if two police officers could not overpower the teen, "maybe they should hire some Blue Bombers to work for them" (Saunders 2008a).

During his testimony, Manuel Raposo, a local business owner who also observed the shooting from his office window, testified that he thought Dumas raised his arm "to clean his face" after being pepper-sprayed. This testimony conflicted with his police statement, in which he described Dumas as lifting his arm in a "stabbing motion." When questioned by the WPS lawyer, Raposo — whose first language is not English — replied that he only referred to it as a "stabbing motion" after the detective taking his statement used that expression.

Testimony from the "involved officers" began with the appearance of Jonathon Mateychuk, who had been on the force for fourteen years. He was working alone as a Community Policing Officer on January 31, 2005. He was the officer who had made the decision to spot-check Matthew Dumas.

According to Mateychuk, he had conducted a number of spot checks of men in the neighbourhood, including someone who looked suspicious because he was wearing a hoodie up over his head despite the rather mild winter weather conditions. On stopping the man, Mateychuk found that "he was a twenty-seven-year-old white male." Mateychuk then spotted Matthew Dumas. He said he decided to pay closer attention to Dumas because the young man kept looking at his police cruiser and the officer's presence seemed to be making him nervous. The young man, according to Mateychuk, seemed to match the description of one of the suspects. He also noticed him adjust something in the chest area of his jacket that had some weight to it. As the young man began to walk away, the officer turned his car around and followed. Seeing him push something up his sleeve, Mateychuk opened his car door and called to him, "and at that point he bolted" (Curtis 2008: 27).

Following Dumas by foot down a back lane and between houses, Mateychuk eventually came upon him in the backyard of Pelletier's house. A large dog was tied up in the yard, barking loudly. Mateychuk took hold of the young man, telling him that he saw him put something up his sleeve and asking why he had run away, but getting no reply. He noticed that the young man was very nervous and shaking, which was making him nervous as well. After taking hold of him and leading him to the lane, Mateychuk began doing a pat-down search and felt a hard object under his coat. Dumas wheeled around and hit the officer in the face. They struggled, "like two hockey fighters spinning around." Mateychuk slipped and fell, losing his hand-held radio in the process. Dumas took off running out onto a nearby sidewalk, and Mateychuk ran after him. It was then that Mateychuk noticed the screwdriver in Dumas's hand, but he continued his pursuit.

Out on the sidewalk, getting within ten feet of Dumas, Mateychuk tried to pepper-spray him, unsuccessfully. When three other officers arrived, Mateychuk warned them that Dumas had a weapon. He pepper-sprayed again — this time within five feet of Dumas, hitting him in the side of the face. Mateychuk, having used up his energy, just kept walking in the direction of Dumas. The other officers, ahead of him and in front of Dumas, began yelling, "Stop, drop the weapon." There was a "barrage of commands constantly being yelled at the male." Mateychuk, out of breath, was not yelling. When Dumas was within only a few feet of the other officer, two shots were fired.

Mateychuk became very emotional during his testimony at the inquest, needing to pause at one point to regain his composure. During his cross-examination, Worme questioned Mateychuk as to why he didn't handcuff Dumas earlier in the pursuit. Mateychuk responded, "The suspect would've bolted towards Dufferin. I would've ended up chasing him." Worme responded with, "That's what happened anyway." Mateychuk also explained that he did not like the idea of being secluded in a backyard with two strangers (Dumas and Pelletier) and a big barking dog, even though it was chained up. He did admit that following Dumas into the backyard instead of waiting for back up "wasn't the smartest thing to do," and that he wished he had waited for more police backup.

When Worme questioned Mateychuk about why he didn't use his police baton to subdue Dumas, the officer replied: "We're not trained to do that. You don't use a baton on someone who's armed with a screwdriver.... It's not a risk any of us are paid to take." When Worme asked him to say what was the most troubling part of the eighteen-year-old's death, Mateychuk responded, "I'll never know why he made the choices he did." He added that he will always ask himself if the outcome would have been different if there were "things I'd done differently" (Saunders 2008b).

On the morning of June 13, Constable Dennis Gburek, the officer who shot Dumas, took the stand to give his testimony. On January 31, 2005, Gburek had been an officer with the wps for just over three years. He and his partner, Constable Wijtek Luer, were patrolling in the North End when the report about the robbery in East Kildonan was broadcast. The two officers stopped three young males, one of whom was holding what turned out to be a toy gun. Constable Gburek then saw another male with a blue hoodie and white baseball cap walking down a back lane. He stopped the young man and did a pat-down search. As he was about to type the youth's name into his computer, he noticed two males in a confrontation down the back lane, and recognized one of them as a police officer. He left to assist the other officer, initially taking his gloves out of his pocket "in case he had to fight" and then taking out his baton "because he was pretty sure he was going to be fighting" (Curtis 2008: 35). When Gburek saw what he thought was a large butcher knife in the young man's hand, he put away the baton and drew his revolver. Now, back out on the sidewalk, as the distance between them decreased — from seventy-five to fifty feet — Gburek began yelling, "Winnipeg Police, stop, police, drop the knife, drop the knife." As he got closer, he realized the young man had a screwdriver, and not a butcher knife. Gburek saw the officer behind the young man pepper-spraying him, but it seemed to have no effect. Realizing that the young man was closing in as Gburek was backing up, he began to yell, "I'm going to shoot you." He told the court that he felt he had no other choice but to pull the trigger. If he did not, he feared he would be stabbed in the neck, above the Kevlar jacket he was wearing.

The shooting was the first time that Constable Gburek had fired his weapon in the line of duty. He told the court that for the past three years since the shooting he had been stressed "to the max" and was waking up with night sweats.

Five other "involved officers" also testified at the inquest. Constable Wijtek Luer had only been on the force for a year and a half when the shooting occurred. He was partnered with Constable Gburek and was busy conducting a spot check of three young males when the shots were fired.

Constable Randy Antonio had logged fifteen years as a police officer as of January 2005. He had been conducting inspections of buildings in the Main Street area when he heard about the robbery over his radio. Antonio was assisting Constable Luer with the spot check of young males when he saw Constable Mateychuk struggling with Dumas in the back lane. Less than one minute later, he heard shots fired and went to the scene to assist. Matthew Dumas was able to speak at that point. All that Constable Antonio could remember him saying was, "He wanted to get out of there. He wanted to go" (Curtis 2008: 43).

Constable Meghan Grenkow was partnered with Constable Randy Dziver. She had only been on the force for two months when the shooting occurred. Grenkow and her partner Dziver arrived on Dufferin Avenue as Constable Gburek was backing away from Dumas with his firearm pointed. She jumped out of the cruiser with her weapon drawn and watched as Dumas "lunged" toward Gburek. After the shooting, Grenkow accompanied an unconscious Matthew Dumas in the ambulance to the Children's Hospital.

Constable Dziver had been on the force for ten years. He and Constable Grenkow were parked on Main Street when they heard over the radio that another officer had seen what he thought were suspects from the robbery. They were then assigned to assist in flooding the area to see if they could find suspects. He testified that he saw an officer, whom he recognized as Constable Gburek, running down Dufferin. He also observed a male come out from between houses on Dufferin onto the sidewalk, followed by another officer. He then parked his cruiser in the middle of the avenue, between the two constables. As he was watching the interaction between Dumas and Gburek, Dziver said that he kept thinking, "He's going to drop it any second, this is going to be over in a minute, he's just going to put it down" (Curtis 2008: 49). After Dumas fell to the ground, Dziver knelt on his legs while two other officers applied handcuffs.

One of those officers was Constable Neil Carrette. With thirty-one years on the force, Carrette was the most seasoned of the officers who were present that afternoon. Positioning himself behind Constable Mateychuk on the sidewalk, Carrette had been hoping for an opportunity to tackle the young man. As the distance closed between Dumas and Constable Gburek and shots were fired, Carrette called for an ambulance and then assisted with Dumas, putting his foot under his head to keep his airway clear because he was having trouble breathing. Carrette became quite emotional during his testimony. When Worme asked him whether the event had anything to do with his retirement three months later, the officer replied, "Possible." He ended his testimony by saying, "It's a terrible thing," and was still wishing that things could have turned out differently.

The inquest also heard testimony from the pathologist who conducted the autopsy, as well as Corporal Greg Gillis, an RCMP officer with expertise in the use of force.

The pathologist, Dr. Charles Littman, testified that the cause of death was massive internal bleeding, and that given the serious nature of the wound, Dumas's death was inevitable. Two other facts were presented during his testimony. Toxicology tests showed that Dumas had marijuana in his blood, but as the pathologist maintained, "I wouldn't say that it was particularly high, indicating that he was a chronic or excessive user of cannabis" (Curtis 2008: 54). Another factor — not included in Judge Curtis's final report — was that the autopsy showed Dumas's right lung to be "hyper inflated," indicating evidence of asthma. When Worme asked the pathologist whether pepper spray could initiate an asthma attack, the doctor's response was that it was possible, but he could not say for sure.

RCMP Corporal Gillis submitted a report entitled "Use of Force Review: Police-Related Shooting of Matthew Dumas," which was filed as an exhibit at the inquest. The report detailed the use of force model adopted by most police forces in Canada. The purpose of the model is to assist officers in the use of a variety of force options and in implementing the related risk assessment process involved in a specific event. The report points out that police officers can apply varying levels of response in dealing with a situation, including: simple police presence; verbal or non-verbal communication (body posture, facial expression, stance); a "soft technique" (touch of a shoulder or putting on handcuffs); grabbing a person; hard physical control (kicking, punching, kneeing, tackling); use of intermediate weapons (pepper spray, baton, Taser); and use of lethal force (a gun). Corporal Gillis told the court that police officers are trained to choose one level of force higher than necessary to ensure that they gain quick and effective control of a situation.

With regard to the robbery incident, Corporal Gillis maintained that with the report of the robbery and the information that the perpetrators had been dropped off in the North End:

> There was an obligation on the police to investigate thoroughly. That would include spreading officers into the area, firstly to see whether or not there are persons in the area that match the basic

> descriptors that have been provided as to those involved directly in the offence and, secondarily, to question people that are in the area to see if there may be further information forthcoming, i.e. such as somebody who might have seen the individuals described getting out of the taxi and noting what direction they took. (Curtis 2008: 60)

In these terms, Corporal Gillis was of the opinion that when Constable Mateychuk saw a male "acting suspiciously," he had a duty to investigate.

On the matter of whether Mateychuk should have handcuffed Dumas in Pelletier's yard, Corporal Gillis said, "That's an option that he could have employed, but we have no way of knowing if that wouldn't have resulted in the assault that occurred a few moments later in the back alley and what the outcome of that would have been" (Curtis 2008: 60). Gillis also noted that officers are trained to consider a distance of twenty-five feet to be a danger zone. As such, neither the use of a police baton nor pepper spray would be considered appropriate responses in the circumstances. In terms of the use of pepper spray, Corporal Gillis indicated that one would expect to see that a person who is pepper-sprayed would "lose focus on the direction that they were moving, the person that they are focused on, that reasonably, they would have dropped an item that was in their hand, stopped movement, maybe gone to the ground … there would have been … a marked departure from their prior behaviour" (Curtis 2008: 62). In Gillis's view, the correct response to the threat of a person with an "edged weapon system" (such as a screwdriver) is to draw the firearm: "The use of force was consistent with accepted police tactical intervention strategies" (Curtis 2008: 62).

With the testimonies of the civilian and police witnesses as well as the pathologist and use of force expert completed, the inquest concluded on Friday, June 20, with closing statements from the three lawyers — inquest counsel Tapper, wps lawyer Carswell, and Worme, counsel for the Dumas family. Judge Curtis was then left with the task of writing up her report, which was released in December 2008.

"AN UNEXPECTED TRAGEDY"

In her report Judge Curtis concluded that the death of Matthew Dumas was "tragic and unexpected." Nevertheless, the judge also held:

> Mr. Dumas had choices along the way. Why he chose the path he did will remain an unanswered question. From the actions of

the officers, it is obviously not the outcome that they would have preferred. Constable Mateychuk got closer than his training told him he should have on Dufferin Avenue when he tried to stop Mr. Dumas by pepper-spraying him. There is ample evidence that Constable Gburek ordered him to drop his weapon on a number of occasions and told Mr. Dumas that he would shoot him. To some witnesses it sounded as though Constable Gburek was begging him to put his weapon down. Most of the witnesses also said that they kept expecting that he would put his weapon down and it would all be over. That did not happen. (Curtis 2008: 66)

The judge also addressed the "undercurrent" to the proceedings: "That racism was the reason Matthew Dumas died." The judge noted that she was "very much alive to the issue" during the proceedings. "At times questions were posed which had the potential to elicit a biased response. It never happened" (Curtis 2008: 67). In the judge's view, "the only time racism became a factor at this inquest was in the last minute of a lengthy submission by Mr. Worme. He compared Matthew Dumas' death to that of J.J. Harper" (2008: 67).

In his closing statement, Worme had noted the "striking correlation" between the two cases: Harper was dressed differently from the suspect that police were seeking. "Like J.J. Harper, Matthew didn't consent to be stopped. Like J.J. Harper, Matthew is in a scuffle with a police officer. Like J.J. Harper, Matthew is shot and is now dead. And the most striking similarity, J.J. Harper and Matthew were Aboriginal." From Worme's standpoint, "race is a fact" of the case. In contrast, the judge held: "The comparison to Mr. Harper's death is not valid.... On an objective analysis of the evidence, I find nothing in the evidence to support the claim that Mr. Dumas' death was a result of racism. Mr. Dumas' behavior and choices drove the events which led to his death on January 31, 2005" (Curtis 2008: 67).

One of the purposes of the inquest was to consider what could be done to prevent similar deaths from occurring in future. While questions were raised during the proceedings regarding the availability of counselling for the civilian witnesses and Dumas family members, as well as the police use of Tasers as an alternative to firearms, the main recommendation offered in the inquest report was for the Winnipeg Police Service to "develop scenario-based training that follows a similar fact-based pattern in order to assess different techniques that may be of use in a similar kind of situation" (Curtis 2008: 68). In a letter to Chief Provincial Court Judge Raymond

Wyant in May 2009, the Manitoba Ombudsman indicated that the WPS "has developed and implemented comprehensive training to a multitude of varying scenarios that include a similar fact base pattern to the Matthew Dumas incident." This training is provided to recruit classes and mandatory for all other police officers. Similar training is provided by the two other police forces in the province, the Brandon Police Service and the RCMP. As such, the Ombudsman deemed that "reasonable consideration" has been given to the recommendation and the files concerning Matthew Dumas have been closed.

"RACE HAD NOTHING TO DO WITH THIS"

The inquest report generated considerable media commentary. Tom Brodbeck (2008), a reporter for the *Winnipeg Sun*, wrote that those who maintained that Matthew Dumas was shot because he was Aboriginal were "using a tragedy to fuel their political agenda and continue to drive a wedge between police and Aboriginal people." Robert Marshall (2008), a retired police officer and regular columnist for the *Winnipeg Free Press*, wrote: "With all the checks and balances that come with such an investigation, racism would have surfaced — if it had been there."

One of the "checks and balances" that Marshall might have had in mind was the role performed by the inquest attorney. Under the Fatality Inquiries Act, "A Crown attorney or other officer or counsel" may be appointed by the minister "to act for the Crown" and may examine witnesses called at the inquest. As AJI commissioners Hamilton and Sinclair (1991b: 85) note, the Act does not specify who is to conduct the inquest. In practice, Crown attorneys conduct the inquest as a "matter of convention." In general terms, the Crown attorney's role is to be the representative of the state and the "guardian of the public interest."

Commenting on the role of the Crown attorney during an inquest, Jeffrey Schnoor, Manitoba's deputy attorney general and deputy minister of justice, notes: "In the advancement of the administration of justice and the public interest, Crown counsel at an inquest should be *impartial and neutral*. He performs a public duty which requires him to ensure that all available relevant evidence is presented in a *fair, impartial and objective manner*" (Schnoor 2009: 12; emphasis added). Schnoor cites relevant case law, including one case in which the court stated, "It is *not* the duty of the Crown at an inquest to have an adversary position" and another case in which it was noted:

> In every inquest the primary advocate for the overall public inter-
> est is the Crown Attorney who acts as counsel for the coroner.
> The history and traditions of that office in this province [Ontario]
> provide a degree of assurance that the Crown Attorney will act as
> an *independent and responsible advocate for the public interest*. (Cited
> in Schnoor 2009: 12; emphasis added)

Robert Tapper was the first person to address the proceedings because the judge had asked him, as attorney appointed to represent the Crown, to make an opening statement. In doing so Tapper breached his role as an impartial and neutral participant in the inquest by making a point of saying that he was "confident" that the judge will find, at the end of the day, that "race had nothing to do with this."

In their discussion of the role of the Crown attorney at an inquest, AJI commissioners Hamilton and Sinclair (1991b: 85) note that "Families of deceased persons should not be put in the position of having to challenge and rebut the 'official version' when the death involves a public agency.... The approach of the person calling the evidence at the inquest must be that there is no 'version.'" Tapper's opening remarks clearly put the Dumas family in the position of having to counter an official version that denied the relevance of race and racism in understanding the event. Donald Worme was attentive to this issue. Outside the inquest courtroom, he commented to the media: "I find it somewhat unusual that there were comments to that effect made by coroner's counsel. I think that there is often a desire that counsel should be more unbiased and should not be offering opinions, particularly at the outset" (CBC News 2008b).

Tapper's opening remarks set the tenor for what was to follow. Thereafter, the focus of the inquest was on the specific events that unfolded — the robbery in East Kildonan, Constable Mateychuk's efforts to apprehend Dumas, and the moments leading up to Constable Gburek firing his gun — with a view to determining whether police officers followed standard operating procedures.

UNPACKING THE OFFICIAL VERSION

The official version of the death of Matthew Dumas, introduced by Tapper at the outset of the inquest and reinforced by Judge Curtis in her report, was that neither race nor racism was pertinent to the case. Nevertheless, this official version rested on particular understandings of race and racism: that race need only be established as an ascribed characteristic of individuals to be relevant; and that racism is an individual matter with a presence that will be obvious.

As evidence to support his argument that "race had nothing to do with this," Tapper pointed out that two of the police officers involved — including Constable Gburek, the shooter — were Métis. The assumption was that racism could not be present because the two officers shared a similar "race" with Dumas. In his closing statement, Tapper reiterated his position, saying that the case was not about "racial prejudice" and that it would be "folly to accuse police of racial profiling." In making this assertion, Tapper seemed to be suggesting that police officers who shared a similar racial background as the citizens they encountered were somehow unaffected by racialization; that is, by the historical and contextual processes by which certain individuals, groups, and nations become differentiated.

One Ontario judge would disagree with that position. Commenting on a case involving an allegation of racial profiling by a Black police officer, the trial judge noted, "It seems that any person of any race could consciously or unconsciously believe that persons of a particular race, his own or others, have a propensity toward criminal activity and thus should be targeted for attention by police" (*R. v. Singh* cited in Tanovich 2006: 18). Similarly, researcher David Harris found that Black Americans experienced differential stops and searches "at the hands of white *and* black officers alike," leading him to conclude that racial profiling is "more than the racism of a few racist whites with badges. Rather it is an institutional problem, and an institutional practice" (cited in Tanovich 2006: 19).

Tapper's assertion that the involvement of Métis officers negated the possibility that race was a factor in the event becomes even more dubious in light of Worme's questioning of the two officers. Both Constable Gburek and Constable Antonio testified that they had never discussed their Métis heritage with other officers, including their partners. The first language of Gburek's partner, Wijtek Luer, was Polish — Luer had emigrated from Poland to Canada in 1986. The two officers had worked together for just over a year prior to the shooting. In the course of his testimony Luer revealed that during that time neither he nor Gburek had talked about their heritage, including what it means to be Métis. Their own race or ethnicity apparently did not have much of a bearing on their everyday work as police officers. Why would that be the case?

As the policing literature amply documents, policing is an occupation — and a culture — characterized by a strong sense of social solidarity among officers and a concomitant social isolation from the citizenry. As

Skolnick (1975: 54) explains, "The dangers of their work not only draws [sic] policemen together as a group but separates them from the rest of the population." The idea that police "are not like other members of society and are being trained to do something that other people know little about," as Sewell (2010: 55) points out, is inculcated into recruits from the earliest stages of their training. Officers are encouraged to define themselves not as members of particular racial or ethnic groups but as members of the police fraternity. The identity of "police officer" takes on a master status, overshadowing racial or ethnic identity. This sense of social solidarity or fraternity was in evidence during the Dumas inquest. On the morning that Constable Gburek was scheduled to testify, the courtroom was full beyond capacity. Winnipeg Police Service officers were in plentiful attendance as a show of support for their comrade.

Moreover, as a paramilitary organization with distinct chains of command, Sewell (2010: 59–60) writes, "Police departments invariably use rules as the key management technique, and those rules are written in great detail into the regulations of the police force. Rules set out virtually all aspects of the way an officer is to behave." Accordingly, *all* officers — regardless of their "race" — will be expected to perform their job according to standard operating procedures. Both the culture and the organization of policing function to override the relevance of the race of an officer.

Judge Curtis was of the view that a "biased response" to questions posed during the inquest would have pointed to the existence of racism, suggesting that racism — if it was indeed present — would manifest itself in a forthright way during the course of the proceedings. Nevertheless, racism is often so muted in appearance that its presence is not obvious or self-evident. This is especially the case with "everyday racism" (Essed 2002), whereby racist beliefs and actions infiltrate everyday life to become part of our common sense and taken-for-granted ways of acting in the world. As Carol Henry and her colleagues (2009: 110) note, one dimension of racism is "its ability to be so subtly expressed or indirectly applied that its targets are not even aware of it. Conversely, racism is sometimes visible only to its victims. It remains indiscernible to others, who therefore deny its existence." The presence of race and racism also becomes less discernible when it takes a systemic form; for instance, when it is embedded in the practices and procedures of an organization.

The official version of the death of Matthew Dumas, therefore, was informed by a "discourse of denial" (Tator and Henry 2006) that failed to acknowledge the cultural, organizational, and systemic manifestations of race and racism. While the focus of the inquest was on whether officers followed their standard operating procedures in responding to the robbery report, the procedures themselves never came under scrutiny. Instead, the inquiry adopted an individualized frame to reach the conclusion that Dumas was the one responsible for his own death. Once again, attending to issues of race and racism as they invade the practice of policing involves moving beyond such individualized frames — including the crude claim that "police are racist bigots" — and exploring the broader context of policing as a racialized activity.

RACIALIZED POLICING IN THE DUMAS CASE

The crucially important step — to go beyond the immediate event and bring into view the broader dynamics present in encounters between racialized groups and the police — requires, as a start, an uncovering of the "mundane processes and related ideas that are part of organizational life" (Holdaway 1997: 384). It also requires taking up an issue the inquest never did adequately address: why a young Aboriginal man like Matthew Dumas was "nervous" about encountering a police officer.

Mundane Processes
One of the "mundane processes" of police work framing the context of the Dumas shooting was the police sweep of the North End neighbourhood. In providing his expert testimony at the inquest, RCMP Corporal Gillis explained that once the robbery had been broadcast over the police radio, officers were called in to conduct a sweep of the area to determine "whether or not there are persons in the area that match the *basic descriptors* that have been provided as to those involved directly in the offence" (Curtis 2008: 60; emphasis added).

In Winnipeg's inner-city communities those kinds of spot checks have become routine events, as testimony provided at the inquest made all too clear. Aboriginal men are regularly stopped by police, sometimes on a weekly basis, and asked to account for themselves. Walking down the street on his way to an appointment at a medical clinic, Stuart Hourie initially made the assumption when he saw a police officer running toward him that *he* was the one under suspicion. Some of the young men stopped by police that afternoon appear to have resented being made subject to (perhaps yet another) spot check. When he stopped one young man and conducted a pat-down search, Constable Gburek described the person as "presenting with attitude" (Curtis 2008: 34).

When Worme pressed Constable Gburek about these spot checks, suggesting to him that he was on the lookout for any Native males who happened to be in the vicinity, the officer objected to this idea, arguing that "ethnic background" would not matter. If a person's clothing matched the description transmitted on the police radio, he would spot-check them. Nevertheless, Constable Luer indicated in his statement that he was unsure of the "basic descriptors," save for the knowledge that the three suspects were Aboriginal: "As we were en route we heard the descriptions of the suspects of the robbery being broadcast. They were basically three native males. The description that sticks most in my mind is a shaved head and bulky blue jacket. However, I am not sure as to that description." Constable Antonio also admitted that his knowledge of the suspects the police were looking for was hazy. As Judge Curtis (2008: 42) summarized, "The only description that he caught was that the suspects were native in appearance, there was a white coat and dark clothing, so he headed off to the area with limited information." Constable Dziver testified that when he and his partner were assigned to assist in flooding the area to see if they could find suspects, "he did not have any particular description that he recalled but was looking for anyone who looked suspicious" (Curtis 2008: 47). From the standpoint of standard operating procedures, then, the officers conducting a sweep of the area were simply on the lookout for "anyone who looked suspicious." In the racialized space of Winnipeg's North End, that translated into the "usual suspects" — young Aboriginal men.

As was the fashion for many young men at the time, Matthew Dumas was dressed in a dark jacket and had on a blue bandana. The main suspect in the robbery was wearing a white Nike parka and a blue toque. Warren had also told the 911 operator that the person carrying the gun "can't be a day over sixteen." Matthew Dumas was eighteen years old. However, Corporal Gillis noted — and the WPS lawyer Carswell and Judge Curtis reiterated — that "clothes can change and guns can be passed along" (Curtis 2008: 67). If clothing descriptions and the likelihood of carrying a gun were *not* the deciding factors, then *what were the criteria* for defining someone as a suspect?

Warren's statement to the 911 operator — "I got three Indians threatening me with a gun" — seems to have set the course for the police sweep of the North End. In other words, the "basic descriptors" of those targeted by police that afternoon were that they were young, male — and Aboriginal. Worme encapsulated this position in a comment made to the media:

> I think it's also become abundantly clear that because of the large Aboriginal population in that particular vicinity, they are all at risk, as Matthew Dumas certainly was. Matthew Dumas was not involved in a crime of any description, but he — simply because he was an Aboriginal youth — had become a suspect and as such ended up where he did. (CBC News 2008c)

Another of the "mundane processes" of police work that framed the context of the Dumas shooting was the use of force. During the inquest much of the focus was on the use of force model utilized by the Winnipeg Police Service and whether the officers involved applied that model appropriately under the circumstances. As Sewell (2010: 110) observes:

> The use of force model makes perfect sense to the armchair critic, but as with police chases, things happen so quickly in real life that often there is little opportunity for an officer's reflection on the options. In virtually every case where an officer pulls a gun and uses it, the officer describes a tense situation in which no alternative seemed possible.

Indeed, as the evidence presented at the inquest indicates, things did "happen so quickly." From the time that Constable Mateychuk first spotted Dumas to the firing of Constable Gburek's police revolver, just over fourteen minutes had elapsed. Gburek estimated that only thirty seconds passed from the time he started moving towards Dumas to when he fired the fatal shots.

In his press conference in February 2005 Police Chief Ewatski commented on the use of force model, noting that police officers use a level of force necessary in response to a person's actions "regardless of that person's race or colour." Given the tense situation that Constable Gburek found himself in at that particular moment, he believed "he had no other choice" (Curtis 2008: 39) but to fire his revolver. Nevertheless, if we widen our gaze to examine the larger picture, one factor that comes into view is the prevailing climate of mistrust — not only of Aboriginal people towards the police, but also of police towards Aboriginal people. This climate of mistrust had a decided bearing on the events that afternoon.

A characteristic of police work is a heightened sensitivity to danger. The nature of the work requires police officers to be "occupied continually with potential violence" (Skolnick 1975: 45). While this sensitivity to danger was no doubt heightened by the knowledge that one of the robbery suspects was in possession of a weapon, it also applied more broadly to the neighbourhood that the police were sweeping and the residents who lived in it. From a policing standpoint, the North End constitutes not only a racialized space — as police were on the lookout for Aboriginal suspects — but a dangerous space populated by potential assailants. Mistrust and suspicion permeated police officers' encounters with North End residents, influencing what Corporal Gillis referred to as the officers' assessment of risk and their deployment of force options.

For instance, one of the issues that emerged during the inquest relating to the use of force model was that Constable Mateychuk did not handcuff Dumas when he apprehended him in Roderick Pelletier's backyard. Had he chosen to do so, it was suggested, the event could have turned out quite differently. This "soft technique" of handcuffing is one used regularly in police encounters with Aboriginal people. Willie Sinclair, for instance, expressed his surprise that Dumas was not handcuffed right away because "Almost everyone who is Anishinabe (aboriginal) gets handcuffed whether they did anything or not" (Saunders 2008a). On questioning, however, Constable Mateychuk indicated that he chose not to handcuff Dumas because he "didn't trust that male," referring to Pelletier, who was also referred to by WPS lawyer Carswell in her closing statement as an "untrustworthy citizen." Pelletier, for his part, said that he was afraid of Mateychuk based on his previous experiences with police, which, according to Worme, "says something about the relationship of police to residents."

The climate of mistrust was also reflected in the use of "forceful" language by police officers towards residents. As Philip Stenning (2003b) notes, the use of force by police officers includes not only physical and lethal force, but also verbal threats and intimidation as a means to secure compliance to their demands. During his testimony Pelletier indicated that Constable Mateychuk had told him to "get the fuck back in your house." He also testified that the officer had said "bad words" to Dumas as he was attempting to apprehend him in Pelletier's backyard. Another Aboriginal resident, Willie Sinclair, had also testified that the same officer had told him to "go back in your fucking house." That type of abusive language, Aboriginal residents of Winnipeg's inner city report, is regularly heard from the mouths of Winnipeg police officers, and it contributes to the climate of mistrust (and animosity) that prevails. Yet, like the officers who testified at the J.J. Harper inquiry, Constable Mateychuk denied using such language during his encounters with Aboriginal residents.

Constable Mateychuk indicated that he made the decision to pursue Dumas because the officer's presence "seemed to be making him nervous"

(Curtis 2008: 26). From a policing standpoint, it was this apparent nervousness that aroused suspicion and justified intervention.

"An Indian Boy in the North End"

At the conclusion of the inquest Tapper commented that it was not possible to know "what was in the head of Matthew Dumas."* He told the court, "We just don't know why Matthew Dumas did what he did. Why was he carrying a weapon?" Tapper's comments encapsulate the individualized frame adopted during the inquest proceedings. If we only knew "what was in his head" on the afternoon of January 31, 2005, a full understanding of the event would somehow follow. The key to the puzzle, in other words, rested with the deceased young man. But given the lack of information provided, Matthew Dumas remained an enigma. Learning more about Dumas — including his previous encounters with police — provides a context that was missing from the inquest proceedings.

At five foot six and weighing 150 pounds, Matthew Dumas was not an imposing figure. As the youngest of five siblings, he was, as his sister Jessica Dumas explained, "the baby in the family." Matthew's family originated from Keeseekoowenin, an Ojibwa First Nation near Riding Mountain, Manitoba. According to Jessica, their great grandparents moved the children around a lot "to keep them out of residential school." They worked all around Manitoba on different farms until the family eventually settled in Winnipeg's North End, where Matthew grew up. His parents separated when he was two years old and he lost contact with his natural father. His mother remarried when Matthew was ten. At the time of his death, Matthew had been alternating between the North End homes of his grandparents and his mother and stepfather, with a bedroom he could use in both houses. He also maintained a close relationship with his older brothers and sisters.

Following the trajectory of many Aboriginal kids growing up in Winnipeg's inner city, Matthew attended a number of schools but did not progress beyond Grade 9. Matthew told one friend that the teachers did not spend enough time with him to enable him to learn, and he found school to be a waste of time. So as a teenager Matthew spent most of his time "chilling with his buddies," which included listening to music, drinking beer, and

---

*   Unless otherwise indicated, quotations in this section are drawn from two sources: an interview conducted with Jessica Dumas by the author, March 9, 2011; and a document detailing interviews with Matthew Dumas's family and friends conducted by a private investigator at the request of the Dumas counsel.

smoking pot. He also spent time hanging out on the streets, which brought him into conflicts with other "crews" (meaning, a tight group of friends) in the North End.

In the summer of 2004 Matthew Dumas was involved in a confrontation on Selkirk Avenue, during which he was stabbed in the arm. Following that incident, he started to carry a knife for protection. As one of his close friends commented, "There are all kinds of people out there that want to hurt him.... 'Cause this North End crew out there don't like us and want to kill us, want to hurt in different ways."

In addition to running into conflicts with North End crews, Dumas also had conflicts with the law. From the age of thirteen he was in and out of youth court and spent time in the youth detention centre on charges ranging from theft of motor vehicle and theft under $5,000 to being unlawfully at large and failure to comply. The charges often stemmed from his involvement in stealing cars to go joyriding and "jacking" people up for their money or belongings when he needed money. While these conflicts suggest that Matthew Dumas was a troubled kid, his friends — including a girlfriend he had been in a relationship with for over a year — described him as "always happy."

Dumas was not so happy, however, when it came to his relationship with the police. According to his friends and his sister, he "hated cops." This animosity appears to have stemmed from his negative experiences with police, one of which involved a Starlight Tour that Dumas and a friend were taken on when they were sixteen. The two boys were picked up by police on Main Street and driven out to Inkster Boulevard and Oak Point Highway on the outskirts of the city, where they were left to walk home. According to his friend, Dumas also "got roughed up lots" by police. So, as his sister Jessica explained, the two boys "didn't want to get picked up by cops, they didn't want to be caught by cops because they know what's going to happen.... They're going to run and take off because that's the way people in the North End see the cops. And people just don't understand that."

Like many other young Aboriginal men in Winnipeg's inner city, Matthew Dumas had negative experiences with police, which engendered mistrust and animosity. Also like other young Aboriginal men, he was not a passive participant. According to one friend, Dumas would often play a game with the police:

Every time he would get into a chase with the cops, or like he would see a cop car driving down the street doing nothing he would grip a snow-

ball and bomb it and he would run. Like, that was the kind of game he
would play with the cops, like, "Come and get me. I bombed your car,
come and get me pigs, come and get me." And he would take off. And
the cops would chase him. That was the kind of game he played with
police. That is how he would get his asthma attacks.

In September 2004 Dumas received his first charge as an adult and spent
time in the Winnipeg Remand Centre. Some people speculated that his
experience of being incarcerated as an adult informed his decision to run
from Constable Mateychuk, that he was fearful of ending up back in jail. In
her report, Judge Curtis also speculated on why Dumas ran from the police
officer: "We also know that there was a warrant out for Mr. Dumas' arrest.
Police at that time were not aware of the warrant. There is no evidence to
show that Mr. Dumas was aware of the warrant, but it may be that he was.
If so, that may be an explanation as to why he ran" (Curtis 2008: 7). Others
called attention to the fact that Dumas was asthmatic (he had an asthma
puffer in his possession at the time of his death), which might have com-
promised his state of mind after running hard to avoid being apprehended
by Constable Mateychuk, being pepper-sprayed several times, and then
encountering officers with their guns drawn, shouting a barrage of commands at him. Still others simply cast Dumas as "angry" and "disturbed."
During his testimony Constable Gburek described the look on Dumas's
face as he was advancing towards him on the sidewalk: "His eyes are big…
they're lit up… big white eyes… he's red in the face… and you can just see
the anger in him… can see his teeth… he's showing his teeth… he's rigid
and… he's got this weird look… it's hard to explain… it's, like, it looks like
he's disturbed" (Curtis 2008: 36).

Jessica Dumas was troubled by the construction of her brother as "angry" and "disturbed." She told me, "He was just a little boy, you know. They
made him sound like this crazed maniac on drugs and nothing could stop
him." That construction did not align with her knowledge of her brother:

There's kids in the North End — and you know, I still call him a kid,
he was just a kid — kids in the North End where some of them can be
really rough, really aggressive and you walk into them and you're like,
okay, you know, you have to watch the way you look at some kids or
whatever, right, because that eye contact and that whatever, all that
stuff. He was not like that at all. Like, he was just, he was a good boy,
you know. There was sure a lot of stuff he could have been mixed up in,

maybe stuff I don't know about, but he's a kid in the North End, you know, he's an Indian boy in the North End. So there's all of everything else that plays into who he was.

Being an "Indian boy in the North End" meant that Matthew Dumas was caught up in a life in which "normal" takes on troublesome properties. Leaving school at an early age, hanging out with friends, getting into trouble, and regular encounters with police set him on a pathway that led to that fateful encounter with a Winnipeg police officer. Certainly his history of conflicts with Winnipeg police officers — including a Starlight Tour and getting "roughed up" — does not absolve his actions. But it does make it more understandable why he would appear to be "nervous" when being scrutinized by a police officer, and why he would run away. Knowing that Matthew felt the need for protection because of hostile encounters with other North End crews also sheds some light on why he was carrying a screwdriver when Constable Mateychuk apprehended him. As his sister explained, "I know good kids in the North End that carry around weapons because they feel like they have to, they have to protect themselves."

TRAGIC—BUT NOT UNEXPECTED

Judge Curtis took the position that there was "nothing in the evidence to support the claim that Mr. Dumas' death was a result of racism." Instead, the judge held that it was Dumas's own behaviour and choices that drove the events that led to his death. This position was premised upon an examination of the immediate events leading up to the discharge of Constable Gburek's firearm. If Dumas had not run from Constable Mateychuk, and if he had simply put down the screwdriver when commanded to do so, his death would have been avoidable. Because of the suspect's own behaviour and choices, police officers were left with little choice of their own. As Constable Dziver testified, Constable Gburek "didn't want to do what he had to do in the end" (Curtis 2008: 48). As with the legal process generally, the matter rested on individualized notions of choice and responsibility. But there is a broader context in which to situate the events that led to the death of Matthew Dumas.

While Judge Curtis was of the view that Dumas's behaviour and choices drove the events that led to his death, the actions that fatal afternoon were actually being determined by broader social and economic forces tied to race and racism — forces that perpetuate the historical, colonialized patterns shaping the lives of Aboriginal people. The resulting conditions of social exclusion and poverty, violence and alcohol use, and entanglement in the net of the criminal justice system have come to dominate the lives of far too many Aboriginal people — and Aboriginal people living in Winnipeg's inner-city communities, as we've seen, are clearly no exception. Yet when these systemic forces become manifested in the form of violence, street gangs, and the street drug and sex trades, the issues are typically framed as a problem "of" Aboriginal people. In other words, those being victimized are the ones held responsible for their plight.

Moreover, it falls on the police, as reproducers of order, to manage and contain the manifestations of this racialized poverty. But in the course of doing so, policing itself takes on a racialized form. Race and racialization have become embedded in the "mundane processes" or standard operating procedures of the police organization. Practices such as sweeps and spot checks of young men because they "fit the description," and the use of physical force and "forceful" language, have become routine features of Aboriginal-police relations. Troublesome police practices — such as Starlight Tours — become commonplace. Not surprisingly, mistrust and animosity shape the encounters between Aboriginal people and the police. Under these conditions the loss of a young Aboriginal man's life is certainly tragic — but not "unexpected."

Indeed, the summer of 2008 proved to be an especially difficult one for relations between Winnipeg's police service and the Aboriginal community. The Dumas inquest was completed at the end of June. On the afternoon of July 22 Michael Langan, a seventeen-year-old Métis man, was Tasered by a police officer after he refused to drop the knife he was holding. Police said they pursued Langan down an inner-city back lane after receiving a report about a smashed window on a Lexus vehicle. Langan became the youngest person in Canada to die as result of being Tasered (CBC News 2008d). Less than two weeks later, in the early hours of August 3, police officers arrested a man after responding to a domestic disturbance call. As they were leaving the house an altercation ensued between the officers and the man's son, twenty-six-year-old Craig McDougall, a member of the Wasagamack First Nation and a nephew of J.J. Harper. McDougall was subsequently shot and killed by police. While police stated that McDougall was in possession of a knife, his family maintained that when he was killed he was holding a cell phone and standing on the other side of a fence (CBC News 2008e, 2008f).

Chapter Eight

RACIALIZED POLICING
AND REPRODUCING ORDER

"Crime control is an impossible task for the police alone," Richard Ericson (1982: 11) writes. "They are expected to handle a phenomenon caused by social, political, economic, and cultural forces beyond their control and have to give the *appearance* that things are (more or less) under control."

Indeed, this "impossible task" of responding to a problem has its source in a much broader context, and that context has a historical dimension. Contemporary Aboriginal-police relations are rooted in the colonial relation between the original inhabitants of the land now called Canada and the role occupied by the North West Mounted Police in managing and containing the Aboriginal population as the emerging settler society took shape. But the unequal power relations between the colonizers and the colonized continue into the present.

In contemporary times colonialism is evidenced by the desperate living conditions in many First Nations communities, where basic necessities such as potable drinking water and adequate housing have taken on the status of a luxury that seems out of reach for too many Aboriginal families. It is also evidenced by the racialized poverty and a culture of despair that character-izes life in inner-city communities, especially in the Prairie provinces, where well-paid jobs are scarce and young Aboriginal men have a greater likelihood of ending up in jail than they do of finishing high school.

It is within this colonial context that police are assigned to do their job — a challenging job that involves much "dirty work" as officers are called upon to deal with all manner of troubles, including people who are in crisis, hurt, sick, intoxicated, angry, and sometimes violent. While crime control has become the leitmotif of modern policing, with the dominating public image of police officers as "crime fighters" and "law enforcers" out to "get the bad guys," at its core policing involves the reproduction of order, the transforming of troublesome situations back to their "normal" state — and the management and containment of troublesome persons — thus preserving the ranks of society. When the social order that the police are reproducing is founded on racism and racial inequality (and other forms of social inequality), policing becomes one of the projects through which race is interpreted and given meaning. It becomes a means by which the racialized order of society is reproduced. In short, policing itself becomes racialized.

While racialized policing emanates from the "impossible task" assigned to police, it also stems from the character of policing itself — for instance, in the cultural frames or stocks of knowledge that police officers draw upon in their everyday work. When particular persons come to be viewed as the "usual suspects," and particular places come to be viewed as spaces of danger and disorder, these frames or stocks of knowledge inform police encounters with Aboriginal people. In the racialized space of the inner city, young Aboriginal men are regularly stopped because they "fit the description," while Aboriginal women are assumed to be involved in the street sex trade. Over time, mistrust and animosity grow, especially as police adopt troublesome practices of their own as a way of dealing with troubled and troublesome people.

THE DENIAL OF A FUNDAMENTAL PROBLEM

Making the claim that policing is racialized is sure to generate controversy and opposition. After all, Aboriginal people who make public their negative experiences with police, such as in the Saskatoon case of Darrel Night, are readily cast as being unbelievable. As well, Aboriginal organizations and their spokespeople are regularly accused of "playing the race card" to advance their own political agenda when they name racism (see Comack and Bowness 2010). Journalists who write about the issue are chastised for engaging in "political correctness," and criminal justice officials who take action on incidents of racialized policing are criticized for being "too soft on crime" or acceding to the demands of "special interest groups" (McLean 2006). The efforts to address what many perceive to be a fundamental problem with relations between Aboriginal people and the police, then, are more often than not met with denials of the problem even existing.

The police participate in this discourse of denial. When the *Toronto Star* published its findings regarding racial profiling, the Toronto chief of police responded by asserting, "We don't do racial profiling" (Rankin et al. 2002a), and the Toronto Police Association launched a $2.7-billion lawsuit against the newspaper for publishing its results. In a similar vein, a few years ago I worked on a project that involved interviews with police officers about safety and security in Winnipeg's inner-city communities (Comack and

Silver 2006, 2008). As part of that project I interviewed Chief of Police Jack Ewatski. At one point in the interview I asked him about something that Aboriginal people were saying: that their young people were being targeted by police and they were often treated roughly and disrespectfully by police officers. The police chief suggested that this perception did not match up with reality. He went so far as to say that this standpoint constituted "urban lore":

> *I am not going to deny the fact that there have been times that police have treated people in a manner that is not acceptable, and when those incidents occur we deal with them, and if we could prove that that is actually the case, that that has happened, then those officers are sanctioned; there's consequences to their actions, too. But I'm also aware of some of the urban lore out there and some of the things of, well, "I heard from a friend of a friend who said that the police came by, beat me up for no reason, and then just dropped me off somewhere." Well, how real is that?*

Despite the police chief's denial discourse, Aboriginal people report that racist, sexist, and disrespectful language, physical violence and assaults, and drop offs and Starlight Tours occur frequently and regularly in their encounters with police — too much so to be disregarded as "myths" or "urban lore."

Similarly, legal professionals and academics who dismiss accounts by Aboriginal people and other racialized groups about their encounters with police as "mere anecdotes" (Gold 2003; Gabor 2004) contribute to this denial discourse. Instead, they privilege official versions and quantitative methodologies as being more valid than qualitative research aimed at gathering individual stories. Nevertheless, as Carol Tator and Frances Henry (2006: 117) comment: "The stories people tell about their lived experiences are more than mere individual communications; they are embedded in a cultural and ideological context. These stories reflect their existing social relations; and while many stories reflect an individual's experiences, taken together they reveal cultural assumptions that transcend the individual."

In his book, *The Truth about Stories: A Native Narrative*, Thomas King (2003: 9) writes, "Stories are wondrous things. And they are dangerous." King is reminding us that the stories Aboriginal people tell of their experiences with the police have the power to inform and transform — so long as we are prepared to *listen to* and *hear* what is being said.

Despite the controversy and opposition surrounding the issue, both the argument and the evidence for how race and racism pervade the practice of policing have been mounted many times before. The Ontario Commission on Systemic Racism in the Criminal Justice System (Ontario 1995: 106) concluded that "systemic racism, the social process that produces racial inequality in how people are treated, is at work in the Ontario criminal justice system.... The criminal justice system tolerates racialization in its practices." The Ontario Human Rights Commission (2003) found that the experience of being racially profiled by police has become routine for people of colour, and the impact of that experience has been profound, with an impact not only on people's trust of police but also on their everyday activities. In its investigation of the shooting death of J.J. Harper, the Aboriginal Justice Inquiry of Manitoba concluded, "Racism exists within the Winnipeg Police Department" (Hamilton and Sinclair 1991b: 93). Similarly, the Royal Commission on the Donald Marshall, Jr. Prosecution deemed racism to be at work in the Sydney, Nova Scotia, police force, and that it was spawned from the "general sense in Sydney's White community at the time that Indians were not 'worth' as much as Whites" (Nova Scotia 1989: 3).

Government-sponsored commissions and inquiries have named the racism in the criminal justice system. They have also been severely critical of police forces for their failure to mount proper investigations when cases of police mistreatment of Aboriginal people come to light. We have seen evidence of this in case after case. AJI commissioners Hamilton and Sinclair deemed the investigation by the Winnipeg Police Department into the death of Harper to be "at best, inadequate. At worst, its primary objective seems to have been to exonerate Const. Robert Cross and to vindicate the Winnipeg Police Department" (1991b: 113). The Royal Commission on the Donald Marshall, Jr. Prosecution called the police investigation into the death of Sandy Seale "entirely inadequate, incompetent and unprofessional" (Nova Scotia 1989: 3). Justice Wright found the police investigation into Neil Stonechild's death to be "insufficient and totally inadequate." According to the commissioner, "the deficiencies in the investigation go beyond incompetence or neglect. They were inexcusable" (Wright 2004: 212, 103). Similarly, Justice Davies was heavily critical of the Vancouver Police Department's treatment of Frank Paul, describing the police investigation into the matter as "fundamentally flawed" (Davies 2008: 18).

Despite the combined weight of all of these pronouncements by government-sponsored commissions and inquiries, the fundamental problem of Aboriginal-police relations persists. At the very least, one would expect public outrage — and not denial — when cases involving racialized policing come to light. But it seems that mainstream society is content to assign the job of ensuring its safety and security to the police. Carsten Stroud (1983: 228) commented years ago on the increasing tendency of society to transfer responsibility for managing social problems to professionals such as the police:

> Canadians seem to be increasingly ready to abdicate personal responsibility, to place the burden of society's problems on "professional" shoulders. We leave our grandparents in nursing homes, we let the poor fall into welfare nets, we create "commissions" and "review boards" and "agencies" to do the things any thinking person once felt ethically obliged to take care of personally. And we surrendered the responsibility for our safety and security of our families to the police forces. Having done so, we [that is, those of us with privilege] slapped our collective hands together and walked off to enjoy our peace as something bought and paid for. The fact that the policeman can't do the job alone seems to be viewed as a breach of contract.

In the neo-liberal climate, calls to "get tough" on crime carry the promise of a quick and ready solution to the problems brought on by the increasing divide between rich and poor and the social unease and anxiety these problems generate. Implicit in the public support garnered for these "get-tough" strategies is the assumption that they will *not* be directed at "Us" — the "ordinary citizen" — but only at "Them" — those deemed to be "trouble." So if police require enhanced powers to arrest, detain, or otherwise control the "criminalized Other," then so be it. If zero-tolerance policing leads to more aggressive tactics to manage squeegee kids, welfare recipients, street-gang members, or other "troublesome" members of society, then so be it. If these strategies extend to include whole communities populated by Aboriginal people and other racialized groups, then so be it. In these terms, the order that the police are reproducing is a racialized order that privileges certain groups over others.

Expecting that police will do this dirty work enables the continued denial of the fundamental problem of racism and ostensibly absolves the rest of us from social responsibility. But this denial comes at considerable cost. As Joyce Green (2006: 158) notes: "While racism is most violently experienced by Aboriginal people, it also mains the humanity and civility of those who perpetuate it, deny it or ignore it. Racism injures the capacity of the body politic to work collaboratively toward common visions." Surely, as Green points out, if all of us who live in this country are ever to realize the necessary sense of social cohesion that will sustain our everyday lives and growth, we must confront and eliminate racism in its every form and every instance.

WHAT IS TO BE DONE?

One strategy for responding to this fundamental problem of Aboriginal-police relations is to encourage Aboriginal people to make formal complaints about their treatment by police. In Manitoba, complaints can be made to the Law Enforcement Review Agency (LERA), created in 1985 under the authority of the Law Enforcement Review Act. According to the Act, any person "who feels aggrieved by a disciplinary default allegedly committed by any member of a police department may file a complaint" with LERA (cited in Hamilton and Sinclair 1991a: 629). However, data provided by LERA suggests that these complaints are not likely to proceed very far. In 2010, for instance, 274 investigations were conducted involving police officers in the province — down from 321 investigations in 2009, 367 in 2008, 422 in 2007, and 560 in 2006. The Winnipeg Police Service accounted for 83 percent of the complaints received in 2010. Processing these cases can be a lengthy undertaking. Of the 274 investigations started in 2010, 103 (37.5 percent) were still ongoing at the end of the year. Of the 171 completed investigations, the vast majority were either dismissed by the commissioner as not supported by sufficient evidence to support a hearing (57 percent) or abandoned or withdrawn by the complainant (32 percent). According to LERA, "In many cases, when a LERA investigator is unable to locate the complainant, a letter is sent to the complainant's last known address asking the complainant to contact the investigator. If contact is not made within 30 days, the complaint is considered abandoned and a registered letter is sent to that effect" (LERA n.d.: 29). Of the remaining complaints, the com-missioner dismissed seven cases (4 percent) as being outside the scope of the Act and one case (.5 percent) as frivolous or vexatious; one case (.5 percent) was resolved informally, and eleven cases (6 percent) resulted in a public hearing before a provincial court judge.

None of the seventy-eight inner-city residents in Winnipeg whom we interviewed about their experiences with police had been successful in launching a LERA complaint. Many of those interviewed believed that there was no point in lodging a formal complaint. As one woman remarked, "You could try, you could do it, but you're not going to get anywhere because you're fighting a whole system." When we asked people why they chose not to report an incident, a typical response was "who's going to believe me?" For people lacking the social capital and acutely aware of their position of disempowerment relative to the power and public support accorded the police, making a formal complaint is often seen as too risky an endeavour. But even when people do try to take action, they can be thwarted. In one of our interviews we had this exchange:

> [*When the cops stop you, do you ever try to get their badge numbers or anything?*]
> *I tried to do that. The cops just walked away.*
> [*They just walked away?*]
> *Yeah.*
> [*And you said, "What's your badge number. I want to write it down." And they just walked away?*]
> *Yeah. Then they threaten to put you in the cop car if you find out the badge number.*

The government-sponsored inquiries and commissions often recommend another strategy: increase the diversity of police forces by recruiting more Aboriginal people (as well as other racialized groups). Manitoba's Aboriginal Justice Inquiry, for example, argued that increasing the representation of Aboriginal people on the Winnipeg Police Department would have the benefit of providing positive role models for Aboriginal youth and enabling the force to be more culturally sensitive to the communities it serves.

When J.J. Harper was killed in 1988, the Winnipeg police force included only eight Aboriginal police officers. In December 1990 that number had increased to 18 Aboriginal officers (out of a total of 1,125). Since Aboriginal people made up 11.8 percent of Manitoba's population at that time, the AJI commissioners recommended that the department hire an additional 115 Aboriginal officers to reach a more equitable number of 133 (Hamilton and Sinclair 1991b: 107). By 1998 the number of Aboriginal officers had increased to 98 (Sinclair 1999: 385). By 2009 there were 141 Aboriginal officers, representing 10.7 percent of the total complement of 1,411 sworn officers employed by the Winnipeg Police Service. The force described another 91 officers (6.4 percent) as "visible minorities" (Winnipeg Police Service 2009: 25).

These figures are encouraging because they suggest a concerted effort on the part of the Winnipeg Police Service to improve the representation of Aboriginal people among its rank and file. Yet this strategy alone will not be enough. As Nicole Lugosi (2011: 308) notes, "Striving for a more proportionate and representative legal system is a good start, but representation alone does not fundamentally challenge the racial hierarchies in the system." Moreover, given that strong internal culture of solidarity in which the identity of police officer overshadows racial or ethnic identities, it is doubtful whether a complement of 10.7 percent can bring about a sea change in the standard operating procedures and everyday practices of policing.

Police forces have also supplemented these efforts to increase diversity by implementing cultural sensitivity training for all of their staff. Typically, these initiatives are aimed more at countering negative stereotypes about Aboriginal people and educating officers about Aboriginal cultures and teachings — and less at "the reality and cultures of *whiteness* as a constructed race and position of privilege" (Lugosi 2011: 313). As Green (2006: 520) notes, on their own, cultural awareness activities, such as having police officers participate in a smudge ceremony, "will not bring about a shift in racist practices or institutions." The broader culture of policing will also have to be addressed, especially in relation to its role in perpetuating troublesome police practices.

Given the command structure and the close working relationships that develop with the force, police are doubtless aware of fellow officers carrying out troublesome practices such as Starlight Tours and the phone book treatment. So why don't they take action to stop them? One of the consequences of the blue wall is that it shields those officers who perpetrate such practices and acts as a barrier to change. Given the strong social bonds that develop within the force, and the edict to "stand by your partner," police are motivated to unite in solidarity to protect their own. They do so at great cost because these actions not only reflect badly on the entire police organization, but also engender mistrust and animosity within the communities that the police are delegated to serve.

Our interviews with inner-city residents in Winnipeg produced examples of positive encounters between Aboriginal people and the police and the professionalism, kindness, and concern that officers can demonstrate as they go about their work. Many more Aboriginal people, however, spoke of the disrespect shown to them by police. In the same way that troublesome police practices create a toxic climate for police-community relations, so too does the use of offensive language by police officers in their interactions with Aboriginal people. The word "fuck" (and its variants) should never be part of a police officer's vocabulary, nor should "squaw," "cunt," or other similarly offensive words. Such abusive language runs counter to the professionalism that police officers are mandated to uphold and should not be tolerated within the force.

Attending to the culture of policing and the language and actions of individual police officers, however, addresses only part of the fundamental problem of Aboriginal-police relations. The structure and organization of police work also needs to addressed. One recommendation that often flows from government-sponsored inquiries and commissions is for police forces to implement community policing as an organizational philosophy and strategy.

The AJI commissioners advocated for a community policing approach, arguing that this model represents a marked improvement over the traditional crime-fighting model, whereby policing is reactive and incident-driven, where the job of police officers is basically about "driving around the streets in a car, isolated from the citizenry, waiting for a dispatcher to call" (Hamilton and Sinclair 1991a: 598). Community policing, in contrast, is decentralized and prevention-oriented. It encourages a partnership between the police and the community; it is flexible and adaptable to Aboriginal cultural standards and accommodating to the wide variation of lifestyles in Aboriginal communities (1991a: 598–99). In the commissioners' view, community policing is "a vital strategy for enabling local residents to have a structured, open relationship with the police" (1991a: 600).

One of the mandates of the Ontario Commission on Systemic Racism in the Criminal Justice System was to investigate and make recommendations on community policing policies and their implementation. The Commission's consultations, however, showed that while community policing had been adopted by local police services, concerns about systemic racism in police practices remained widespread. In particular, community members expressed "fear that racial equality is not on the community policing agenda" (Ontario 1995: 337). Similarly, even though police forces across the country have implemented community policing initiatives, concerns have emerged about the extent to which these initiatives have had an impact on the hierarchical structure and bureaucratic organization of the services. Writers have pointed to difficulties in effectively implementing community policing initiatives in neighbourhoods where the residents are not in a position to participate actively in the kind of ownership and co-operation envisioned by the model. Commentators have also noted that individual

police officers have tended to resist efforts to implement community policing because they consider the model to be akin to social work and therefore
at odds with the "real" police work of fighting crime (Linden, Clairmont, and
Murphy 2000; Greene 2000; Hebert 2001). The advent of more aggressive
models, such as zero-tolerance policing, has also shifted the focus of policing
away from the more co-operative approach involved in community policing
and back to the traditional model of police as "crime fighters."

Government-sponsored commissions and inquiries have also led to another recommendation around the need for improvements in investigation
processes and procedures in cases of alleged police wrongdoing. Critical of
the state of race relations in the province, the Ontario Race Relations and
Policing Task Force (Ontario 1989) made fifty-seven recommendations for
its improvement, including the creation of the Special Investigations Unit.
In 1990 Ontario became the first province to establish an independent
civilian oversight body responsible for carrying out criminal investigations
involving the police. Appointed and funded by the provincial government,
the siu is responsible for investigating allegations of wrongdoing involving
serious injury and death caused by police officers.

Ontario's siu became subject to considerable public scrutiny after its
inception, including at least seven reports, one of which was produced by
the Ontario Ombudsman in 2008. Entitled *Oversight Unseen* (Marin 2008),
the report called the independence of the agency into question, especially
given the use of former police officers as investigators. It also noted that
the public perception of the siu was akin to "a toothless tiger and muzzled
watchdog" (Marin 2008: 74). David MacAlister, principal researcher for
the B.C. Civil Liberties Association, summarizes some of the concerns
raised in the report:

> In some instances, police refused to cooperate with siu investiga-
> tors. Delays in being notified of cases requiring siu involvement
> were compounded by delays in interviewing witnesses. Decisions
> made by the siu not to charge police officers are not subject to ex-
> planation in a public venue, causing further concern. A significant
> concern was the deference given to the police by siu investigators
> during their investigations. There was a reluctance to insist on po-
> lice cooperation. The internal culture of the siu was found to have
> been adversely affected by the large number of ex-police officers
> on staff. (MacAlister 2010: 16)

Other provinces have also established civilian oversight bodies to deal with allegations of police wrongdoing. In Manitoba the Aboriginal Justice Inquiry noted that "Manitoba compares poorly with other western provinces in its regulation of police activities" (Hamilton and Sinclair 1991a: 624) and highlighted "the need for independent investigations of serious incidents involving the police, especially those where possible criminal acts are alleged against the police, or where a person dies or suffers serious injury in an incident involving the police" (Hamilton and Sinclair 1991a: 628). Yet it was almost two decades before the provincial government undertook a revision of its Provincial Police Act. The impetus for this revision came not from a concern to remedy the fractured relations between Aboriginal people and the police but from an inquiry into a traffic death caused by an off-duty police officer.

In the early morning of February 25, 2005, a light pickup truck driven by thirty-one-year-old Derek Harvey-Zenk, a constable with the Winnipeg Police Service, crashed into the back of a car driven by forty-year-old Crystal Taman. On her way to work, Taman had been sitting at a controlled intersection on a highway near the perimeter of Winnipeg, waiting for the light to change. She was killed instantly. It was later revealed that Constable Zenk had spent the previous evening at a local bar with a group of fellow officers from his North End police district. Leaving the establishment at around 2:30 a.m., several of the officers continued the party at the residence of a police sergeant. Zenk was on his way home at 7:00 a.m. when the crash occurred (Salhany 2008).

Constable Zenk was initially charged with impaired driving causing death, criminal negligence causing death, refusing a Breathalyzer test, and dangerous operation of a motor vehicle causing death. But a plea agreement was struck in which he pleaded guilty to a lesser offence of dangerous driving causing death in exchange for a conditional sentence of two-years-less-a-day to be served at his home (CBC News 2007). Public outcry over the plea bargain and allegations that the police investigation had been botched led the Manitoba justice minister to pass an order-in-council in December 2007 establishing an inquiry into the case. The Taman Inquiry, which overlapped the inquest into the death of Matthew Dumas, ran for eight weeks in 2008.

In his report, Commissioner Roger Salhany, a retired Ontario superior court justice, deemed the initial investigation into the accident by the East St. Paul Police Service to be "riddled with incompetence" (Salhany 2008: 7). Officers were found to have falsified their notes and engaged in a "cover-up" in an effort to protect one of their own (Salhany 2008: 11). The commissioner also deemed the subsequent Winnipeg Police Service investigation to have been conducted "so poorly… that it cast light on a broader systemic problem. It showed the perils of having police officers investigate, or even interview, other police officers from their own force in criminal cases" (Salhany 2008: 8). The commissioner therefore recommended that a special investigation unit independent of all police enforcement agencies in Manitoba be established "for the purpose of investigating any alleged criminal activity of a member of the police service" (Salhany 2008: 14).

In March 2009 the Manitoba government introduced changes to the Provincial Police Act. The Act provides for the establishment of a civilian-led Manitoba Police Commission to oversee policing throughout the province. Civilian boards will have the authority to hire and fire police chiefs and set the tone for policing in their respective communities. Police will no longer investigate their own officers in the event of serious criminal allegations, such as a police-involved shooting death. Nevertheless, police officers will still play a role in the investigation. They can be either current or former police officers selected by a civilian director. The current police officers would be seconded from their police service. As Manitoba's justice minister Dave Chomiak noted at the time, the assignment of police officers to the investigative unit has the potential to generate controversy, but "to be logical, that's what it will probably have to be. Investigators don't sort of grow on trees" (Owen 2009).

In August 2011 the province announced the appointment of Inspector Brian Cyncora, a thirty-year-veteran of the Winnipeg Police Service, as the first executive director of the Manitoba Police Commission. The composition of the Commission's board had previously been announced. Criminologist Rick Linden was appointed to head the board; other commissioners included an Aboriginal representative as well as Robert Taman, the husband of Crystal Taman (Owen 2011). While reporter Bruce Owen (2009) opined that Manitoba's new Provincial Police Act will "effectively tear down the 'blue wall' that has separated many Manitobans from their police officers," whether that will in fact be the case remains to be seen.

Strategies such as encouraging Aboriginal people to make formal complaints, increasing the racial diversity of police forces, implementing cultural sensitivity training for officers, attending to the disrespect (such as the use of offensive language) shown to Aboriginal people by the police, and improving investigative processes and procedures when acts of police wrongdoing arise could most likely go a long way towards improving relations between Aboriginal people and the police. But those strategies alone will not remedy the fundamental problem; they fail to address its roots. What is required is a dramatic shift in how we frame the problem of Aboriginal-police relations.

REFRAMING THE PROBLEM

How a problem is framed will govern the particular ways of responding to it. For instance, the current trend is to frame the problems confronting inner-city communities in criminal justice terms, as located in the prevalence of crime, violence, and street gangs in these communities. With this framing, "law and order" strategies such as zero-tolerance policing and heightened surveillance and containment make sense. If, however, the problem is reframed as being rooted in the impoverished social and economic conditions in these communities, then crime, violence, and street gangs become symptoms of a deeper problem that requires solutions beyond "fighting crime" to ameliorate them.

One rationale for shifting how the problem is framed is the costs incurred by criminal justice interventions. Crime control is an incredibly expensive venture. According to Sewell (2010: 141), "Police services eat up almost a quarter of the property tax revenues of many municipalities, and those governments find themselves under increasing financial pressure." Despite declining crime rates, spending on police forces rose by 41 percent per capita across the country between 1999 and 2009 (Morrow 2011). While salaries take up some 80 percent of police budgets (Linden, Clairmont, and Murphy 2000), the use of expensive technologies only adds to that burden. For instance, the purchase of a helicopter by the Winnipeg Police Service cost the city $3.5 million, while the Province of Manitoba contributes $1.3 million annually in operating costs (CTV Winnipeg 2011). As the first contact point in the criminal justice system, police are also involved in funnelling individuals into what Angela Davis (2000) called the "prison industrial complex." Mass incarceration involves huge financial costs for the state. In the effort to advance its "law and order" agenda, the Canadian government has poured considerable monies into shoring up its penitentiary system. The annual budget of the Correctional Service of Canada increased by 86.6 percent after 2005–6. Expenditures in this area were projected to rise to $3.178 billion by 2012–13 (Piche 2011).

Another powerful rationale for reframing the problem is the human and social capital that is at stake. In the Manitoba context, Michael Mendelson (2004: 8) argued that "the increasing importance of the Aboriginal workforce to Manitoba… cannot be exaggerated. There is likely no single more critical economic factor for [the Prairie] provinces." Manitoba's Aboriginal population is predicted to grow from about 159,000 in 2001 to 231,000 by 2017 (Loxley 2010). These figures suggest that Aboriginal youth will be an important resource for the province — but only if current conditions of racialized poverty and social exclusion are addressed. In this respect, inner-city communities where Aboriginal people are to be found in large proportions are the site of a growing number of community-based organizations whose mandate is to attend to the complex material, cultural, and emotional needs of the residents (see, for example, Silver 2006c; CCPA-MB 2007).

By and large these community-based organizations — many of which are Aboriginal-driven — adopt a community development approach that involves strategies by which people participate directly or through organizations that they control in bottom-up planning and community action (Wharf and Clague 1997). Community development, in other words, is geared towards enabling communities to overcome poverty and social exclusion in ways of their choosing. As Jim Silver and his colleagues (2006: 134) explain:

> Community development involves the continuous process of capacity-building: building upon and strengthening local resources to generate well-being among community members. ... Community development is based on the premise that community members need to gain control of resources to generate economic well-being. The general goal of community development is to benefit those who have been marginalized from the current economic system.

Aboriginal community development is even more comprehensive. It is aimed at decolonization, or the process of undoing colonialism by attending to the devastating effects that it has wreaked on Aboriginal people, in terms not only of their material circumstances but also their identity. In contrast to criminal justice strategies that focus on punishment, discipline, and control, Aboriginal community development focuses on healing, wellness, and capacity-building. Honouring Aboriginal traditions, values, and cultures becomes an important part of this healing process. So too does reclaiming a sense of self-worth and pride that has been systematically stripped from Aboriginal people by colonial strategies manifested in the residential schools, the reserve system, and the Indian Act, and dominant discourses that Other them as "welfare recipients" and "criminals." By adopting a holistic approach that focuses on strengthening the individual, the family, and the community, Aboriginal community-based organizations aim to move Aboriginal people out of and beyond colonialism's straitjacket (see Silver et al. 2006).

Non-Aboriginal people are also implicated in this process of decolonization. Similar to the strategies adopted by the women's movement, Aboriginal community development is constituted as being carried out "by" and "with" Aboriginal people because Aboriginal people (as in women's struggles for equality) ultimately need to claim their entitlements through their own organizations. But just as men are not absolved of their responsibility in making change to realize substantive equality for women, non-Aboriginal people have a role to play as allies, walking beside and not in front of or behind Aboriginal people in their quest for change (Silver et al. 2006: 156). The police too could play a role in this project of decolonization and community development, albeit a very different role than has traditionally been designed for them.

COMMUNITY MOBILIZATION

Given that police have occupied a central role in the reproduction of or-der — more specifically, in the dreadful task of policing the conflict and abuses that arise from the particular forms of poverty and social exclusion that our society has created — reframing the problem and re-envisioning the strategies for resolving it open up new possibilities for the role of the police in the form of community mobilization.

Although most modern police forces tend to adopt a blended approach in which a variety of policing models are employed, typically the core strat-egy involves the traditional crime-fighting model of policing, with other initiatives (community policing, specialized units, and the like) positioned as a supplementary or secondary consideration. The traditional model of policing sets the police up as an outside force sent into troubled and troublesome communities to quell disorder. Rather than being an outside force, police need to be a more integral part of the communities they are mandated to serve. One way of doing so is to shift their organizational focus from crime-fighting to community mobilization.

Community mobilization involves working in close partnership with community-based organizations and social service agencies engaged in a wide variety of neighbourhood revitalization initiatives. It involves police officers walking the beat, getting to know people and the community, de-veloping relationships, using conflict resolution and problem-solving skills, earning the trust of people. It involves the police working *with* the community to collectively build safer and healthier neighbourhoods (Comack and Silver 2006). Clearly, the role of police as crime fighters would not disappear within this model of policing, but it would be a subsidiary to the refashioned core strategy of community mobilization.

Working in close contact with community members would enable police to know where the problems are, and to intervene, at least in some cases, before problems occur. In these terms, police would become part of a process of "asset-based community development" (Kretzmann and McKnight 1993). While the traditional approach to inner-city communities is to see them through a "deficit lens" — that is, solely in terms of their problems — an "asset-based" approach identifies and builds upon the strengths of a neighbourhood. In this way, the role of police as "reproducers of order" would be transformed. Rather than reproducing the status quo, police could participate in the fashioning of a new form of social order; one not founded on race and racism — and racialized policing.

A common response to the argument that race and racism invade the practice of policing is that the presence of racism in a police force merely reflects the racism in the wider society and is therefore not a special matter of concern. AJI commissioners Hamilton and Sinclair (1991b: 111) disagree:

> Police officers occupy a unique and powerful position in our society. They have the ability to interfere with the freedom of citizens and are called upon to protect society from the misdeeds of its members. The position of police officers provides them with opportunities to intrude into our lives — a right denied to all others. We have every right to expect and demand from them that they fulfill their responsibilities fully, fairly and in a manner that does not discriminate against anyone on account of race. It is not acceptable for any member of society to do that, but it is even more unacceptable for a police officer to do so.

Police alone cannot solve the problems that trouble Aboriginal communities and their residents. But policing *can* be part of a long-term solution that involves decolonization and community mobilization and revitalization. At the very least, making such change requires political will. But it starts with the recognition that a fundamental problem exists in Aboriginal-police relations — a problem rooted in colonialism, poverty, and social exclusion.

Appendix

A NOTE ON METHODOLOGY

The experiences and standpoints of Aboriginal people featured in chapter 6, "Policing Winnipeg's Inner-City Communities," were drawn from interviews conducted in 2008 and 2009 for a study undertaken in collaboration with Nahanni Fontaine, who was then justice director of the Southern Chiefs' Organization, which represents 34 First Nations communities in Manitoba. When we advertised the study on an Aboriginal radio station and posted advertisements at various inner-city locales, our initial hope was to secure interviews with 24 Aboriginal people; as it turned out, many more people than that contacted us about participating in the study, and we eventually completed 78 interviews.

Several inner-city agencies — including the John Howard Society office, Nine Circles (a clinic for HIV-positive people), Sage House (a drop-in centre for women and transgenders involved in the street sex trade), Resource Assistance for Youth (RaY), the Indian and Métis Family Centre, the Indian and Métis Friendship Centre, and Onashowewin (which offers a restorative justice program) — supported our project by providing venues where the interviews could be carried out. We also did interviews at coffee shops and a local hospital when those places turned out to be convenient for the participants. In one case I met with a mother and her two daughters at their home. In each case participants received honorariums of $25 in acknowledgement of their contribution to the study.

In accordance with ethical standards for conducting social science research, participants signed consent forms that detailed the purpose of the study — to gather the stories of Aboriginal people about their experiences with police — and were provided with assurances of confidentiality in handling and reporting the information (for example, pseudonyms have been used for the people interviewed). During the interviews (which were recorded and later transcribed), participants were asked about the nature and extent of their contact with police, starting from their earliest experiences. When participants had only a few experiences to relay, their interviews tended to be short (around 15 minutes), while others spoke at greater length in interviews lasting over one hour. On average, interviews were about 25 minutes in duration.

The 78 people interviewed for the study constituted a diverse group. Almost half (38) were female, 47 percent (37) were male, and the remaining 3 people identified themselves as transgendered. The participants ranged in age from 15 to 65, with a mean age of 37. During the interviews many people spoke of their difficult and unsettled childhoods. Like many other Aboriginal people, some of them had been separated from their parents and taken into care as children. Often they were shifted between several different foster and group homes when they were younger. Some of them were affiliated with street gangs as youth, and many disclosed problems with drugs and/or alcohol, which brought them into conflict with the law. Several of the women and transgenders had experience working in the street sex trade, and their encounters with police often occurred in that context. Participants were also forthcoming about their law violations. Some had spent time in the youth detention centre, and some had served sentences as adults in jail and prison. When talking about their experiences with police, some participants admitted to their own responsibility in generating conflicts. As one 23-year-old man commented, "When I was younger I treated them like shit, so they treated me like shit."

Collectively, the stories told by these 78 people have great weight. It is difficult to dispute their veracity when they are lined up next to each other. It also becomes harder to dismiss the stories as fabrications when people tell them in such detail. Sitting across from the people I was talking to, I could see that their faces and body language often revealed as much as their words. In one interview a young man began to get very nervous and breathless as he was talking about an experience with a police officer. Noticing his discomfort, Nahanni and I stopped the interview and shifted the discussion, acknowledging how difficult this retelling was for him. Even though his experience had happened a few years before, he was still feeling its impact. I am therefore ever mindful of the courage it takes for people to come forward to tell their stories — especially in the face of the silencing and social censuring that often accompanies their efforts.

REFERENCES

Adam, B.A. 2000. "Large Crowd Attends Candlelight Vigil." *Saskatoon Star Phoenix*. At <injusticebusters.com/index.htm/cops/htm> February 18.

Anderson, A.B. 2005. "Socio-Demographic Study of Aboriginal Population in Saskatoon." Bridges and Foundations Project. University of Saskatchewan. At <bridgesandfoundations.usask.ca/reports/sociodemo_reportfinal.pdf>.

Anderson, R. 2010. *2006 Aboriginal Population Profile for Saskatoon*. Ottawa: Statistics Canada. At <statcan.gc.ca/pub/89-638-x/2010003/article/11080-eng.htm>.

Banton, M. 1987. "The Classification of Races in Europe and North America: 1700–1850." *International Social Science Journal* 39 (1).

Barnsley, P. 2002. "Starlight Cruise Cops Get Eight Months." *Windspeaker* 19 (9).

Barrett. S.R. 1987. *Is God a Racist? The Right Wing in Canada*. Toronto: University of Toronto Press.

Bayley, D.H. 2005. "What Do the Police Do?" In T. Newburn (ed.), *Policing: Key Readings*. Portland: Willan Publishing.

BCCLA (British Columbia Civil Liberties Association). n.d. "Frank Paul Inquiry." At <bccla.org.policeissue/frankpaul.html>.

Becker, H. 1963. *Outsiders: Studies in the Sociology of Deviance*. New York: The Free Press.

Bittle, S., N. Quann, T. Hattem, and D. Muise. 2002. *A One-Day Snapshot of Aboriginal Youth in Custody Across Canada*. Ottawa: Department of Justice Canada. At <dsp-psd.pwgsc.gc.ca/Collection/J2-266-2002E.pdf>.

Bittner, E. 2005. "Florence Nightingale in Pursuit of Willie Sutton: A Theory of the Police." In T. Newburn (ed.), *Policing: Key Readings*. Portland: Willan Publishing.

Blackstone, C., and N. Trocmé. 2004. "Community Based Child Welfare for Aboriginal Children: Supporting Resilience through Structural Change." At <cecw-cepb.ca/sites/default/files/publications/en/communityBasedCWA-boriginalChildren.pdf>.

Bopp, M., J. Bopp, and P. Lane. 2003. *Aboriginal Domestic Violence in Canada*. Ottawa: Aboriginal Healing Foundation.

Braidwood, T. 2010. *Why? The Robert Dziekanski Tragedy*. Braidwood Commission on the Death of Robert Dziekanski. British Columbia. At <braidwoodinquiry.ca/report/P2Report.php> May 20.

Brass, M. 2004. "Starlight Tours." CBC. At <cbc.ca/news/background/aboriginals/

starlighttours.html> July 2.

Broad, D. 2000. *Hollow Work, Hollow Society? Globalization and the Casual Labour Problem in Canada.* Halifax: Fernwood Publishing.

Broad, D., J. Cruikshank, and J. Mulvale. 2006. "Where's the Work? Labour Market Trends in the New Economy." In D. Broad and W. Antony (eds.), *Capitalism Rebooted? Work and Welfare in the New Economy.* Halifax: Fernwood Publishing.

Brodbeck, T. 2008. "The Facts Are Clear: Race Reflex Makes a Bad Thing Worse." *Winnipeg Sun*, December 14.

Brodeur, J.P. (ed.). 1998. *How to Recognize Good Policing: Problems and Issues.* Thompson Oaks, CA: Sage Publications.

Brown, J., N. Higgitt, C. Miller, S. Wingert, M. Williams, and L. Morrissette. 2006. "Challenges Faced by Women Working in the Inner City Sex Trade." *Canadian Journal of Urban Research* 15 (1).

Brown, L., and C. Brown. 1978. *An Unauthorized History of the RCMP.* Toronto: James Lorimer.

Brownridge, D. 2003. "Male Partner Violence against Aboriginal Women in Canada: An Empirical Analysis." *Journal of Interpersonal Violence* 18 (1).

Bruser, D. 2010. Troubled Neighbourhood Desperate for Change. *Toronto Star.* At <thestar.com.printarticle/761305> February 7.

Buddle, K. 2011. "Urban Aboriginal Gangs and Street Sociality in the Canadian West: Places, Performances, and Predicaments of Transition." In H.A. Howard and C. Proulx (eds.), *Aboriginal Peoples in Canadian Cities: Transformations and Continuities.* Waterloo: Wilfrid Laurier University Press.

Burton, Randy. 2004. "Inquiry Confirms Worst About Police." *The Star Phoenix.* At <injusticebusters.com/04/Stonechild_Neil.shtml> October 27.

____. 2001. "Keep the Racial Fires Burning." *Saskatoon Star Phoenix*, November 1.

Campaign 2000. 2010. *Report Card on Child and Family Poverty in Canada: 1989–2010.* At <campaign2000.ca/reportCards/national/2010EnglishC2 000NationalReportCard.pdf>.

Canada. 2002. *Convention against Torture and Other Cruel, Inhuman or Degrading Treatment or Punishment: Fourth Report of Canada* (April 1996–April 2000). Ottawa: Minister of Public Works and Government Services. At <dsp-psd. pwgsc.gc.ca/Collection/CH4-43-2002E.pdf>.

Canadian Panel on Violence Against Women. 1993. *Changing the Landscape: Ending Violence: Achieving Equality.* Ottawa: Minister of Supply and Services Canada.

Carter, S. 1999. *Aboriginal People and Colonizers of Western Canada to 1900.* Toronto: University of Toronto Press.

Castagna, C. 2005. "Shooter Métis, Lawyer Notes." *Winnipeg Sun*, February 4.

CBC News. 2008a. "Winnipeg Police Apologize to Rapper for Gunpoint Pullover." At <cbc.ca/news/arts/music/story/2008/06/07/winnipeg-rapper-apology.

html> June 7.

____. 2008b. "Inquest Begins into Police Shooting of Winnipeg Teen." At <cbc. ca/canada/manitoba/story/2008/06/09/dumas-inquest.html> June 9.

____. 2008c. "'I Did Not Want to Pull the Trigger': Officer at Dumas Inquest." At <cbc.ca/canada/manitoba/story/2008/06/13/dumas.html> June 13.

____. 2008d. "'Nobody Deserves to Die that Way,' Dad Says of Teen Hit with Taster." At <cbc.ca/news/canada/manitoba/story/2008/07/25/langan-father.html> July 25.

____. 2008e. "Winnipeg Police Shooting Angers First Nation." At <cbc.ca/canada/manitoba/story/2008/08/04/police-shooting.html> August 4.

____. 2008f. "Knife Seized at Scene of Shooting Death, Police Chief Says." At <cbc. ca/canada/manitoba/story/2008/08/05/simcoe-shooting.html> August 5.

____. 2007. "No Jail Time for Ex-Cop who Killed Woman in Car Crash." At <cbc. ca/news/canada/manitoba/story/2007/10/29/harveymordenzenk.html> October 29.

____. 2004. "Saskatoon Fires Police Officers in Stonechild Case." At <cbc.ca/ news/canada/story/2004/11/12/stonechild041112.html> November 12.

CCPA-MB (Canadian Centre for Policy Alternatives–Manitoba). 2007. *Step by Step: Stories of Change in Winnipeg's Inner City.* At <policyalternatives.ca/ sites/default/files/uploads/publications/Manitoba_Pubs/2007/State_of_ the_Inner_City2007.pdf>.

Chaco, J., and S. Nanco (eds.). 1993. *Community Policing in Canada.* Toronto: Canadian Scholars' Press.

Chan, J. 1996. "Changing Police Culture." *British Journal of Criminology* 36 (1).

Chan, W., and K. Mirchandani. 2002. "From Race and Crime to Racialization and Criminalization." In W. Chan and K. Mirchandani (eds.), *Crimes of Colour: Racialization and the Criminal Justice System in Canada.* Peterborough: Broadview Press.

Chettleburgh, M.C. 2007. *Young Thugs: Inside the Dangerous World of Canadian Street Gangs.* Toronto: Harper Collins.

Cheung, L. 2005. *Racial Status and Employment Outcomes.* Research Paper #34. Ottawa: Canadian Labour Congress.

Clairmont, D. 1991. "Community-Based Policing: Implementation and Impact." *Canadian Journal of Criminology* 33 (July–October).

Closs, W.J., and P.F. McKenna. 2006. "Profiling a Problem in Canadian Police Leadership: The Kingston Police Data Collection Project." *Canadian Public Administration* 49 (2).

Collin, C., and H. Jensen. 2009. *A Statistical Profile of Poverty in Canada.* Ottawa: Library of Parliament. At <parl.gc.ca/Content/LOP/ResearchPublications/ prb0917-e.htm#a9>.

Comack, E. 2008. *Out There/In Here: Masculinity, Violence, and Prisoning.* Halifax: Fernwood Publishing.

_____. 1996. *Women in Trouble: Connecting Women's Law Violations to Their Histories of Abuse.* Halifax: Fernwood Publishing.

_____. 1986. "'We Will Get Some Good Out of This Riot Yet': The Canadian State, Drug Legislation and Class Conflict." In S. Brickey and E. Comack (eds.), *The Social Basis of Law.* Toronto: Garamond Press.

Comack, E., and G. Balfour. 2004. *The Power to Criminalize: Violence, Inequality and the Law.* Halifax and Winnipeg: Fernwood Publishing.

Comack, E., and E. Bowness. 2010. "Dealing the Race Card: Public Discourse on the Policing of Winnipeg's Inner-city Communities." *Canadian Journal of Urban Research* 19 (1).

Comack, E., L. Deane, L. Morrissette, and J. Silver. 2009. "If You Want to Change Violence in the 'Hood You Have to Change the 'Hood: Violence and Street Gangs in Winnipeg's Inner City. A Report Presented to Honourable Dave Chomiak, Manitoba Minister of Justice and Attorney General, September 10." Winnipeg: CCPA-MB.

Comack, E., and M. Seshia. 2010. "Bad Dates and Street Hassles: Violence in the Winnipeg Street Sex Trade." *Canadian Journal of Criminology and Criminal Justice* 52 (2).

Comack, E., and J Silver. 2008. "A Canadian Exception to the Punitive Turn? Community Reponses to Policing Practices in Winnipeg's Inner City." *Canadian Journal of Sociology* 33 (4).

_____. 2006. *Safety and Security in Winnipeg's Inner-City Communities: Bridging the Community-Police Divide.* Winnipeg: CCPA-MB.

Commission on First Nations and Métis Peoples and Justice Reform. 2004. *Legacy of Hope: An Agenda for Change.* Volume 1. At <justicereformcomm.sk.ca>.

Commission on Systemic Racism in the Ontario Criminal Justice System. 1998. "Racism in Justice: Perceptions." In V. Satzewich (ed.), *Racism and Social Inequality in Canada: Concepts, Controversies and Strategies of Resistance.* Toronto: Thompson Educational Publishing.

Coolican, L. 2002. "Inquest in Hands of Jury: Jurrors Must Weigh Conflicting testimony of Wegner's Final Hours." *Saskatoon StarPhoenix.* At <injusticebusters. com/index.htm/Wegner.htm> February 13.

_____. 2001a. "Naistus Last Seen on Street with Beer: Native Man Wandering with Open Liquor 'Prime Target' for Police Pickup, Family's Lawyer Says." *Saskatoon StarPhoenix,* November 2.

_____. 2001b. "Inquest Upsets Family: 'No Answers That Would Close the Wounds': Uncle." *Leader Post* (November 5): A1.

Craig, T. 1991. "Family Suspects Foul Play." *Saskatoon StarPhoenix,* March 4.

CTV News. 2005. "Blacks Stopped More Often by Police, Study Finds." At <ctv. ca/CTVNews/CanadaAM/20050526/kingston_policereport_050526/> May 26.

CTV Winnipeg. 2011. "Police Helicopter Used More Than 50 times During

First Week." At <winnipeg.ctv.ca/servlet/an/plocal/CTVNews/20110210/ wpg_helicopter_110210/20110210/?hub=WinnipegHome> February 10.

Curtis, K.M. 2008. *The Fatality Inquiries Act*. Report by Provincial Judge on Inquest Respecting the Death of Matthew Adam Joseph Dumas. Winnipeg: The Provincial Court of Manitoba. At <manitobacourts.mb.ca/pdf/dumas_inquest_report.pdf> December 9.

Das Gupta, T. 2009. *Real Nurses and Others: Racism in Nursing*. Winnipeg and Halifax: Fernwood Publishing.

Dauvergne, M., and J. Turner. 2010. "Police-Reported Crime Statistics in Canada, 2009." *Juristat* 30 (2).

Davies, W.H. (Commissioner). 2008. *Alone and Cold: The Davies Commission Inquiry into the Death of Frank Paul*. Interim Report (February 12). Vancouver, British Columbia. At <frankpaulinquiry.ca/report/>.

Davis, A. 2000. *The Prison Industrial Complex and Its Impact on Communities of Color*. Videocassette. Madison: University of Wisconsin.

Deane, L. 2006. *Under One Roof: Community Economic Development and Housing in the Inner City*. Halifax: Fernwood Publishing.

Deane, L., D. Bracken, and L. Morrissette. 2007. "Desistance within an Urban Aboriginal Gang." *Probation Journal* 54.

Dei, G. 2009. "Speaking Race: Silence, Salience, and the Politics of Anti-Racist Scholarship." In M. Wallis and A. Fleras (eds.), *The Politics of Race in Canada*. Toronto: Oxford University Press.

DIAND (Department of Indian Affairs and Northern Development). 2003. *Backgrounder: The Residential School System*. Ottawa: Indian and Northern Affairs Canada. At <ainc-inac.gc.ca/gs/schl_e.html>.

Dickie, D.J., and H. Palk. 1957. *Pages from Canada's Story*. Toronto: J.M. Dent and Sons.

Dion, S. 2005. "Aboriginal People and Stories of Canadian History: Investigating Barriers to Transforming Relationships." In C. James (ed.), *Possibilities and Limitations: Multicultural Policies and Programs in Canada*. Halifax, NS: Fernwood Publishing.

Dumaine, F., and R. Linden. 2005. "Future Directions in Community Policing: Evaluation of the Ottawa Police Service Community Police Centres." *The Canadian Review of Policing Research* 1. At <crpr.icaap.org/index.php/crpr/article/view/43/49>.

Dyer, R. 1997. *White*. London: Routledge.

Elliot, J.E., and A. Fleras. 1996. *Unequal Relations: An Introduction to Race and Ethnic and Aboriginal Dynamics in Canada* (second edition). Toronto: Oxford University Press.

Ennab, F. 2010. "Rupturing the Myth of the Peaceful Western Canadian Frontier: A Socio-historical Study of Colonization, Violence, and the North West Mounted Police, 1873–1905." Master's Thesis, Department of Sociology,

University of Manitoba. At <mspace.lib.umanitoba.ca/handle/1993/4109>.

Ericson, R. 1982. *Reproducing Order: A Study of Police Patrol Work*. Toronto: University of Toronto Press.

Essed, P. 2002. "Everyday Racism: A New Approach to the Study of Racism." In P. Essed and D. T. Goldberg (eds.), *Race Critical Theories*. Oxford: Blackwell Publishers.

Fielding, N. 2005. "Concepts and Theory in Community Policing." *The Howard Journal* 44, 5.

_____. 1995. *Community Policing*. Oxford: Clarendon Press.

Fitzgerald, R., M. Wisener, and J. Savoie. 2004. *Neighbourhood Characteristics and Distribution of Crime in Winnipeg*. Ottawa: Canadian Centre for Justice Statistics. Catalogue no. 85-561-MIE.

Fontaine, N. 2006. "Surviving Colonization: Annishinaabe Ikwe Gang Participation." In G. Balfour and E. Comack (eds.), *Criminalizing Women: Gender and (In)justice in Neo-liberal Times*. Halifax: Fernwood Publishing.

Fridell, L., R. Lunney, D. Diamond, and B. Kobu. 2001. *Racially Biased Policing: A Principled Response*. Washington, DC: Police Executive Research Forum.

Gabor, T. 2004. "Inflammatory Rhetoric on Racial Profiling Can Undermine Police Services." *Canadian Journal of Criminology and Criminal Justice* 46 (4).

Galabuzi, G.E. 2009. "Social Exclusion." In D. Raphael (ed.), *Social Determinants of Health: Canadian Perspectives* (second edition). Toronto: Canadian Scholars' Press

Garland, D. 2000. "The Culture of High Crime Societies: Some Preconditions of Recent 'Law and Order' Policies." *The British Journal of Criminology* 40.

Gibbins, R., and R. Ponting. 1986. "Historical Background and Overview." In R. Ponting (ed.), *Arduous Journey*. Toronto: McLelland and Stewart.

Gillmor, D. 1988. "The Shooting of J.J. Harper." *Saturday Night* (December).

Gilroy, P. 1991. *There Ain't No Black in the Union Jack: The Cultural Politics of Race and Nation*. Chicago: University of Chicago Press.

Gold, A. 2003. "Media Hype, Racial Profiling, and Good Science." *Canadian Journal of Criminology and Criminal Justice* 45 (3).

Grabosky, P.N. 1999. "Zero Tolerance Policing." *Trends and Issues in Crime and Criminal Justice*. Canberra: Australian Institute of Criminology (January).

Gray, J. 2004. "Officers Make Racist Remarks on Tape." *Globe and Mail*, January 21.

Graydon, J. 2008. "Canadian Aboriginal Reserves in Crisis: Long-term Solutions Are Needed to Stop the Cycle of Poverty." At <suite101.com/content/canadian-reserves-in-crisis-a78339>.

Green, Joyce. 2006. "From *Stonechild* to Social Cohesion: Anti-Racist Challenges for Saskatchewan." *Canadian Journal of Political Science* 39 (3).

Greene, Jack. 2000. "Community Policing in America: Changing the Nature, Structure, and Function of the Police." *Criminal Justice* 3.

Greene, Judith. 1999. "Zero Tolerance: A Case Study of Police Policies and

Practices in New York City." *Crime and Delinquency* 45 (2).

Hall, S. 1997. "The Spectacle of the 'Other.'" In S. Hall (ed.), *Representation: Cultural Representations and Signifying Practices*. Milton Keynes: Open University.

____. 1978. "Racism and Reaction." In *Five Views of Multi-Racial Britain*. London: Commission for Racial Equality.

Hall, S., C. Critcher, T. Jefferson, J. Clarke, and B. Roberts. 1978. *Policing the Crisis: Mugging, the State and Law and Order*. London: MacMillan.

Halyk, S. 2004. *Submission of the Federation of Saskatchewan Indian Nations to the Commission of Inquiry into the Death of Neil Stonechild*. Saskatoon, Saskatchewan. At <justice.gov.sk.ca/stonechild/finalsubs/FSIN-finalsub.pdf>.

Hamilton, A.C., and C.M. Sinclair (Commissioners). 1991a. *Report of the Aboriginal Justice Inquiry of Manitoba. Volume 1. The Justice System and Aboriginal People*. Winnipeg: Queen's Printer.

____. 1991b. *Report of the Aboriginal Justice Inquiry of Manitoba. Volume 2. The Deaths of Helen Betty Osborne and John Joseph Harper*. Winnipeg: Queen's Printer.

Harris, D. 2002. *Profiles in Injustice: Why Racial Profiling Cannot Work*. New York: New Press.

Harvey, E. 2003. *An Independent Review of the Toronto Star Analysis of Criminal Information processing System (CIPS) Data Provided by the Toronto Police Service (TPS)*. At <torontopolice.on.ca/publications/files/reports/harveyreport.pdf>.

Henry, F. 1994. *The Caribbean Diaspora in Toronto: Learning to Live with Racism*. Toronto: University of Toronto Press.

Henry, F., and C. Tator. 2006. *The Color of Democracy: Racism in Canadian Society*. Toronto: Thomas-Nelson.

____. 2002. *Discourses of Domination: Racial bias in the Canadian English-Language Press*. Toronto: University of Toronto Press.

____. 2000. Racist Discourse in Canada's English Print Media. Toronto: Canadian Race Relations Foundation.

Henry, F., C. Tator, W. Mattis, and T. Rees. 2009. "The Ideology of Racism." In M. Wallis and A. Feras (eds.), *The Politics of Race in Canada*. Toronto: Oxford University Press.

Herbert, S. 2001. "Policing the Contemporary City: Fixing Broken Windows or Shoring up Neo-liberalism?" *Theoretical Criminology* 5 (4).

Hoffman, M.A. 2011. "Canada's National Use-of-Force Framework for Police Officers." *The Police Chief* (April). At <policechiefmagazine.org/magazine/index.cfm?fuseaction=display_arch&article_id=1397&issue_id=102004>.

Holdaway, S. 2003. "Police Relations in England and Wales: Theory, Policy, and Practice." *Police and Society* 7 (1).

____. 1997. "Some Recent Approaches to the Study of Race in Criminological Research." *British Journal of Criminology* 37 (3).

Hopkins-Burke, R. 1998. "The Socio-political Context of Zero Tolerance Policing Strategies." *Policing: An International Journal of Police Strategies and Management* 21 (4).

Hubbard, T. 2004. *Two Worlds Colliding*. National Film Board of Canada

Huey, L. 2007. *Negotiating Demands: The Politics of Skid Row Policing in Edinburgh, San Francisco, and Vancouver*. Toronto: University of Toronto Press.

Hutchinson, B. 2000. "Frozen Ghosts." *Saturday Night* (August).

Innes, M. 1999. "'An Iron Fist in an Iron Glove?' The Zero Tolerance Policing Debate." *The Howard Journal* 38 (4).

Jackson, M. 1989. "Locking up Natives in Canada." *University of British Columbia Law Review* 23.

Jakubowski, L. 2006. "'Managing' Canadian Immigration: Racism, Ethnic Selectivity, and the Law." In E. Comack (ed.), *Locating Law: Race, Class, Gender, Sexuality Connections* (second edition). Halifax: Fernwood Publishing.

James, C.E. 2008. "'Armed and Dangerous'/'Known to Police': Racializing Suspects. In C. Brooks and B. Schissel (eds.), *Marginality and Condemnation: An Introduction to Criminology* (second edition). Halifax and Winnipeg: Fernwood Publishing.

____. 1998. "'Up to No Good': Blacks on the Streets and Encountering Police." In V. Satzewich (ed.), *Racism & Social Inequality in Canada: Concepts, Controversies & Strategies of Resistance*. Toronto: Thompson Educational Publishing.

Johnson, A. 2005. "Privilege as Paradox." In P. Rothenberg (ed.), *White Privilege: Essential Readings on the Other Side of Racism*. New York: Worth Publishers.

Johnson, H. 1996. *Dangerous Domains*. Toronto: Nelson.

Jones, T., and T. Newburn. 2002. "Learning from Uncle Sam? Exploring U.S. Influences on British Crime Control Policy." *Governance: An International Journal of Policy, Administration, and Institutions* 15 (1).

Justice as Healing. 1998. "Sentencing Circle: A General Overview and Guidelines." Native Law Centre 3 (3). At <usask.ca/nativelaw/publications/jah/1998/Sent_Circle_Guidelines.pdf>.

Katz, S. 2007. "CrimeStat Website Launched." At <http://www.winnipeg.ca/police/press/2007/02feb/2007_02_02.stm> February 2.

____. 2006. "We Can Slash the Crime Rate." *Winnipeg Sun*, May 28.

Kazemipur, A., and S.S. Halli. 2000. *The New Poverty in Canada: Ethnic Groups and Ghetto Neighbourhoods*. Toronto: Thompson.

Kelling, G. 1974. *The Kansas City Preventive Patrol Experiment*. Washington, DC: Police Foundation.

Kerstetter, S. 2002. "Top 50% of Canadians Hold 94.4% of Wealth, Bottom Half 5.6%." *The CCPA Monitor* 9 (6).

King, T. 2003. *The Truth about Stories: A Native Narrative*. Toronto: House of

Anansi Press.

King, W.R., and T.M. Dunn. 2004. "Dumping: Police-initiated Transjurisdictional Transport of Troublesome Persons." *Police Quarterly* 7 (3).

Knockwood, I. 2001. *Out of the Depths: The Experiences of Mi'kmaw Children at the Indian Residential School at Shubenacadie, Nova Scotia* (third edition). Halifax: Rosewood.

Kossick, D. 2000. "Death by Cold." *Canadian Dimension* 34 (4).

Kretzmann, J.P., and J.L. McKnight. 1993. *Building Communities from the Inside Out: A Path toward Finding and Mobilizing a Community's Assets.* Evanston, IL: The Asset Based Community Development Institute, Institute for Policy Research.

La Prairie, C. 2002. Aboriginal Over-Representation in the Criminal Justice System: A Tale of Nine Cities." *Canadian Journal of Criminology* 44 (2).

____. 1994. *Seen But Not Heard: Native People in the Inner City.* Ottawa: Aboriginal Justice Directorate, Minister of Justice and Attorney General of Canada.

Lambert, S. 2005. "Winnipeg Shooting Heightens Tensions." *Winnipeg Free Press*, February 8.

Langton, J. 2007. "The Dark Lure of 'Pain Compliance.'" *Toronto Star*. At <thestar.com/printarticle/281499> December 1.

Larner, W. 2000. "Neo-Liberalism: Policy, Ideology, Governmentality." *Studies in Political Economy* 63 (Autumn).

Larocque, E. 2000. "Violence in Aboriginal Communities." In K. McKenna and J. Larkin (eds.), *Violence Against Women: New Canadian Perspectives*. Toronto: Inanna.

Latimer, J., and L.C. Foss. 2004. *A One-Day Snapshot of Aboriginal Youth in Custody Across Canada: Phase II*. Ottawa: Department of Justice Canada. At <justice.gc.ca/eng/pi/rs/rep-rap/2004/yj2-jj2/yj2.pdf>.

Leighton, B. 1994. "Community Policing in Canada: An Overview of Experience and Evaluations." In D. Rosenbaum (ed.), *The Challenge of Community Policing: Testing the Promises.* Thompson Oaks, CA: Sage Publications.

LERA (Law Enforcement Review Agency). n.d. *Annual Report 2010.* Winnipeg: Manitoba Justice. At <gov.mb.ca/justice/lera/annual_report/pdf/2010/2010-annual_report.pdf>.

Lezubski, D., J. Silver, and E. Black. 2000. "High and Rising: The Growth of Poverty in Winnipeg." In J. Silver (ed.), *Solutions that Work: Fighting Poverty in Winnipeg.* Halifax: Fernwood Publishing.

Linden, The Honourable S. (Commissioner). 2007. *Report of the Ipperwash Inquiry.* Toronto. At <attorneygeneral.jus.gov.on.ca/inquiries/ipperwash/report/index.html>.

Linden, R. 2000. *Criminology: A Canadian Perspective* (fourth edition). Toronto: Harcourt Brace.

Linden, R., D. Clairmont, and C. Murphy. 2000. "Aboriginal Policing in Manitoba: A Report to the Aboriginal Justice Implementation Commission." Winnipeg:

Manitoba Justice. At <ajic.mb.ca/consult.html>.

Linder, D. 2001. "The Trials of Los Angeles Police Officers in Connection with the Beating of Rodney King." At <law2.umkc.edu/faculty/projects/ftrials/lapd/lapdaccount.html>.

Loxley, J. 2010. *Aboriginal, Northern, and Community Economic Development: Papers and Retrospectives.* Winnipeg: Arbeiter Ring.

Lugosi, N. 2011. "'Truth-Telling' and Legal Discourse: A Critical Analysis of the Neil Stonechild Inquiry." *Canadian Journal of Political Science* 44, 2.

Lynch, T. 2000. "'We Own the Night' Amadou Diallo's Deadly Encounter with New York City's Street Crimes Unit." CATO *Institute Briefing Papers* No. 56. Washington, DC: CATO Institute March 31.

MacAlister, D. 2010. *Police-Involved Deaths: The Failure of Self-Investigation. Final Report.* Vancouver: British Columbia Civil Liberties Association. At <bccla.org/othercontent/Police_involved_deaths.pdf>.

MacKinnon, S. 2009. "Tracking Poverty in Winnipeg's Inner City: 1996–2006." *State of the Inner City Report 2009.* Winnipeg: CCPA-MB.

Makin, K. 2003. "Police Use Racial Profiling, Appeal Court Concludes." *Globe and Mail*, April 17.

Mannette, J. 1992. *Elusive Justice: Beyond the Marshall Inquiry.* Halifax: Fernwood Publishing.

Manning, P. 1989. "Occupational Culture." In W.G. Bailey (ed.), *The Encyclopedia of Police Science.* New York: Garland.

Marin, A. 2008. *Oversight Unseen: Investigation into the Special Investigation Unit's Operational Effectiveness and Credibility.* Toronto: Ombudsman Ontario. At <ombudsman.on.ca/Ombudsman/files/8a/8acb8114-b212-42b5-8221-3d5e4e95a3f1.pdf>.

Marshall, R. 2008. "If It Was Racist, It Would Be Known." *Winnipeg Free Press*, December 14.

McCalla, A., and V. Satzewich. 2002. "Settler Capitalism and the Construction of Immigrants and "Indians" as Racialized Others." In W. Chan and K. Mirchandani (eds.), *Crimes of Colour: Racialization and the Criminal Justice System in Canada.* Peterborough: Broadview Press.

McEvoy, M., and J. Daniluk. 1995. "Wounds to the Soul: The Experiences of Aboriginal Women as Survivors of Sexual Abuse." *Canadian Psychology* 36.

McIvor, S., and T. Nahanee. 1998. "Aboriginal Women: Invisible Victims of Violence." In K. Bonnycastle and G. Rigakos (eds.), *Unsettling Truths: Battered Women, Policy, Politics, and Contemporary Research in Canada.* Vancouver: Collective Press.

McLean, C. 2006. *When Police Become Prey: What Lies Behind Starlight Tours.* Silver Harvest Productions.

McLeod, H. 2004. "A Glimpse at Aboriginal-Based Street Gangs." A Report for the Royal Canadian Mounted Police "D" Division, Winnipeg, Manitoba for the National Aboriginal Policing Forum held in Ottawa, Ontario. Hosted by Pacific Business and Law Institute, September 22 and 23.

McLeod, J. 2000. *Beginning Postcolonialism*. New York: Palgrave.

McNairn, K. 2004. "Retracing Rodney Naistus's Footsteps Up to the Day He Died." At <injusticebusters.com/04/Naistus_Rodney.shtml>.

____. 2000. "Natives Step Forward to Challenge Authorities." *Saskatoon StarPhoenix*, March 10.

Melchers, R. 2003. "Do Toronto Police Engage in Racial Profiling?" *Canadian Journal of Criminology and Criminal Justice* 45 (3).

Mendelson, M. 2004. *Aboriginal People in Canada's Labour Market: Work and Unemployment, Today and Tomorrow*. Ottawa: Caledon Institute of Social Policy.

Miles, R. 2000. "Apropos the Idea of 'Race'... Again." In L. Black and J. Solomos (eds.), *Theories of Race and Racism*. London: Routledge.

____. 1993. *Racism after 'Race Relations.'* London: Routledge.

____. 1989. *Racism*. Milton Keynes: Open University Press.

Miles, R., and R. Torres. 2007. "Does 'Race' Matter? Transatlantic Perspectives on Racism after 'Race Relations.'" In T. Das Gupta, C.E. James, R. Maaka, G-E. Galabuzi, and C. Andersen (eds.), *Race and Racialization: Essential Readings*. Toronto: Canadian Scholars Press.

Milloy, J. 1999. *A National Crime: The Canadian Government and the Residential School System, 1879 to 1986*. Winnipeg: University of Manitoba Press.

Monture, P. 2007. "Racing and Erasing: Law and Gender in White Settler Societies." In S. Hier and S. Bolaria (eds.), *Race & Racism in 21st-Century Canada*. Peterborough: Broadview Press.

Monture-Angus, P. 1995. *Thunder in My Soul: A Mohawk Woman Speaks*. Halifax: Fernwood Publishing.

Morash, M., and J.K. Ford (eds.). 2002. *The Move to Community Policing: Making Change Happen*. Thousand Oaks, CA: Sage Publications.

Morrow, A. 2011. "What Price for Law and Order?" *Globe and Mail*, January 8.

Mosher, C.J. 1998. *Discrimination and Denial: Systemic Racism in Ontario's Legal and Criminal Justice Systems, 1892–1961*. Toronto: University of Toronto Press.

Moyer, S. 1992. "Race, Gender and Homicide: Comparisons between Aboriginals and Other Canadians." *Canadian Journal of Criminology* 34.

Murphy, C. 1993. "The Development, Impact and Implications of Community Policing in Canada." In J. Chacko and S. Nancoo (eds.), *Community Policing in Canada*. Toronto: Canadian Scholar's Press.

National Collaborating Centre for Aboriginal Health [NCCAH]. 2009–2010. *Poverty as a Social Determinant of First Nations, Inuit, and Métis Health*. At nccah-<ccnsa.ca/docs/fact%20sheets/social%20determinates/NCCAH_ fs_poverty_EN.pdf>.

Nettelbeck, A., and R. Smandych. 2010. "Policing Indigenous Peoples on Two

Colonial Frontiers: Australia's Mounted Police and Canada's North-West Mounted Police." *The Australian and New Zealand Journal of Criminology* 43 (2).

Newburn, T. 2002. "Atlantic Crossings: 'Policy Transfer' and Crime Control in the USA and Britain." *Punishment and Society* 4 (2).

Nickel, R. 2005. "Justice Rejects Call to Reopen Night Case MP Wanted Second Look into Case Against Ex-Cops." *Saskatoon StarPhoenix*. At <injusticebusters. com/05/Night_Darrell.shtml> January 29.

Noël, A. 2009. "Aboriginal Peoples and Poverty in Canada: Can Provincial Governments Make a Difference?" Paper presented at the Annual Meeting of the International Sociological Association's Research Committee 19, Montreal, August 20. At <cccg.umontreal.ca/RC19/PDF/Noel-A_ Rc192009.pdf>.

Nova Scotia. 1989. *Royal Commission on the Donald Marshall, Jr., Prosecution: Digest of Findings and Recommendations.* (Chief Justice T. Alexander Hickman, Chairman). At <gov.ns.ca/just/marshall_inquiry/_docs/ Royal%20Commission%20on%20the%20Donald%20Marshall%20Jr%20 Prosecution_findings.pdf>.

OHRC (Ontario Human Rights Commission). 2003. *Paying the Price: The Human Cost of Racial Profiling.* Inquiry Report. Toronto: Ontario Human Rights Commission.

Omni, M., and H. Winant. 1994. *Racial Formation in the United States.* New York: Routledge.

____. 1993. "On the Theoretical Status of the Concept of Race." In C. McCarthy and W. Crichlow (eds), *Race, Identity and Representation in Education.* London: Routledge.

Ontario. 1995. *Report of the Commission on Systemic Racism in the Ontario Criminal Justice System.* (Margaret Gittens and David Cole, Co-Chairs). Toronto: Queen's Printer.

____. 1992. *Report of the Advisor on Race Relations to the Premier of Ontario* (Advisor: Hon. S. Lewis). Toronto: Advisor on Race Relations.

____. 1989. *The Report of the Race Relations and Policing Task Force* (Clare Lewis, Chair). Toronto: Task Force on Race Relations and Policing.

Ontario Native Women's Association. 1989. *Breaking Free: A Proposal for Change to Aboriginal Family Violence.* Thunder Bay, Ontario.

Owen, B. 2011. "Police Inspector Changes His Hat." *Winnipeg Free Press,* August 13.

____. 2009. "Police Act Tears Down 'Blue Wall.'" *Winnipeg Free Press,* April 15.

____. 2005. "'In-Your-Face' Blitz Unveiled." *Winnipeg Free Press,* October 26.

Paoline, E.A. 2003. "Taking Stock: Toward a Richer Understanding of Police Culture." *Journal of Criminal Justice* 31.

Parker, J. 2003. "Police Union Draws Mayor's Ire: 'Come Clean' with Complaints, Maddin Says." *Saskatoon StarPhoenix,* June 9.

Perreault, S. 2011. "Violent Victimization of Aboriginal People in the Canadian Provinces, 2009." *Juristat* (March).

____. 2009. "The Incarceration of Aboriginal People in Adult Correctional Services." *Juristat* 29 (3).

Perreaux, L. 2000. "Decade-Old Death Resurfaces." *Saskatoon StarPhoenix*, February 22.

Pettipas, K. 1995. *Severing the Ties that Bind: Government Repression of Indigenous Religious Ceremonies on the Prairies.* Winnipeg: University of Manitoba Press.

Piche, J. 2011. "Tracking the Politics of 'Crime' and Punishment in Canada." At <tpcp-canada.blogspot.com/2011/06/what-austerity-and-small-government.html>.

Ponting, J.R. 1998. "Racism and Stereotyping of First Nations." In V. Satzewich (ed.), *Racism and Social Inequality in Canada: Concepts, Controversies and Strategies of Resistance.* Toronto: Thompson Educational Publishing.

Pratt, J. 1999. "Governmentality, Neo-Liberalism and Dangerousness." In R. Smandych (ed.), *Governable Places: Readings on Governmentality and Crime Control.* Brookfield, VT: Ashgate.

Rankin, J. 2010a. "Race Matters: Blacks Documented by Police at High Rate." *Toronto Star.* At <thestar.com/printarticle/761343> February 6.

____. 2010b. "Story Behind the Numbers." *Toronto Star.* At <thestar.com/printarticle/761069> February 6.

____. 2010c. "Police Ponder How Best to Collect Race Data." *Toronto Star.* At <thestar.com/printarticle/765605> February 15.

Rankin, J., J. Quinn, M. Shephard, J. Duncanson, and S. Simmie. 2002a. "Singled Out" *Toronto Star*, October 19.

____. 2002b. "Police Target Black Drivers." *Toronto Star*, October 20.

Rankin, J., J. Duncanson, J. Quinn, M. Shephard, and S. Simmie. 2002c. "Black Arrest Rates Highest." *Toronto Star*, October 26.

Rankin, J., J. Quinn, M. Shephard, S. Simmie, and J. Duncanson. 2002d. "Life and Death on Mean Streets. *Toronto Star*, October 27.

Razack, S. 2007. "When Place Becomes Race." In T. Das Gupta, C. E. James, R. Maaka, G-E. Galabuzi and C. Andersen (eds.), *Race and Racialization: Essential Readings.* Toronto: Canadian Scholars' Press.

____ (ed.). 2002. *Race, Space and the Law: Unmapping the White Settler Society.* Toronto: Between the Lines.

____. 2000. "Gendered Racialized Violence and Spatialized Justice: The Murder of Pamela George." *Canadian Journal of Law and Society* 15 (2).

RCAP (Royal Commission on Aboriginal Peoples). 1996. *Report of the Royal Commission on Aboriginal Peoples.* Ottawa: Indian and Northern Affairs Canada. At <ainc-inac.gc.ca/ch/rcap/sg/sgmm_e.html>.

Reber, S., and R. Renaud. 2005. *Starlight Tour: The Last, Lonely Night of Neil Stonechild.* Toronto: Random House Canada.

Reiman, J., and P. Leighton. 2010. *The Rich Get Richer and the Poor Get Prison: Ideology, Class and Criminal Justice* (ninth edition). Toronto: Pearson.

Reiner, R. 1992. *The Politics of the Police* (second edition). London: Harvester Wheatsheaf.

Ritzer, G. 2004. *The McDonaldization of Society.* Thousand Oaks, CA: Pine Forge.

Roberts, D. 2000. "The Saskatoon Police and the Frozen Bodies: Officers Suspended After Deaths of Native Men." *Globe and Mail.* At <injusticebusters.com/index.htm/cops2.htm> February 17.

Rose, N. 1996. "Governing Advanced Liberal Democracies." *British Journal of Criminology* 40.

Rosenbaum, D. (ed.) 1994. *The Challenge of Community Policing: Testing the Promises.* London: Sage.

Salhany, The Honourable R. (Commissioner). 2008. *Report of the Taman Inquiry.* Manitoba: Taman Inquiry into the Investigation and Prosecution of Derek Harvey-Zenk. At <tamaninquiry.ca/pdf/taman_inquiry_A.pdf>.

Sanders, J. 2006. "Sightless Eyes: Recent Events Show the City's Leaders Lack the Vision to Fix It." *Uptown Magazine,* May 18.

Sangster, J. 2001. *Regulating Girls and Women: Sexuality, Family and the Law in Ontario, 1920–1960.* Toronto: Oxford University Press.

Sapers, H. 2007. *Annual Report of the Office of the Correctional Investigator 2006–2007.* Ottawa: Minister of Public Works and Government Services Canada. At <oci-bec.gc.ca/rpt/pdf/annrpt/annrpt20062007-eng.pdf>.

Saunders, C. 2008a. "Dumas Witness Feared for his Life." *Winnipeg Free Press,* June 11.

____. 2008b. "Dumas Set on Escape: Officer." *Winnipeg Free Press,* June 13.

Schnoor, J. 2009. "Written Submission of the Government of Manitoba—Funding Request Made on Behalf of the Estate and Family of Brian Lloyd Sinclair." Provincial Court of Manitoba in the Matter of: The Inquest into the Death of Brian Lloyd Sinclair. At <eponymedia.com/ignoredtodeathmanitoba.ca/Chartrand%20Report%20Document%20Record%20-%20FINAL.pdf> November 16.

Seshia, M. 2005. *The Unheard Speak Out.* Winnipeg: CCPA-MB.

Sewell, J. 2010. *Police in Canada: The Real Story.* Toronto: James Lorimer.

Shearing, C., and R. Ericson. 1991. "Culture as Figurative Action." *British Journal of Sociology* 42 (4).

Sherman, L. 1974. "The Sociology of the Social Reform of the American Police: 1950–73." *Journal of Police Science and Administration* 2.

Silver, J. 2010. "Segregated City: A Century of Poverty in Winnipeg." In P. Thomas and C. Brown (eds.), *Manitoba Politics and Government.* Winnipeg: University of Manitoba Press.

____. 2006a. Building a Path to a Better Future: Urban Aboriginal People." In J. Silver (ed.), *In Their Own Voices: Building Urban Aboriginal Communities.*

Halifax and Winnipeg: Fernwood Publishing.

____. 2006b. *North End Winnipeg's Lord Selkirk Park Housing Development: History, Comparative Context, Prospects*. Winnipeg: CCPA-MB (June).

____ (ed.). 2006c. *In Their Own Voices: Building Urban Aboriginal Communities*. Halifax and Winnipeg: Fernwood Publishing.

Silver, J., P. Ghorayshi, J. Hay, and D. Klyne. 2006. "Sharing, Community and Decolonization." In J. Silver (ed.), *In Their Own Voices: Building Urban Aboriginal Communities*. Halifax and Winnipeg: Fernwood Publishing.

Simpson, S. 2010. "Black in Kingston: Youth Perspectives on 'Blackness' and Belonging in a Small Ontario City." Master of Education thesis, Queen's University, Kingston, Ontario. At <catspaw.its.queensu.ca/jspui/bitstream/1974/6259/1/Simpson_Stephanie_C_201012_MEd.pdf>.

Sinclair, G. 1999. *Cowboys and Indians: The Shooting of J.J. Harper*. Toronto: McClelland and Stewart.

Skelton, I., C. Selig, and L. Deane. 2007. "CED and Social Housing Initiatives in Inner-City Winnipeg." In J. Loxley, J. Silver and K. Sexsmith (eds.), *Doing Community Economic Development*. Halifax and Winnipeg: Fernwood Publishing.

Skolnick, J. 1975. *Justice without Trial: Law Enforcement in a Democratic Society* (second edition). New York: John Wiley.

Smith, C. 2007. *Conflict, Crisis, and Accountability: Racial Profiling and Law Enforcement in Canada*. Ottawa: Canadian Centre for Policy Alternatives.

Smith, G. 2004. "The Death of Neil Stonechild: Judge Rejects Police Version of Events One Cold Night in Saskatoon but No Charges are Planned." *Globe and Mail*, October 27.

Smylie, J. 2009. "The Health of Aboriginal Peoples." In D. Raphael (ed.), *Social Determinants of Health* (second edition). Toronto: Canadian Scholars' Press.

Snider, L. 2006. "The Disappearance of Corporate Crime." In E. Comack (ed.), *Locating Law: Class.Race/Gender/Sexuality Connections*. Halifax and Winnipeg: Fernwood Publishing.

____. 1998. "Towards Safer Societies." *The British Journal of Criminology* 38, 1 (Winter).

Solomos, J. 1988. *Black Youth, Racism and the State: The Politics of Ideology and Policy*. Cambridge: Cambridge University Press.

South Wind. 2007. "Matthew Dumas Family Launches Civil Suit against Winnipeg Police." Winnipeg: Southern Chiefs' Organization.

____. 2005. "Family of Matthew Dumas Outraged at the Findings of the Winnipeg Police Services Investigation." Winnipeg: Southern Chiefs' Organization.

Spence, C. 2004. *An Analysis of Race Relations in Saskatoon: The Contributions of the Housing Sector*. Department of Sociology, University of Saskatchewan. At <bridgesandfoundations.usask.ca/reports/analysis_racerelations.pdf>.

Statistics Canada. 2011. *Family Violence in Canada: A Statistical Profile*. Catalogue no. 85-224-X. At <statcan.gc.ca/pub/85-224-x/85-224-x2010000-eng.pdf>.

____. 2008. *Aboriginal Peoples in Canada in 2006: Inuit, Métis and First Nations, 2006 Census.* At <12.statcan.ca/census-recensement/2006/as-sa/97-558/pdf/97-558-XIE2006001.pdf>.

____. 2005. "Crime Statistics." *The Daily,* July 21.

Stenning, P. 2003a. "Policing the Cultural Kaleidoscope: Recent Canadian Experience." *Police & Society* (7).

____. 2003b. "Police Use of Force and Human Rights in Canada." In P. Stenning (ed.) *Police Use of Force and Human Rights in Canada.* Vancouver: Criminology Research Centre, Simon Fraser University. At <sfu.ca/crc/fulltext/pufrep.pdf>.

Stenning, P., C. Birkbeck, O. Adang, D. Baker, T. Feltes, L. Gerardo Gabaldón, M. Haberfeld, E. Paes Machado, and P. Waddington. 2009. "Researching the Use of Force: The Background to the International Project." *Crime, Law and Social Change* 52.

Stroud, C. 1983. *The Blue Wall: Street Cops in Canada.* Toronto: McClelland and Stewart.

Talbot, C.K., C.H.S. Jaywardene, and T.J. Juliani. 1983. *The Thin Blue Line.* Ottawa: Crimecare, Inc.

Tanovich, D. 2006. *The Colour of Justice: Policing Race in Canada.* Toronto: Irwin law.

____. 2003–2004. "E-Racing Racial Profiling." *Alberta Law Review* 41.

Tator, C., and F. Henry. 2006. *Racial Profiling in Canada: Challenging the Myth of 'A Few Bad Apples.'* Toronto: University of Toronto Press.

Toronto Police Service. 2003. "Independent Review Final Report." At <toronto-police.on.ca.print.php?sid=386>.

Toronto Star. 2010a. *Toronto Star Analysis of Toronto Police Service Data – 2010. Advanced Findings.* At <media.thestar.topscms.com/acrobat/dd/49/f22a053a43cd98df18c4650f56d7.pdf>.

____. 2010b. "The Chief on Race, Crime and Policing." February 6. At <thestar.com/printarticle/761112>.

United Way Winnipeg. 2010. *Eagle's Eye View: An Environmental Scan of the Aboriginal Community in Winnipeg* (second edition). Winnipeg.

Vellacott, M. 2004. "Don't Judge Too Soon." At <injusticebusters.com/04/Vellacott.shtml> August 31.

Wacquant, L. 2008. *Urban Outcasts: A Comparative Sociology of Advanced Marginality.* Cambridge: Polity Press.

____. 2006. "The 'Scholarly Myths' of the New Law and Order Doxa." *Socialist Register.*

Ward, W.P. 1978. *White Canada Forever: Popular Attitudes and Public Policy Towards Orientals in British Columbia.* Montreal: McGill-Queen's University Press.

Westley, Wm. 2005. "Responsibilities of the Police." In T. Newburn (ed.), *Policing:*

Key Readings. Portland: Willan Publishing.

Wharf, B., and M. Clague (eds.). 1997. *Community Organizing: Canadian Experiences*. Toronto: Oxford University Press.

Williams, T. 2001. "Racism in Justice: The Report of the Commission on Systemic Racism in the Ontario Criminal Justice System." In Susan C. Boyd, Dorothy E. Chunn, and Robert Menzies (eds.), *(Ab)using Power: The Canadian Experience*. Halifax: Fernwood Publishing.

Wilson, J. 1975. *Thinking About Crime*. New York: Basic Books.

Winant, H. 1998. "Racism Today: Continuity and Change in the Post-Civil Rights Era." *Ethnic and Racial Studies* 21 (4).

Winnipeg Free Press. 2011. "Mounties Face Perjury Charges in Taser Death." At <http://www.winnipegfreepress.com/canada/mounties-face-perjury-charges-in-taser-death-121433119.html> May 7.

Woolford, A. 2009. *The Politics of Restorative Justice: A Critical Introduction*. Halifax and Winnipeg: Fernwood Publishing.

Wortley, S. 2007. *Police Use of Force in Ontario: An Examination of Data from the Special Investigations Unit*. Research Project Conducted on Behalf of the African Canadian Legal Clinic for the Ipperwash Inquiry. At <attorneygeneral.jus.gov.on.ca/inquiries/ipperwash/policy_part/projects/pdf/AfricanCanadianClinicIpperwashProject_SIUStudybyScotWortley.pdf>.

Wortley, S., and J. Tanner. 2005. "Inflammatory Rhetoric? Baseless Accusations? A Response to Gabor's Critique of Racial Profiling Research in Canada." *Canadian Journal of Criminology and Criminal Justice* 47 (3).

____. 2004. "Racial Profiling in Canada: Survey Evidence from Toronto." *The Canadian Review of Policing Research* 1 (1).

____. 2003. "Data, Denials and Confusion: The Racial Profile Debate in Toronto." *Canadian Journal of Criminology and Criminal Justice* 45.

WPS (Winnipeg Police Service). 2009. *Annual Report*. At <winnipeg.ca/police/annualreports/2009/2009_wps_annual_report_english.pdf>.

____. 2006a. "Operation Clean Sweep." At <winnipeg.ca/police/>.

____. 2006b. "Statement from Chief of Police J.J. Ewatski on Receipt of Calgary Police Review: Officer-Involved Shooting of Matthew Dumas." Media Release. At <winnipeg.ca/police/press/2006/08aug/2006_08_09.stm> August 9.

____. 2005a. "Police Related Shooting Investigated." Media Release. At <winnipeg.ca/police/press/2005/02feb/2005_02_01.stm> February 1.

____. 2005b. "Shooting Investigated." Media Release. At <winnipeg.ca/police/press/2005/01jan/2005_01_31.stm> January 31.

____. 2005c. Video of Chief Ewatski's Media Statement. At <winnipeg.ca/police/press/2005/07feb/2005_02.stm> February 7.

Wright, Justice D.H. (Commissioner). 2004. *Report of the Commission of Inquiry into Matters Relating to the Death of Neil Stonechild*. At <justice.gov.sk.ca/

stonechild/finalreport/Stonechild.pdf>.

Yalnizan, A. 2011. "A Problem for Everyone." *National Post*, September 21.

York, G. 1990. *The Dispossessed: Life and Death in Native Canada*. London: Vintage.

Zakreski, D. 2000. "Witness Recalls Native Man Struggling with Police: Man who Sparked Internal Probe Tells Horror Story." *Saskatoon StarPhoenix*, February 18.

CASE LAW CITED

R. v. Gladue [1999] 1 S.C.R. 908

R. v. Munson [2001a] 214 Sask. R. 262.

R. v. Munson [2001b] 212 Sask. R. 305.

R. v. Munson [2001c] 212 Sask. R. 29.

R. v. Munson and Hatchen [2003] SKCA 028.

R. v. Park [1995] 2 S.C.R. 836